BRAINWORKS

SUCCESS SMARTS UNLIMITED

ARLENE TAYLOR PHD

Success Resources International
Napa California

Editors:

Edward Cherney BS
Bruce Harlow MD
Margie Penkala AS
Leona Glidden Running PhD

Computer assistance with illustrations:

George DiRienzo PhD, Midnight Graphics

Web Master:

Michael S. Johnson BA

Typestyle: Times New Roman

Library of Congress Catalog Card Number: 96-92428

ISBN Number: 1-887307-96-6 $15.00 Softcover

Published by:
Success Resources International
Napa California

Also by Arlene Taylor

Back to Basics
Timely Tips for Building Bona Fide
Boundaries and Optimum Self Esteem

Thresholds to Thriving
A Power Pack of Practical Prescriptions
co-authored with Lorna L. Lawrence PhD

Gender Graphics
Understanding and Appreciating
Male/Female Differences

SHARE YOUR SUCCESS STORY WITH OTHERS

Taylor is collecting stories of individuals whose lives have been enhanced through participating in one of her research projects, attending one of her seminars (e.g., *Whole-brained Success Strategies, Brainworks Unlimited*[TM]), studying some of her resources, completing the Benziger Thinking Styles Assessment, or "you name it." There is no limit to the number of words.

Are you willing to share your experience? What have you learned through these educational opportunities? How has this knowledge made a positive difference in your life? Have you been able to solve a specific problem? Have some of your puzzling questions been answered? Have your relationships been enhanced? Have you made a career shift or successfully tweaked your existing job? Have you embraced new opportunities? Have you developed (or deleted) some specific behaviors from your lifestyle? Have you handled conflict in certain situations more effectively? Have you avoided problems when, previously, you might not have?

Some of these success stories will be published. In order to preserve confidentiality, names will be changed before your story is shared, unless you provide written permission to use your first and/or last name and state of residence.

Be an inspiration and encouragement to others.
Write to:

Arlene Taylor
P.O. Box 2554 Napa CA 94558-0255
FAX: 707•648•1965

TABLE OF CONTENTS

NOTHING NEW UNDER THE SUN

Whenever a new discovery is reported to the
scientific world, we hear, *it may not be true.*

Later on, when the truth of the new discovery has
been demonstrated beyond question, we hear,
it may be true, but it's not really important.

Finally, when enough time has elapsed so that
the importance of the discovery is beyond
question, we hear, *it may be important—
but it's no longer new . . .*

—Montaigne

FOREWORD

Some years ago I heard about Arlene Taylor and her lectures on the brain and thinking styles. I was naturally curious, albeit somewhat skeptical. More recently I became involved with these concepts when my two sons completed the thinking styles assessment in their search for personal understanding and educational direction. As a result, I believe that Jon and Peter have a better sense of who they are and of their innate capabilities.

When my wife Cheryl and I enrolled in *Brainworks Unlimited*™, completed the assessments, listened to Arlene, and then interacted with each other and with friends who were there, we realized in a new way that there were reasons behind our personalities and abilities. We found in these concepts a great tool to expand thinking, to foster understanding, and to allow for acceptance.

In these pages you now hold in your hands, you'll find the keys to many unopened doors as you interact with Arlene. You will sense her enthusiasm and become energized by it. You will better understand yourself and your fellow humans. You can then opt for acceptance rather than criticism and, I would hope, grow toward wholeness. You may also open wounds in this process and decide to change your direction.

As an internal medicine specialist, my education included studies in neurology and psychology but my first love has always been in areas of human behavior. It would have been wonderful to have the synthesis of this research when I went to school, but since I am still *in school* I have been able to incorporate this evolving science into my practice.

So to summarize:

> *When I say some things not really foreseen,*
> *It isn't because I'm somewhere between*
> *A saint and a demon . . .*
> *I'm human, I mean!*

Thank you, Arlene, for your work!

Thomas E. Stiles, M.D.

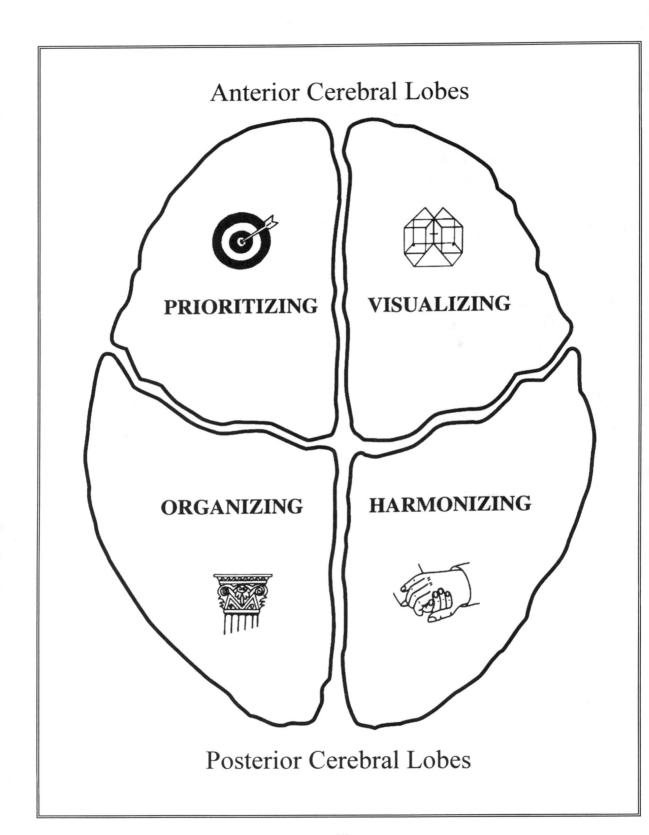

IN THE DECADE OF THE BRAIN

Introduction

Attempting to explain human behavior and brain function is nothing new. Human beings have been at it for years, perhaps eons. Some of the explanations have been expressed in terms of *models*; representations designed to portray complex data in a way that can be more easily understood. In reviewing a variety of models, it became obvious that one pattern stood out—descriptions usually occurred in a quadrantal pattern. This is consistent with the four segments that comprise the cerebrum.

One of the earliest recorded attempts to map brain function was by Hippocrates, in the fifth century BC. In an effort to help his patients understand themselves and the connection between emotions and health, Hippocrates described four basic temperament types and named them the: Choleric, Phlegmatic, Sanguine, and Melancholy. Galen, in the second century AD, also utilized this model, the labels of which are still in vogue today.

Some time later, the Native American Medicine Wheel, representative of a cultural-religious model, also utilized a quadrantal pattern. It characterized individuals by the four directions: North, Buffalo; South, Mouse; West, Bear; and East, Eagle. According to this description, human beings are each born at a specific location on the wheel. Their task in life is to move through all four positions, learning something from each. It was recognized that one would always be most comfortable at one's birth position on the wheel.

In the 1930s, C. G. Jung observed and described behavioral differences in terms of thinking, sensing, feeling, and intuition. Jung's model formed the basis for inventories such as the Myers-Briggs and Keirsey-Bates. In the 1980s, Benziger's *working model of brain function* grew out of a physiological update to the work of Jung.

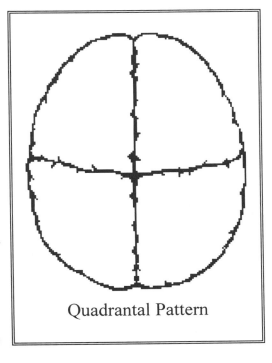

Quadrantal Pattern

I presented my first lecture on the brain in 1967. It's interesting to look back and realize how dramatically the database has exploded since then, especially during the past few years. Now in this, the decade of the brain—so proclaimed by former President George Bush—state-of-the-art research projects utilizing positron emission tomography, and other imaging technologies, have opened a window on the brain that was never thought possible.

The body of knowledge encompassing brain function has been greatly expanded by individuals such as Pribram, Gazzoniga, Andreasen, Cytowic, Benziger, Luria, Restak, Asimov, Ornstein, Sobel, Sapolsky, Haier, and Sacks—to name just a few. It has been stimulating to follow the flow of research data, more and more of which is being made available in nontechnical language, and to practically apply the wealth of information to everyday living.

The *Brainworks Unlimited*™ and *Whole-Brained Success Strategies* seminars were specifically designed to help participants identify and honor their innate giftedness, catch a glimpse of what is possible in terms of brain function, and to incorporate the information into their personal and professional lives. This cutting-edge information has enhanced my life beyond measure. It can do the same for you. The knowledge you gain can enhance all your relationships and help you to thrive. If you are already thriving, it can help to make it last. Remember that the goal is not to rigidly conform to a specific brain-function model, but to recognize and honor your own innate giftedness as well as that of others.

Seminar participants have repeatedly asked for copies of material presented in my seminars. This syllabus, including a number of the overhead illustrations, is a response to those requests. The illustrations are set up in an identical format so that the thinking styles and the practical applications are consistently displayed in the same position.

Those of you who have had me score and interpret your BTSA (Benziger Thinking Styles Assessment) will already be familiar with the terminology Benziger uses: *frontal left/right modes* and *basal left/right modes*. Some may find it easier to use terminology such as: *upper left/right* and *lower left/right*, as would be depicted on a chart. I often use the terms: *prioritizing, organizing, harmonizing, and visualizing thinking styles.*

Anterior Cerebral Lobes

Frontal Left Mode	Frontal Right Mode
Basal Left Mode	Basal Right Mode

Posterior Cerebral Lobes

Anterior Cerebral Lobes

Prioritizing Thinking Style	Visualizing Thinking Style
Organizing Thinking Style	Harmonizing Thinking Style

Posterior Cerebral Lobes

At the end of each chapter you will find a collection of *Brain Builders*. Some will be very easy; others may be more difficult. The *Creativity Corner* provides an opportunity for you to depict whatever is especially relevant to you. Try drawing a picture, creating an affirmation, writing a poem . . .

I have made every effort to present brain-function information as clearly and accurately as possible. Terminology, meanings, and personal understanding can vary, however. Data may be interpreted differently by different individuals. This information is not intended to take the place of appropriate professional (medical or psychological) care. The author, contributors, and editors do not take responsibility for the improper application of the concepts presented herein.

My thanks to each of you who have participated in the research projects and/or who have inspired me with attendance at my seminars. Many thanks to Dr. Katherine Benziger, Dr. Bruce Harlow, Dr. Leona Glidden Running, Dr. Thomas Stiles, and others who have graciously favored me with their expertise and encouragement.

It's what's under the *hat* that really matters . . .

Anterior Cerebral Lobes

PRIORITIZING

VISUALIZING

ORGANIZING

HARMONIZING

Posterior Cerebral Lobes

Chapter One
Spotlight on the Brain

Imagine a headquarters edifice three times larger than the Empire State building in New York City. And suppose that housed within this immense structure was electronic circuitry equal to that of all the radio and television stations in the entire world. Envision that this electronic circuitry required all of the electrical energy produced by Niagara Falls to operate it, and the entire Niagara River to keep it cool. What is it? The human brain, of course. Scientists estimate this is what it would take to duplicate functions comparable to those of the human brain—were it possible. And even then, the colossal computer might still not be able to decide whether to have hash browns and eggs, or oat cereal and prunes, for breakfast.

As noted in the introduction, the nineties have been declared the decade of the brain. How fitting a prelude to our transition into the next millennium. No doubt, the brain's superb engineering is more than adequate to launch us into the 21st century, but we, individually, must take responsibility for *gearing* up.

What do we mean when we speak of *the brain*? It consists of all the nervous tissue protected by the bony skull. Labyrinthine and multifaceted, it is progressively becoming more and more understandable as research continues to peel back fascinating layer after fascinating layer of hidden treasure.

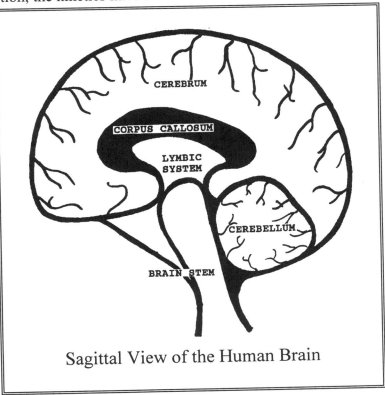

Sagittal View of the Human Brain

If we would cut the human brain in half, we could see some divisions even without the aid of a microscope. For example, we could see the brain stem, an energy-generating plant connected to the spinal cord. We could also see the medulla oblongata, wherein great trunk nerves cross over and produce that well-known phenomenon whereby each side of the brain controls the opposite side of the body. Sitting above the brain stem like a little French cap, we might locate the limbic system containing important regulatory structures with interesting names such as Amygdala and Hippocampus. This group of brain organs is more commonly referred to as the pain/pleasure center.

The largest portion of nervous tissue is the cerebrum. It is divided by the longitudinal fissure into the right and left hemispheres. Many of us recall having heard at least some *right brain/left brain* information as early as the 1970s. These hemispheres, in turn, are divided by the central fissure, thereby defining four cerebral sections.

Cerebral Fissures

The hemispheres are connected by a group of nerve fibers called the Corpus Callosum. To obtain an idea of the approximate size of your cerebral hemispheres, clench both hands into fists. Place your fists together, knuckles touching, with your thumbs toward your body. If you have small hands as I do, don't despair. If you have the hands of a wide-receiver, no need to feel especially elated. In most cases, intelligence is related not to absolute brain size, but rather to how we use what we have.

The cerebrum is composed of layers of tissue. Imagine that your skin and veins represent the outer layer called the cortex. Stretched out flat, the cortex would be about an eighth of an inch thick and would cover two and a half square feet of area. The more folds and creases in the cortex, the more information it has stored. A baby's brain is nearly as smooth as its bottom because it has not yet experienced a great deal of *learning*.

Interestingly, left-handed males are believed to have the thickest layer of cortex; females of either handedness, the next thickest layer; followed by right-handed males. In theory, the thicker the cortex the greater the potential for intelligence. If you happen to be a right-hander as I am, don't succumb to despondency. Believe me, you will never run out of potential!

One more comparison. Imagine that there is a gray glove on your left hand and a white glove on your right hand. This will give you an idea of the slight color variation between the two halves of the cerebrum. The left hemisphere has slightly more *gray* matter to help us handle the facts, figures, and dates that are so valued by our society. Many of its functions require the separation and organization of facts in an orderly, linear, sequential manner.

The right hemisphere is a slightly lighter color because more of its neurons are myelinated—coated with a covering that facilitates the rapid conduction of impulses from one thinking cell to another. The myelin sheath allows many of the right-brain functions to occur almost simultaneously. This is extremely valuable when we need to see the big picture, to perceive the entire problem at once, or initiate fight/flight in a dangerous situation.

DEFINITIONS

In order to utilize our brainpower more efficiently, we need to examine some of the database relating to the functioning of the human brain in general, and then move on to learn as much as we can about our own in particular. As we begin this exploration, there are two concepts that I wish to define. The first involves the use of the term *different*. As I use that word it means *unlike* and refers to biological, cultural, societal, psychological, and physiological phenomena. It doesn't imply inferiority or superiority and has nothing to do with good or bad.

The second addresses the concept of generalizations—research findings (gleaned in large sample studies) that hold true *on the average*. The conclusions drawn from research often apply more to groups of people than to specific individuals. There are always exceptions to the rule because human beings are so unique. Therefore, as you process this information you may occasionally think, "I'm not like that; this doesn't apply to me." Indeed, you may differ. That does not invalidate the research, however. Think of generalizations as a starting point, a frame of reference to help stimulate your thinking and perhaps answer puzzling questions that have been simmering on the back burner of your mind for years.

BRAIN AND BODY LEADS

Because of what is now known about brain function, it is becoming increasingly possible to assign generalized responsibility for specific skills to each of the four cerebral sections. These categories define, in effect, four thinking styles. Researchers such as Benziger and Sohn report that most of us are born with a biochemical predisposition for processing information (thinking) in one of the cerebral sections. This preference is referred to as *brain lead*.

The concept of brain lead is consistent with preferences (leads) we observe in other parts of the body. For example, most people have a preference for using one hand over the other. Assuming that we have two hands, our lead hand is the one we usually use for eating, brushing our teeth, combing our hair, and throwing a ball. (Handwriting cannot definitively be used to determine handedness because some individuals were forced to switch from their innate preference and learned to write with their opposite hand.)

We have other natural body leads, as well. Fold your hands, fingers interlocking, in your usual way. Your lead thumb will be on top. Next, move your fingers one position so that you fold your hands with the opposite thumb on top. How does that feel? The first time I folded my hands in this opposite manner, it felt so unnatural I glanced down to see whose hand I was holding!

Cross your arms in front of your chest. Your lead arm is on top. Recross your arms with your lead arm on the bottom. How does that feel? Some of you may need some help! Practice folding your hands and your arms both ways until both positions feel relatively comfortable. With time, we can learn to override our natural preference, but will generally feel more comfortable when using it.

Do you know which eye is your lead eye? If not, try this simple exercise. Make a circle with each hand by joining the tips of your thumb and index finger. Superimpose the circles with your arms as far out in front of you as possible. Search out an object to look at and center it in the middle of your newly-formed *spyglass*.

Keeping your arms and fingers as still as possible, close one eye. If the object is still in the center of the circle, your lead eye is open. If the object appeared to *move* to the edge or even outside of the circle, you opened your nonlead eye. Our brain usually selects the eye with the highest acuity as our lead eye. It generally handles about ninety percent of our focusing. The nonlead eye helps to provide depth and three-dimensional perception. (When wearing glasses, your lead eye may be different.)

Most of us have a lead foot and a lead leg, as well. To determine footedness, observe with which foot you lead when you climb stairs or step off a curb. Which shoe do you put on first? Which leg goes into your hosiery or pant legs first? I was explaining this to my husband early in our marriage, and he was a bit skeptical. Casually I suggested, "Tomorrow morning, why don't you try getting dressed by putting the opposite leg into your trousers first? See if it makes any difference." He took me at my word—and fell flat on the floor. (Well, almost!) We did have a good laugh. Often we fail to realize how strongly and automatically we are influenced by these innate leads.

The majority of individuals have *lateral dominance*, a term meaning that all leads (e.g., arm, hand, foot, eye) are on the same side of the body. Some studies suggest that approximately thirty percent of the population exhibit *mixed dominance* in which the leads are mixed up, some occurring on one side of the body, some on the other. Usually, this does not cause any difficulty. In fact, mixed dominance can have its advantages in a sport such as baseball. Batters who have their lead hand, arm, leg, and foot on the same side of the body, but who have their lead eye on the opposite side, usually have higher batting averages.

One way in which we can exercise our brain is by consciously cultivating ambidexterity—switching hands to perform certain tasks. For example, try switching hands when you comb your hair, brush your teeth, open doors, write down telephone numbers, or hold a fork. The possibilities are endless. You may have some surprises! Many of us do not realize how automatically, and consistently we use body leads for certain activities until we consciously try to switch. Use your imagination, and enjoy watching your ability and coordination improve.

I have had some of my best chuckles during attempts to switch hands for certain activities. For example, the first time I tried to brush my teeth while holding the toothbrush in my left hand, there was more toothpaste on the mirror than on my teeth. Even though I didn't enjoy cleaning the mirror, the laughter served to boost my immune system function!

THE CEREBRUM

The cerebrum is composed of eight lobes, four in each hemisphere. There are two anterior lobes and six posterior lobes. The two anterior cerebral lobes are responsible for many of our intellectual functions: perception, strategic planning, logical decision-making, focusing attention, adapting to new situations, and regulating complex behaviors. They are abstract (conceptual) in their thought processing, and are able to deal with ideas that are separate from objects or things.

The two anterior lobes are hard-wired, so to speak, to the powerful energy source, in the core of the brain, which energizes their thinking ability. They conceptualize sensed information received through the sensory systems, as well as information obtained directly from the environment.

The six posterior lobes, three on each side, are the repository for sensed information. They touch, smell, taste, see, and hear the environment in an immediate and concrete (realistic) way:

- The occipital lobes (visual cortex) analyze optical information for position, movement, shape, and orientation. They house the visual sensory system.
- The temporal lobes enable us to translate sounds into meaning. They house the auditory sensory system. They also contain important memory banks.
- The parietal lobes help us to recognize, connect with, and use objects in our environment. They house the kinesthetic sensory system.

In general, the right hemisphere is innovative, musical, relational, and collegial. It is global in perspective and not particularly time-based. According to Gazzaniga, the right hemisphere contains mechanisms that enable us to soak up the raw material of sensory experiences. It can receive and deal with information that is received *any side up* or *all at once.* The right hemisphere is able to interpret *symbols:* representational characters that are more generalized and inclusive than signs. Birth, as a symbol, can mean the entrance of a specific individual into this world, or it can represent any number of new beginnings—along with corresponding feelings of hope and joy. Symbols often evoke a deep emotional response, usually related to one's own perceptions, beliefs, and experiences. The American flag is a symbol. Those who love America, salute the flag; those who dislike America, burn it.

Stereotypically, the left hemisphere is linear, sequential, and time-oriented. It is involved with goal setting and goal achievement and tends to dominate the right side of the brain if allowed to do so. It prefers to receive information *vertically and right-side-up*. According to Gazzaniga, the left hemisphere contains mechanisms for processing complex sensory data. This part of the brain is constantly trying to find the correlation between events we encounter in the world. It also constantly assesses who we are and where we stand in relation to others.

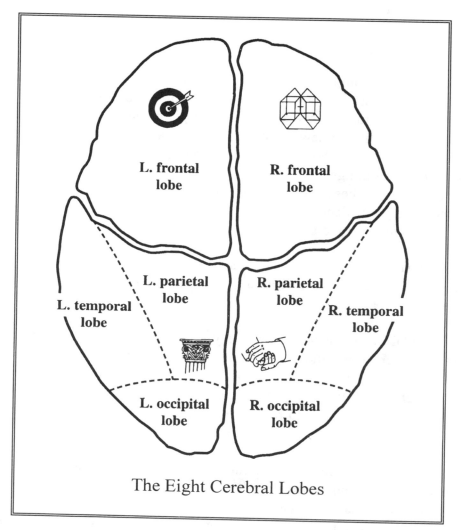

The Eight Cerebral Lobes

The left hemisphere is able to interpret *signs*—representations that usually have a specific, predetermined, and consistent meaning. For example, the legend on a highway map lists the signs that can help us to determine what route we will take to our destination. Signs are rather neutral in meaning. When we see a plus (+) sign we know that it simply means something is to be added. This does not, in and of itself, evoke much emotion unless, perhaps, we're adding a million dollars to our bank account!

METAPHORIC FOUR-ROOM HOUSE

Some individuals like to picture the cerebrum as a four-room house, each room representing one of the four thinking styles. Some even like to imagine specific items in each room to help them recall some of the characteristics of each thinking style. You can enter any room and move from one room to another through connecting doorways. From the organizing room, you can move through one doorway into the harmonizing room, or through the other doorway into the prioritizing room. In order to reach the visualizing room, however, you must first pass through either the harmonizing, or the prioritizing room. There is no diagonal hallway that permits direct access between either the harmonizing and prioritizing rooms, or between the organizing and visualizing rooms.

Prioritizing room	Visualizing room
• Machines and mechanical tools • Research equipment such as computers • Charts and graphs • Framed awards • Abstract photographs of arrows • A list of goals and objectives • A written five-year plan • Structured music playing in the background (e.g., Bach)	• Plenty of flat surfaces on which to *stack* • A computer to assist with innovative creativity • A wide range of reading materials • Large sheets of paper with pencils and markers • Caricatures and cartoons • A bulletin board with pins • Jazz or baroque music playing in the background
Organizing room	Harmonizing room
• Filing cabinets with appropriate folders and labels • A computer to keep track of information • A *to do* list • A selection of *how to* books or procedure manuals • A dictionary • A calendar • Helpful items (e.g., pencils, paper clips, calculator) • Martial music playing in the background	• Decorations that include photos of family/friends, candles, stuffed animals • Comfortable chairs with a cozy afghan • A computer for personal use • Inspirational books and pictures • Smiley stickers • Colorful marking pens • Objects from nature (e.g., plants) • Musical instruments • Rhythmical or *folk* music playing in the background

Metaphorically, some individuals like to spend the majority of their time in just one of these four rooms. They tend to avoid activities in the other three rooms, and tend to procrastinate when they can't avoid them. We refer to these individuals as quarter-brainers. Approximately thirty-five percent of the population fall into this category. They are the *specialists* in our society. Often, they can perform outstandingly well when engaged in activities that utilize their preferred thinking style.

Other individuals prefer to divide the majority of their time between two of the four rooms, usually adjacent rooms. We refer to these individuals as half-brainers. Approximately fifty-five percent of the population fall into this group. Some individuals have become accustomed to using the two rooms diagonally opposite from each other. This is not a normally-occurring pattern; and, of course, it takes more energy to run back and forth through a connecting room.

About five percent of the population enjoy dividing their time among three of the four rooms on a regular basis. We can refer to them as tri-brainers. Actually, most of us have the potential to become tri-brainers, and to easily access the functions of the cerebral sections on either side of our brain lead. Developing the fourth thinking style, the one opposite our lead, takes more effort. I like to picture a spread eagle positioned in my lead.

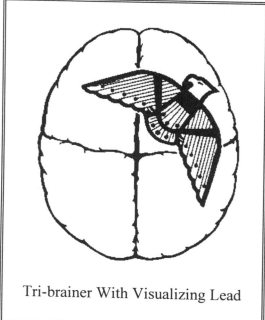

Tri-brainer With Visualizing Lead

The remainder divide their time among all four rooms, either because they have worked hard to develop functions in all four rooms, or because they do not have a clear preference for one room over the others. These individuals are often seen as the generalists in our culture; the ones who seem to be good at a little bit of everything, although they may not perform any of the tasks as outstandingly as would a specialist.

On the down-side (and there always is one) tri-brainers and whole-brainers may actually have a bit more trouble making decisions because it's as if there are three or four *chiefs* each pressing for a preferred choice in any given situation. However, these individuals can learn to delegate responsibility for making the decision to the thinking style best suited for the task at hand.

THE NEURONS

In order to better understand what underlies innate brain lead, we need to review a bit of anatomy and physiology. There are two main types of cells in the brain: glial cells that form the supportive and protective parts of the system, and neurons that form the functional (cognitive) part. Neurons are specialized cells that have a very limited ability to repair themselves, but a highly developed propensity to transmit information.

Imagine that your hand resembles a neuron. Let your palm represent the cell body. Your thumb can be the axon—the main nerve fiber by which information leaves the neuron (and which in some parts of the human nervous system can reach a length of three feet).

Your remaining four fingers can represent the other cell extensions called dendrites, whose job is to collect incoming information. They are quite short, usually under a millimeter in length, but play a vital part in our ability to think. In a brain that has been challenged through mental exercise, a thousand of these little dendrites (each covered with dendritic fibers, resembling the teeth on a comb) may sprout from a single neuron.

In some forms of mental retardation, it is believed that these dendrites (or the dendritic fibers) are either missing or reduced in numbers. Consequently, in such cases, the brain can be exposed to information, but learning does not take place. If scientists knew how to stimulate the defective neurons to grow adequate numbers of dendrites and dendritic fibers, some forms of retardation could be remedied.

A tiny space (synaptic gap) separates the end of one axon from the dendrite receptors of an adjacent neuron. The synaptic gap is filled with fluid in which are dissolved chemicals called neurotransmitters. Although hundreds of neurotransmitters have been identified, each synaptic gap usually contains only three to five at any given time.

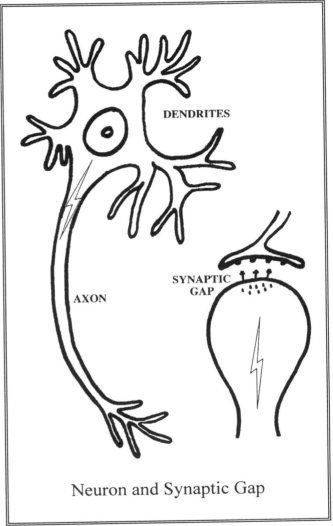

Neuron and Synaptic Gap

Here are three examples:

- **Acetylcholine,** the most common neurotransmitter, is associated with the speed of information exchange. Nicotine, amphetamines, caffeine, and cocaine (to name just a few) are believed to affect acetylcholine in one way or another. Choline, found in soybean products such as lecithin, is a precursor (building block) for this neurotransmitter.

- **Dopamine** is a neurotransmitter associated with autonomic muscle movement, and with our ability to sense pleasure. In Parkinsonism, there is a deficiency of dopamine; in Schizophrenia, an excess. Certain drugs such as nicotine, alcohol, caffeine, cocaine, opiates, barbiturates, as well as a variety of addictive behaviors, activities, and processes, are believed to influence relative dopamine levels within the brain. (Refer to my Brain Reward Systems audiotapes for additional information on neurotransmitters and addictive behaviors.)

- **Serotonin** is associated with sleep induction, with regulation of mood, and with our ability to feel joyful. Decreased levels of serotonin are associated with depression and with sleep irregularities. Some studies suggest that habitual patterns of negative thinking can decrease serotonin levels within the brain—a good reason for evaluating our mind-set and learning new patterns of thinking, if so indicated. Some forms of meditation are believed to increase serotonin levels.

In order for thinking to take place, information must be shared between neurons. This requires a combination of electrical and chemical transmission, because the neurons don't actually touch each other. Information crosses the neuron by means of electricity. Yes, the brain has its own electrical generating plant! Speeds of electrical transmission can range from one mile per hour to one-hundred fifty miles per hour. When the impulse reaches the end of the axon, one or more neurotransmitters are released. Their job is to ferry the information across the synaptic gap. Dendrites on the other side pick up the information and pull it into the neuron. The process is repeated as necessary.

BIOCHEMICAL ADVANTAGE

Researchers have identified a reduced resistance to the transmission of information across the synaptic gaps in our innate brain lead. This biochemical advantage means that, in general, information moves more easily between neurons. Think of it as just *flying* across the synaptic gap. Potentially, we can learn more quickly, achieve higher levels of competence, and expend less metabolic energy when utilizing skills governed by our brain lead. Of course, this helps to boost our self-esteem, because we feel *smart* when we perform tasks or attempt to learn skills that use preferred functions. We may even feel like we are playing rather than working, because we accomplish these tasks so much more easily.

Outside our innate brain lead, metabolic energy expenditure is a different story. Studies by Dr. Richard Haier suggest that we may expend up to one hundred times more metabolic energy when utilizing nonpreferred functions. No wonder we tend to procrastinate certain tasks and/or feel exhausted after we finish them. The tasks we hate the most may be the ones that require utilization of the thinking style diagonally opposite from our brain lead. Remember, there is no direct neuronic pathway between the two. Watch for new research reports in this area.

Brain lead pushes us toward two different types of relationships; relationships that mirror our brain lead and those that complement our brain lead. Relationships that mirror our own lead and build our self-esteem are usually the ones we have with our closest friends. We speak the same language, as it were. We often like and dislike the same things. When circumstances result in our not being able to see each other for a time, and then we're able to get together again, it's almost as if there had been no intervening time. We quickly pick up right where we left off. Why? Because we approach life from the perspective of the same thinking style.

Brain lead also pushes us toward relationships that complement our brain lead and that increase our chances for long-term survival. We usually select our life partners, and even our career associates, from this complementary group. "Now I understand why I get along better with my best friend than with my spouse," some of you groan. "Why don't we partner with our best friends?" Sometimes we do in a second marriage, or when partnering occurs later in life. Initially, however, the brain usually *selects for wholeness*. It knows we need the entire range of cerebral functions, and it knows wherein lie our strengths and weaknesses. Consequently, it nudges us toward partnering with individuals who have strengths to complement our weaknesses. Understanding this predisposition can reduce our tendency to feel frustrated when confronted with others who *differ* from us. It gives us the conscious option not only to collaborate, but also to honor each other's differences.

It says here that

brain lead pushes us

toward two types of

relationships . . .

♣♣ with those who are like us
(best friends)

♣♠ with those who are different
(life partners)

. . . that's good to know!

BRAIN BUILDERS

Points to Ponder

- The human mind, once stretched to a new idea, never returns to its original dimensions. —Oliver Wendell Holmes

- Two key concepts I have learned in this section:

  _____

  _____

- Two facts I've discovered about myself while studying this section:

  _____

  _____

- One way in which I am now applying this information:

  _____

  _____

  _____

- The largest portion of brain tissue is the _____.

- The limbic system is sometimes referred to as the _____ _____ center.

- **T F** Brain lead refers to an innate preference for processing information in one of the thinking styles over the other three.

- **T F** Brain lead pushes us toward two different types of relationships.

- **T F** The neurons are separated by a space known as the synaptic gap.

Brain Teasers

1.	2.	3.	4.
G R A N D	HE AD	N W O D	iiii iiii o o

Creativity Corner

DOMAIN AND METHOD

PRIORITIZING THINKING STYLE

- ◆ Domain
  - Analyzing for functionality
  - Setting/achieving goals
  - Establishing priorities
  - Problem solving based on data

- ◆ Method
  - Logical (inductive/deductive) reasoning

VISUALIZING THINKING STYLE

- ◆ Domain
  - Abstract pattern comparison
  - Imagining change
  - Developing new ideas/products
  - Creative problem solving

- ◆ Method
  - Dynamic 3-D internal picturing

ORGANIZING THINKING STYLE

- ◆ Domain
  - Bounded shapes
  - Grasping/manipulating
  - Speech sounds (words)
  - Procedures
  - Routines

- ◆ Method
  - Sequencing

HARMONIZING THINKING STYLE

- ◆ Domain
  - Harmony
  - Connection/touch
  - Nonspeech sounds (tones, music)
  - Affirmation
  - Relationship development

- ◆ Method
  - Comparing relationally

Chapter Two
The Four Thinking Styles

No thinking style is better than another; no particular brain lead good or bad. Each style differs from the others, however. Each is a specialist in its own field, with valuable strengths and corresponding weaknesses; each looks at life from its own perspective; each perceives the environment somewhat differently; and each has its own method of processing information (sometimes referred to as *domain* and *method*, or *what* and *how*).

The competencies that we learn most easily, and that we perform most effectively over time, are those that are congruent with our preferred thinking style.

ORGANIZING THINKING STYLE

The organizing thinking style is concrete (realistic), present tense, sensory, and sequential. This section of the cerebrum is gifted not only at identifying bounded shapes, but at storing and recalling the labels for them. This includes the names of people who are, after all, bounded shapes. This part of the brain pushes us to grasp and manipulate bounded shapes. We've all observed little children who pick up objects and, in the process, drop some of them. Later on as adults, however, these are the same individuals who may be the most likely to wash and dry your heirloom stemware without a single mishap.

Prioritizers	Visualizers
Organizers	Harmonizers

The left temporal lobe has a preference for speech sounds and is especially tuned to decode nouns and verbs: nouns, because they are labels for bounded shapes; and verbs, because they tell us what to do with them. Wernicke's Area, the sensory-motor center, enables us to hear, identify, decode, and interpret words at rates of up to one thousand per minute. Since most people speak at a rate of about one hundred words per minute we can understand why our minds sometimes tend to *wander* when we are listening to someone who is speaking very slowly, or when we are listening to information that we do not perceive as interesting, or as very important to our lives.

Templates in this, our native language center, help us to recognize language presented to us in visual, written, or gestured form (e.g., American Sign Language). These functions enable us to assemble letters into words, and words into thoughts; to use a language form with proper spelling, punctuation, and complete sentence structure; to develop the skills of printing and handwriting. That is, we learn to move a bounded shape (pen) across a bounded shape (paper) and draw bounded shapes (letters/numbers).

These organizing functions also enable us to learn and recall the building blocks of music (e.g., chord structure, time signatures, measure divisions). When we sight-read music, we compare musical *signs* (e.g., notes) against our memory-bank files of learned information. The more automatically and quickly we make these comparisons, the better our sight-reading.

This section of the cerebrum is skilled at *loading a piece of software*, if you will, and then running the program accurately, over and over. In other words, it can sequence a set of actions into a routine, and then repeat it accurately. It doesn't like to be interrupted in this process, because interruptions can decrease efficiency. Those of us who learned to drive a stick-shift vehicle initially loaded the software that enabled us to drive for hours without consciously thinking of which gear to use. If, however, the lights of the car in front of us flash red, the automatic program is interrupted, and we must quickly make a decision regarding the preferred gear. In a similar way, we can perform activities of daily living and think about something else at the same time. Imagine what it would be like to brush your teeth and have to consciously and continually think about every single movement!

We sometimes refer to this thinking style as *foundational*, because we begin developing its valuable contributions almost at birth. Early in a child's life, adult-child conversations might sound something like this:

- What is that animal? *A dog.* Right. What is the dog doing? Oh boy! Why now?

- What's your name? *Marc, spelled with a "c."* Yes, that's a great name. No, I have no idea why your parents named you that.

- Point to your nose. No, that's my nose. What sticky fingers you have!

- Hold your spoon this way. Why is it that the mouthpiece always seems easier to grasp?

We ask these questions over, and over, and over again as we attempt to help children to identify, label, and manipulate bounded shapes. In our culture, we also emphasize facts, figures, dates, and details. We ask:

- How old are you? *Three fingers wave in the air.* (This might relate to the question; then again, it might not!)

- What color is your ball? *Brown.* (It was red until it fell in the mud.)

- How many ears do you have? *Two.* (I can't tell you how many times in childhood someone informed me that humans have two ears and only one tongue. I think that fact was supposed to prod me to decrease the number of times I used the word *why*.)

- If you have one apple, and I give you mine, how many do you have? *One.* (Oh, I see you ate yours. This was meant to be a theoretical question but I got a factual answer.)

Characteristics of organizers

Organizers typically exhibit characteristics that relate to the way in which they prefer to interact with their environment. Pat is an example. People who like Pat describe her as cautious, conservative, detailed, and thorough. She goes *by the book*; one reason she is such an excellent key-punch operator. Her work is virtually mistake-free unless, that is, she is frequently interrupted. In that case, her production may decline, and her errors escalate. She tends to approach problem solving from a rules perspective, and leans toward decisions that are rational, predictable, dependable, and proven. Her solutions tend to be practical, though somewhat conservative and traditional. She can be talked into compromising, when necessary, and is not above manipulation in an attempt to preserve the status quo. Those who think differently from Pat say that she is stuck in a rut and boring. Indeed, without balanced input from the rest of the cerebrum, Pat may not be as open to change, or to learning new information, as would be beneficial to her.

Individuals with this innate brain lead can be stereotypically described as:

- Dependable and sequential. They approach life sequentially (from part-to-whole) and process information in a structured manner (step-by-step). They prefer to do *first things first,* and tend to think in terms of linked ideas, one thought directly following another. They can be depended upon to follow a routine accurately.

- Practical and predictable. They are very practical; the ones most likely to be carrying an umbrella when the rain hits in the middle of the afternoon. They are also very predictable, usually holding tenaciously to their likes and dislikes. A friend of mine asserts that she could go on a TV quiz-show and accurately answer the questions for her partner who exhibits this thinking style.

- Adept at tracking time and money. They (organizers) usually possess a very good sense of time. They try to complete work projects on time. They want to be *on time* and expect the same of others. They often have a budget—and stick to it carefully. (Individuals with a different lead may not be able to spell the word budget, much less follow one!)

- Traditional. They like to maintain traditions. I wish I had understood this earlier in my life. Several years ago I arrived at the home of a good friend for our annual Thanksgiving potluck, cranberry soufflé in hand—not with the dish of candied sweet potatoes that I had traditionally contributed for the past three years. To say that the hostess was not pleased would be putting it mildly. "You always bring sweet potatoes," she lamented. "My menu calls for sweet potatoes. Now what will we do?" There wasn't much to be done except proceed without them. Looking back at that experience, I now recognize some additional, and preferred, options. I might have either contacted her in advance or brought both dishes. Live and learn!

- Hating change. Organizers want to maintain the status quo and, consequently, usually resist change with a passion. They may be motivated to change if it becomes a matter of life and death. Even then, they do not want to be rushed—crisis or not. They are more likely to change when it is presented as less a matter of change, and more a matter of efficiently incorporating practical and efficient strategies into existing procedures. They can actually experience increased stress during times of change, or when interrupted. Consequently, they may dig in their heels, refuse to change, and even sabotage the efforts of others to initiate change. These are the individuals who like to get all the furniture organized, and except for moving it occasionally to vacuum, would just as soon leave everything as is, thank you very much. After all, it takes energy to move bounded shapes, and organizers are very conserving of energy. Telling them to try something different, *for a change,* won't earn you big points.

- Avoiding conflict. In general, they are uncomfortable with conflict because it represents a potential for change. Therefore, in situations of conflict, they will often try to invoke rules and regulations in an attempt to maintain the status quo.

The organizing functions enable us to develop routines, and to follow them accurately and almost automatically. Their conservative and traditional approach to life helps to keep us from running off after every harebrained idea. This promotes completion which prevents us from jumping from one task to another without completing any of them. These functions also help us to deal with reality (the way things are), and to experience a sense of belonging when we are in familiar surroundings. The creativity of this thinking style centers around a desire to maintain order and efficiency within the environment.

The weakness of this thinking style derives from a tendency to maintain the status quo at all costs. Because it can be so unbending in its efforts to avoid change, and because it is so reticent to look at new options, it can miss out on some of life's opportunities. It may be viewed by others as somewhat boring and stuck in a rut.

FIND ONE DIFFERENCE IN EACH SECTION

HARMONIZING THINKING STYLE

The harmonizing thinking style—while also concrete (realistic), present tense, and sensory—is particularly collegial and relational. Its specialty involves comparing and assessing the small patterns created by the relationships between two or more bounded shapes. Consequently, this section of the brain enables us to recognize faces quickly and to read nonverbals. Faces, for example, are simply composites of bounded shapes (e.g., eyes, eyebrows, ears, noses, mouths, chins). Without the ability to recognize faces, we might arrive home from work and have no idea whether or not the people in our home belonged there.

Prioritizers	Visualizers
Organizers	**Harmonizers**

An ability to *read* nonverbal body language also stems from this function. Imagine that you are looking at a person whose forehead is wrinkled in a frown, whose hand is on the hip with the elbow angled away from the body, and whose foot is stamping the ground. Even without the advantage of audible speech, you could quickly figure out that this individual is upset.

Some researchers estimate that fifty-five percent of the message in a two-person communication derives from facial cues and body language; thirty-five percent from voice tone and rhythm, and only ten percent from actual words. This part of the cerebrum is sensitive to the congruence of verbal and non-verbal language, and can often distinguish between what people express verbally and what they really mean. The way in which something is said may be more important than the actual content of the words.

The right temporal lobe contains templates for processing nonspeech sounds: musical notes; the *music* of speech (e.g., tone of voice, tempo, speed, inflection); nature sounds such as the wind sighing through the trees, a babbling brook, or the distant call of a whippoorwill. It is particularly sensitive to sounds that might indicate a danger to the individual—sounds that might require the fight/flight response. It prefers harmonious sounds, so can become annoyed by unpleasant or irritating sounds such as the incessant dripping of water, rattling window screens, jangling keys, the scrape of a fingernail across a chalkboard, or the continual yapping of a dog.

Some of you may have read the book entitled *The Man Who Mistook His Wife for a Hat.* In it, Dr. Sacks describes a stroke patient who had lost the ability to recognize his wife's face. This was disconcerting, to say the least. The doctor suggested that the wife always wear a specific hat when she visited her husband in the hospital. The patient was told that he would know his wife by her distinctive chapeau. Indeed, that's exactly what happened. An undamaged portion of the patient's brain recognized the hat and connected it with his wife.

I was interested to learn that a tiny cluster of cells, recently identified within the right temporal lobe, is believed to help us assign *meaning* to spiritual experiences. While we can get to religion through any part of the cerebrum, we may need the skills of the harmonizing thinking style to develop a meaningful spiritual relationship with a Higher Power.

Characteristics of harmonizers

My friend, Hector, an accomplished chef, possesses an innate harmonizing lead. Those who value his strengths describe him as deeply spiritual, musical and very intuitive in his desire to nurture others. They value the way in which he is able to reach out and touch people in a sensitive and caring manner, both verbally and physically.

> The face, the index of a feeling mind. —Crabbe

Hector approaches problem solving from a collegial, peacemaking perspective. Directed toward preserving harmony and decreasing or avoiding conflict, his decisions are likely to be somewhat subjective and based on feelings. With an emphasis on interpersonal interactions, his solutions are designed to please the largest possible number of individuals. He would like everyone to be comfortable and happy—especially his nuclear and work families.

Those who don't like Hector say he's too gullible, really a *soft touch*, even too compliant for his own good. Some accuse him of being overly concerned with emotions, and overly sensitive to everything. According to at least one of his relatives, Hector's spouse wears the pants in their family. Hector is very easygoing, and doesn't seem to mind that his partner takes the lead in many of their decisions.

Individuals with this innate brain lead can be stereotypically described as:

- Collegial and relational. They are concerned about how others feel. Because of this, they place great emphasis on connecting with others, instinctively reaching out to comfort, encourage, and nurture. You may find them doodling smiley-faces on written notes, cards, and letters.

- Reading body language well. They not only read body language well, but have an ability to duplicate specific behaviors. Consequently, they may enjoy acting in skits and dramatic plays. The ability to *act* involves bringing one's nonverbal body language (gestures, costume, facial expressions), as well as one's words and voice sounds, into *harmony* with whatever character one is trying to portray. The better individuals can do that, the better actors or actresses we deem them to be. When we are learning to speak a foreign language, this part of the brain lends invaluable assistance with its expertise for assessing and matching the rhythms, tempo, and inflections of the new lingo. In childhood, harmonizers often like to play *dress-up* and may change clothes several times a day. In adulthood, they often enjoy shopping—their term for trying on clothes to see what feels good, looks good, and might fit a particular occasion harmoniously.

- Sensitive and sentimental. They are sensitive not only to their own feelings, but to the feelings of others, as well. They can be very nurturing to themselves and to others. They often enjoy activities that create memories, and tend to celebrate for almost any reason.

For example, they enjoy potlucks with friends. As one seminar participant said, "It doesn't get much better than eating wonderful bounded shapes in the company of your favorite bounded shapes!" That about sums it up.

- Musical. They (harmonizers) enjoy music, and often like to sing, play musical instruments (preferably by ear), and attend musical concerts. They may also enjoy movement, tapping their toes in tempo with rhythmic sounds. Some enjoy dancing or exercising to music.

- Acquiescing to change. They will usually agree to change, especially in a crisis situation, or when they understand the ways in which the change will benefit all concerned. Because they are interested in personal growth (especially if it leads to increased harmony and decreased conflict), they often want to improve and desire to help others improve. In general, they approach change slowly. They want to talk about it, be involved, and have everyone included in the process. They are adept at helping to smooth the implementation of change, although their concerns for harmony can sometimes delay the process.

- Hating conflict. They hate conflict because they perceive that it interferes with harmony, and collegial relationships. They'll usually try to arrange a collaborative solution. In their pursuit of harmony, they may overcomply to the point of violating conscience.

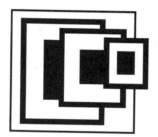  

The harmonizing functions enable us to connect with others, with the environment, and with a Higher Power. The creativity of this thinking style centers around a desire to achieve harmony within the environment (sounds, odors, colors, textures), among individuals, and between individuals and their environment. It is concerned with retaining (or avoiding) memories that contain a strong emotional component. Consequently, it is sometimes called the guardian of *feelings*. It prefers to process information in a feeling manner, and prefers to act from the basis of feelings rather than facts.

The weakness of this thinking style arises from a tendency to become inappropriately concerned with feelings and relationships. It may be viewed by others as too sensitive. Somehow it expects people to get along all the time, and these unrealistic expectations can cause trouble. Its fear of causing upsets or of hurting another's feelings can lead to the avoidance of necessary confrontation. It can experience stress when its relationships are not harmonious, or when it doesn't have the relationships it desires. It can miss out on some of life's opportunities because of a tendency to become immobilized due to the processing (and sometimes overprocessing) of feelings, or due to an inability to manage emotions and feelings effectively.

VISUALIZING THINKING STYLE

The visualizing thinking style is abstract (conceptual), simultaneous, spontaneous, synthesizing, spatial, intuitive, and innovative. It is gifted at scanning the environment for large patterns created by bounded shapes. It picks up information in a global fashion, and, second for second, can take in huge amounts of information. It can also compare abstract patterns when no tangible bounded shapes are present. It compares these patterns for the purpose of identifying trends, and for imagining the appropriate change that is indicated.

Prioritizers	**Visualizers**
Organizers	Harmonizers

The right frontal lobe is the home of mental imaging (visualization), a function that frightens some individuals. One woman told me she wouldn't even *think* of visualizing. I chuckled because we all do it, most of us on a daily basis. When we don't realize this, we unfortunately may use this skill in a negative manner. For example, we may imagine ourselves failing at something and we may tell ourselves: "I know I am going to mess up. This is not going to work." Often this negativity results in a self-fulfilling prophecy. When we understand visualization, we are much more likely to use it consciously and positively. We can picture ourselves as being successful at whatever task we need to accomplish. This doesn't mean we won't make mistakes, or that we can avoid practice, but we usually act in accordance with what we imagine to be so.

Some healthcare professionals are capitalizing on this innate mental ability, and are teaching cancer patients to visualize their white blood cells as fighters that attack and destroy tumors. They are teaching children with severe asthma to visualize their bronchial tubes expanding, thus allowing air to flow freely into their lungs. They are teaching people with depressive-thinking habits to visualize happy internal pictures. To some degree, our bodies do act out what our minds see internally. Study after study is verifying the close connection between brain and body—between the mental pictures we create and our physical health.

The visualizing functions help us to think in pictures, patterns, and metaphors rather than in words. Visualizers can learn to recognize words and to read by memorizing the shape of words as created by the letters, but may find it difficult to *spell* accurately. Furthermore, they usually do better when they can view the whole word or the whole problem. Therefore, phonics can be a challenge. They tend to communicate through *gestures*. These may be in the form of *mime*, body position, hand or arm movements, facial expressions, tears, or any number of other subtle, and not-so-subtle, types of body language. One man described his arm movements as attempts to *draw* pictures in the air to communicate what he was seeing internally.

Visualizers also excel at looking at things in a new way. Many of the inventions and artistic creations we enjoy today came into being as an individual with this brain lead asked a new question such as:

* Mightn't there be a faster way to accomplish this task?
* I wonder what would happen if we did such and such?
* Just because it hasn't ever been done before, why not try it now?
* What would this tune sound like with different harmony, or rhythm, or time signature?
* Is a *David* hiding in this block of granite?
* Why shouldn't I paint with a new pigment?
* Who made that rule?
* What do you mean there is only one way to approach this?
* If birds can fly, why can't we?

Visualizers prefer *flexible storage*—material filed in stacks around the environment—and don't like their stacks moved. This system is not *messy*, you understand, although it may appear so to those with a different thinking style. The bottom line is, *if it's out of sight, it's out of mind.* Information filed away in a cabinet, out of the line of vision, may be forgotten. Flexible storage makes it easier to integrate vague data for which there are yet no exact labels. It also helps in the processing of bits of information whose precise application in the project is yet unclear.

Characteristics of visualizers

Angie, a real estate agent, possesses an innate visualizing preference. She is an innovative problem solver, and approaches challenges from a global perspective. Her decisions tend to be intuitive and change-oriented; her solutions spontaneous and visionary. People who like Angie describe her as being very intuitive about new products. Those who don't like her say she has very little understanding of the concepts of budgets and hierarchy. Consequently, they tend to dismiss many of her solutions as impractical and unrealistic. Some of her coworkers enjoy her sense of humor; some complain that she is unpredictable, and that her artistic flair is somewhat inappropriate in a professional setting. Nevertheless, they concede that she usually grasps the big picture quickly, and, in retrospect, her ideas have often proved to be correct, even though they were not accepted at the time.

Individuals with this innate brain lead:

* Enjoy problem solving—innovatively. They are energized by solving problems. They may enjoy putting puzzles together, working geometry problems, solving trigonometry riddles, creating architectural designs, or drawing petrochemical diagrams. When insufficient data are available, or when there is no *track record*, so to speak, they often follow intuitive hunches. In such situations, they can often put together *gum-and-baling-*

wire solutions. They may work in fits and starts, often turning to a completely different activity while continuing to brainstorm. Their internal imagining may result in a wide spectrum of artistic creations and inventions ranging from bounded shapes to processes, and relating to any field.

- Identify trends. They possess the ability to analyze abstract patterns of information in a way that enables them to identify trends. You may hear them say something like, "Based on what is happening now, in order to be where we need to be in five years, this is what we need to do." The problem often is, however, that what they envision may be ten to fifteen years ahead of time in terms of what individuals with a lead in one of the other thinking styles may perceive. Consequently, visualizers can become discouraged and disillusioned. This can be especially true in artistic arenas. Many of our towering geniuses in the arts died sick, penniless, and heartbroken—only to have their work venerated and sold for millions of dollars a couple of hundred years later. There are endless examples of scholars, inventors, writers, and poets who were considered radicals or worse but whose contributions were eventually embraced with awe and not a little amazement. Examples include Gallileo who was excommunicated because he postulated that the world was round; and Florence Nightingale, who dared to establish the profession of nursing—a career-choice shunned by others of her own class.

- Foster humor. They have been called the guardians of comedy. Visualizers often possess an off-the-wall, sometimes bizarre, sense of humor. This enables them to chuckle at themselves and at the vagaries of life. They can find something funny in almost every situation—a quality that can prompt them to laugh when no one else is laughing. This tendency may be viewed by others as insensitivity, however, and as a lack of social appropriateness. They can deal with the absurd, and can learn through absurdities. While most people can eventually find some humor in a joke or cartoon, these individuals make this connection intuitively, and almost instantly. You may also find them using prosody (the addition of voice inflections or body language to put a different *twist* on what is actually said). For example, a raised eyebrow accompanying the words, "That's a brilliant idea," can portray a sarcastic opposite.

> From whatever place I write, expect that part of my *travels* will consist of excursions in my own mind. —Coleridge

- Create artistically. They can create artistically in almost any arena imaginable: painting, drawing, sculpting, writing stories/books/poems, photography, acting, composing, carving, *throwing* clay, architectural designing, entrepreneurialism, and so on. You may have seen individuals on a city street corner drawing caricatures of tourists; creating a likeness with exaggerated characteristics—often rather humorous exaggerations. They can process information that is received horizontally or upside down; one basis for Betty Edward's book, *Drawing on the Right Side of the Brain.*

- Dislike conflict. They (visualizers) don't like conflict, and may not like to discuss it verbally, either. Perhaps this is because their thinking style springs from internal pictures. If they can't avoid conflict, they may try to solve the problem quickly, using an unusual solution. If this doesn't work, they may withdraw physically and emotionally. Or, if pushed hard enough, they may suddenly switch to another thinking style and draw upon its skill as a last resort. They may access the prioritizing thinking style and try to argue, control, or negotiate; they may move into the harmonizing thinking style and try to placate by complying; they may even fight from the organizing thinking style and invoke rules and regulations.

- Love change. They can envision and create change. In fact, they enjoy it so much that at times they are wont to create change just for the variety—a predisposition that can appear very unpredictable, and even unstable, to others. Their motto could well be "a change is as good as a rest." They can be very spontaneous, bouncing from one project to another, from one idea to another, from one joy to another, even from one relationship to another. If the change is futuristic, innovative, and presents new perspectives in problem solving—so much the better. They are intuitive, dynamic, energetic, spontaneous, and sometimes leap before they look. This penchant for change can be acted out through the pursuit of travel, acting, or being a swinger; through expanding their horizons by associating with others who are different from them; through a continual pursuit of *learning* new information; even through moving to a new location and/or changing careers. They tend to want to change the environment in order to meet personal needs, rather than adapting to what already exists. This can provoke conflict with others who want to maintain the status quo.

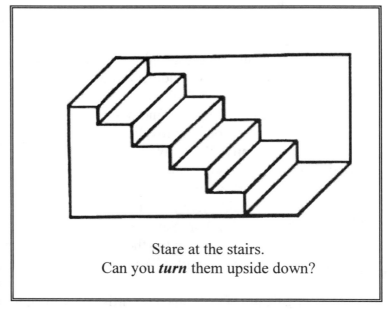

Stare at the stairs.
Can you *turn* them upside down?

The visualizing functions enable us to see the big picture. By comparing large amounts of data, visualizers are able to identify trends, and brainstorm desirable changes. They can mentally image what things will look like when the change is implemented, and are willing to take a risk and embrace the change.

Visualizers are not only visionary, they can inspire others to want to change and grow, as well. They are *creative* in the way in which they internally manipulate three-dimensional objects and abstract ideas. They often work best when they can come up with an ingenious innovation, get the project started, whip up enthusiasm among coworkers, and then leave the actual completion to someone else. They can experience stress when they are not allowed artistic freedom; when they are expected to conform to rigid rules and regulations; when they must try to repeat detailed routines accurately.

The weakness of this thinking style stems from a tendency to dislike rules, regulations, and routines. Consequently, it can quickly become bored, especially with details and repetition. This may explain why, in some studies, the majority of high-school dropouts were found to be students with this brain lead. They tried to fit into the organized routine of the average school environment, and simply found it too difficult, boring, or punishing. Unmanaged, the visualizer's giftedness in mental imaging can also be a weakness. As someone succinctly explained, "If you already picture the project completed in your mind's eye, why ever would you want to actually see the project through to completion? Let someone else do the detail work!"

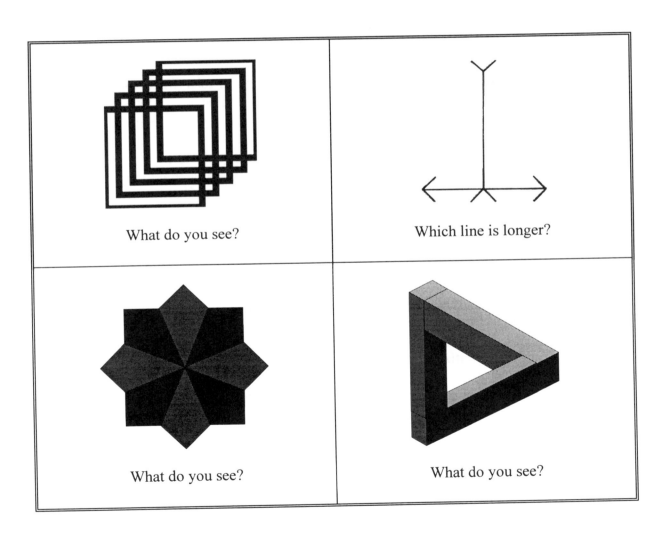

What do you see?

Which line is longer?

What do you see?

What do you see?

PRIORITIZING THINKING STYLE

The left frontal lobe houses the prioritizing thinking style which is also abstract (conceptual). It can handle abstract thinking, as well as the abstracting of information. The hallmark of this thinking style is its ability to make objective nonemotional decisions based on an inductive/deductive style of reasoning—often referred to as *logic*. This data-based type of thinking is prized in research. (The other three thinking styles are capable of making *rational* decisions—decisions that are reasonable, but not derived from inductive/deductive reasoning.)

Prioritizers ◎	Visualizers
Organizers	Harmonizers

This part of the brain enables us to take in and analyze information, from the environment, for the purpose of setting and achieving goals. We are able to assess different variables, classify them into groups, or rank them in order of importance; as well as weigh options, and select those most suited to accomplish the task at hand.

This part of the cerebrum helps us to focus on facts and scientific evidence. It excels at using numbers as in arithmetic, algebra, statistics, and calculus; and it likes to be correct. It definitely wants to minimize risk. Therefore, it is usually very deliberate when making decisions, and wants to have all the necessary data available—in black and white. Many department heads have met with their chief financial officer only to have their budget requests denied because of insufficient data, or because they were unable to argue their case persuasively. What this usually means is that they failed to present their request in a *logical* data-based format.

Prioritizing functions (including those orchestrated by Broca's Area, the primary speech center), enable us to understand the structure of language. For example, we can analyze it and figure out the verbs versus the adverbs; the nouns versus the adjectives; the dangling participles; the past, present, and future tenses. Prioritizers tend to think in words, and use language to communicate their decisions. They may also like to argue, criticize, and debate just for fun, finding such activities absolutely energizing.

Characteristics of prioritizers

Dennis, the financial vice president of a large health club, possesses an innate prioritizing lead. Those who value his skills describe him as analytical, factual, decisive. They say he has well-defined goals, stays on target, loves to achieve, and knows how to make both time and money work to his advantage. Dennis approaches problem solving from a logical perspective. He tends to make objective, nonemotional, resource-efficient decisions based on data. His solutions are usually fiscally sound and definitely geared to help him win. Those who do not like Dennis refer to him as a workaholic. They say he comes across as calculating and critical. A few complain that he is overly competitive (even exploitative at times), turning everything into a win-lose scenario. Dennis, of course, plans to win and, in the process, he can appear abrasively authoritarian.

Individuals with this innate brain lead:

- Set and pursue goals. They possess the potential ability to manage willpower, to follow through on their conscious choices, to do whatever it takes to realize their goals, and to *win*. The slogan *just say no* was likely coined for these individuals. Willed behavior is different from behavior that results from impulse or reflex. Willed behavior involves the establishment of goals, the evaluation of alternative courses of action, and the selection of the strategies most likely to result in success. They are also able to inhibit behaviors that don't contribute to perseverance and success in the face of obstacles and frustration.

- Seek to be in charge. They want to wield social and organizational power, and like to be in charge. They prefer to make all major decisions or at least select the individual who will. Overall, their desire is to direct the process for identifying, analyzing, and selecting the best options for success—based, of course, on hard data. They want to set the direc-

tion for themselves as individuals, for the family, for the corporation, for the nation, for the world, for outer space—if not for the universe! Some people joke that you can get these individuals to serve on almost any committee if you just *let them be the chair*.

- Analyze logically. They want to figure out how things work. These are the little children who want to dismantle the typewriter, or take the clock apart to see what makes it tick. They excel in diagnostic thinking. They can become the mechanics who discover what is wrong with broken machines and fix them. Or the physicians who diagnose disease in a sick body and come up with treatment recommendations. Many prioritizers excel at research; creating hypotheses and developing strategies to test them.

- Use tools. They like to use tools and machines of all kinds. These can range from a golf club to help them win the tournament to a computer to help them manipulate figures and project the profit margin for the year. In terms of hobbies or leisure activities they may enjoy repairing cars, appliances, machines, or buildings. They enjoy using tools in building, wood working, and making things like a kite. Because they use words as tools for communication, they often enjoy campaigning in politics or joining a debate club. They can offend others with their decisive,

> The brain is an apparatus with which we think that we think. —Bierce

somewhat abrupt, conversational style. This is usually unintentional. They usually cut right to the heart of the issue, and are oblivious to their impact on others. Some like to play the *devil's advocate*, just for the sheer pleasure it gives them. Two lawyers or two physicians who appear to be engaged in a heated argument may simply be polishing the art of verbal fencing—and enjoying every minute of it!

- Accept conflict. They (prioritizers) often view conflict as part of the game plan leading to success. If highly extroverted as well, they may welcome conflict in the form of competition. When conflict is undesirable, they want to make the decisions that will end it, and can invoke authoritative, coercive, or even exploitative power. While willing to confront, they may not recognize the feelings of others and may even approach conflict somewhat abrasively.

- Avoid change. In general, they don't want to change just for the sake of changing. Their philosophy can be summed up in the words, "If it ain't broke, don't fix it." They will embrace change, however, in the face of crisis—as long as the change is logical, fiscally sound, and facilitates the attainment of their goals. Once they decide change is necessary, they want to make the decisions and lead out in the change. They can expedite the process, although they tend to become impatient and may unwittingly offend others.

The functions of the prioritizing thinking style enable us to make tough decisions and to select the best options in a given situation. They provide us with the ability to set a direction in life, to prioritize the steps that need to be taken in order to be successful, and to actually accomplish what we set out to do. The *creativity* of this thinking style is exhibited in the way in which it sets and pursues goals.

The weakness of this thinking style stems from a tendency to pursue goal attainment at all costs, a trait that can encourage workaholism. In addition, prioritizers may be viewed by others as insensitive. In their attempts to assign tasks to others based on an analysis of who can do what best, they may be viewed as *people users.* There is usually nothing inherently sinister going on, however. They just want to reach their goals as quickly as possible and with a minimum of risk. They can actually experience stress when not allowed to make decisions, to set and achieve goals, and to lead. If not balanced by the competencies in the other thinking styles, prioritizers can blow up when frustrated or under stress—like a volcano that builds up a head of steam and then periodically erupts. This characteristic can be quite disconcerting to others.

FOUR DIFFERENT WORLDS

I sometimes compare the concept of thinking styles to a barbershop quartet. Although four individuals are singing, the sound differs depending on who is singing the lead. In a similar way, we all use parts of the cerebrum on a daily basis. The thinking style we prefer, however, depends upon our individual brain lead.

Recently, I was discussing the concept of brain lead with a courtroom attorney. Part way through our conversation he said, "That explains why four different individuals can present testimony, and each story sounds like it's from a different planet!" He related a court session he had attended not long ago. The case involved a two-vehicle accident. Four witnesses had been subpoenaed to give testimony. "I'll bet we were looking at four different brain leads," the attorney continued, and summarized the four witnesses as follows:

- Witness one (organizer) reported conversation that had been overheard at the accident site as well as details related to the bounded shapes (the little red sports car had virtually been flattened by the huge semitrailer rig), and cited the rules of the road that had been broken.

- Witness two (harmonizer) described the relationship of the vehicles to each other in terms of position (the sports car had all but disappeared under the semi), cited the injuries of the victims, mentioned the groans emitted by the wounded, and described the weather—drizzle accompanied by biting wind.

- Witness three (visualizer) speculated on the possible actions of each driver that had resulted in the wreck, and readily teared up when relating the death of the sports-car driver.

- Witness four (prioritizer) was critical of signage on that portion of the highway, told the judge he should *throw the book* at the truck driver, and made mention of the fact that the highway patrol had asked for blood-alcohol tests.

Four different points of view; each one contributing information not readily absorbed or perceived by the others. At present, our legal system is set up to determine who is right and who is wrong; who is telling the truth and who is lying. How interesting it might be if the system, instead, sought for the collective truth based on four different perspectives because each thinking style has something very special to contribute.

ACCESS

As mentioned earlier, we can access any thinking style, drawing from the unique functions each contributes. Ideally, we can choose to access any style, at any given moment, based on the need. That's one of the benefits of developing competencies throughout the cerebrum. In essence, we build *highways* that permit us to access all functions regardless of brain lead (although the metabolic energy required will differ). Ideally, we can also engage in whole-brained teamwork. Definite benefits, such as exponentially improved outcomes, can result when a select caucus of brains (all four thinking styles represented) collaborate. Both ideals are definitely attainable. A lack of individual access to a particular thinking style, or a lack of representation of a specific thinking style in group interactions, holds implications for potentially diminished outcomes.

Unbalanced, each one of us is at risk for exhibiting less-than-desirable behaviors. For example:

- Organizers want consistency, predictability, and routine but they don't have to become stubborn, proliferate rigid rules, avoid all change/spontaneity, and miss opportunities for personal growth.

- Harmonizers crave harmony and collegiality, but they don't have to exhibit a victim stance by constantly appeasing, overcomplying, or violating conscience in an attempt to avoid all conflict and confrontation.

- Visualizers desire innovation, the opportunity to risk creatively, and freedom from restrictions; but they don't have to break the law, flaunt societal conventions, and avoid all details.

- Prioritizers aspire to set and attain goals, but they don't have to become workaholic, run roughshod over others in their quest for control, insist upon making all of the decisions in every situation, and run the risk of becoming an offender.

Brain lead does not constitute an absolute mandate for stereotypical action. Understanding our innate preferences and the way in which we tend to approach interactions with the environment and with others does not leave us without free choice. Depending upon the situation, we may select functions from a nonlead style to enhance those of our preference in order to realize more effective outcomes. We may make a concerted effort to develop competencies in all thinking styles; we can learn to recognize those times when teaming up with those who are gifted in our areas of weakness can be efficacious. These strategies can not only improve our outcomes, they can also be fun to implement.

> Half a brain is better than none;
> A whole brain is second to none.
> —Cherney

In general, society rewards thinking styles differently by gender. Males are rewarded for exhibiting prioritizing competencies; females for harmonizing skills. Because of our westernized industrial-type economy, we all get to practice organizing skills. With very few exceptions, neither males nor females are rewarded for visualizing strengths—until a couple of hundred years after their demise. Then, their creative contributions may be venerated and ascribed astronomical value.

SOCIETAL REWARDS BY GENDER

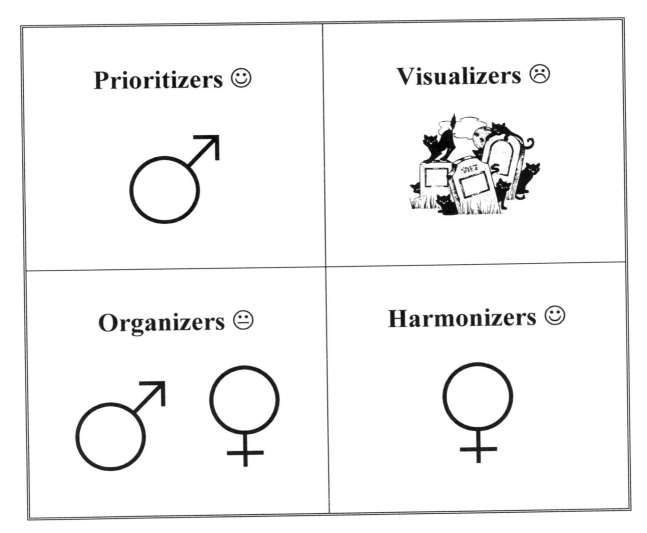

Individuals whose innate brain lead does not match societal expectations may experience subtle and not-so-subtle pressure to conform. This process can begin at a very young age and can include role-modeling, specific verbal directives, lack of opportunity or support for choices that fall outside of approved expectations, and outright punishment. In general, females are pushed to exhibit competencies in the harmonizing thinking style; males, in the prioritizing. (In our culture, everyone is given opportunity to practice organizing skills, and are expected to evidence some level of competency). The higher one's level of extroversion, the greater the risk of excessive/prolonged adaption. (Refer to Chapter Seven for examples.)

BRAIN BUILDERS

Points to Ponder

- No great improvements in the lot of mankind are possible, until a great change takes place in the fundamental constitution of their modes of thought. —John Stuart Mill

- Two key concepts I have learned in this section:

  _____

  _____

- Two facets I've discovered about myself while studying this section:

  _____

  _____

- One way in which I am now applying this information:

  _____

  _____

- Neurons are the _____ cells of the brain.

- All thinking styles are of equal _____, although they may be rewarded differently by society.

- Unfortunately for some individuals, society generally rewards thinking styles differently based on _____.

- **T F** The concept of a *brain lead* is consistent with preferences we observe in other parts of the body.

- **T F** Cultivating ambidexterity is not helpful to brain development.

- **T F** Brain lead pushes us toward two different types of relationships.

Brain Teasers

1.	2.	3.	4.
S M T W T __	# OF SQUARES?	STAND I	

Creativity Corner

THE FACES OF ALERTNESS

Chapter Three
Extroversion/Introversion

In our culture, the words extroversion and introversion have often been used to define external behaviors; the degree to which people like other people, and whether or not a person is outgoing or shy in terms of communicating with others. More properly, these terms describe the brain's level of alertness. Each human brain comes wired with a built-in alertness factor that can be expressed as an E:I ratio—falling somewhere along a continuum that stretches from the extremely extroverted brain at one end to the extremely introverted brain at the opposite end. Our individual E:I ratio may be as important to our sense of *self* as brain lead. In fact, we may only be able to make the best use of innate giftedness when the environment matches our brain's innate level of alertness.

EXTROVERSION/INTROVERSION CONTINUUM

12:0 11:1 10:2	9:3 8:4	7:5 6:6 5:7	4:8 3:9	2:10 1:11 0:12
15% EXTREME EXTROVERTS	HIGH EXTROVERTS	BALANCED E:I RATIO	HIGH INTROVERTS	15% EXTREME INTROVERTS

- Fifteen percent of the population are extremely extroverted. They seek stimulation in order to feel alert because their brain is too *sleepy.*

- Fifteen percent of the population are extremely introverted. They back away from stimulation because their brain is too wide *awake.*

- The remaining seventy percent of the population fall between these extremes. Their needs for stimulation reflect their individual position on the continuum.

EXTREME EXTROVERTS

Extreme extroverts, about fifteen percent of the population, are believed to be born with a brain that innately requires a great deal of stimulation to keep it alert and interested. We can say that their brain is too *sleepy* or that the diameter of their metaphoric camera lens is very small. Their lower-than-average level of alertness causes them to seek for higher-than-average levels of stimulation in order to feel vibrantly alive. They may try to obtain this stimulation in a wide variety of ways: through competitive activities, through connecting with large groups of people, or through positioning themselves where the *action* is. They are focused outwardly in that they are intent on influencing their environment, whatever that is (natural, human, mechanical), and in return, the brain receives the stimulation it craves in order to feel comfortable.

Their need for stimulation often pushes them toward competition. They can view most situations as an opportunity to *win*. They wouldn't think of playing a game of tennis or volleyball without keeping score. Keeping score provides additional stimulation to the

brain. (An exception might be an extremely extroverted harmonizer who manifests E:I ratio through behaviors that promote harmony.)

For a couple of years after graduating from college, I played the ukulele with the San Juan Valley Singers. Decades later I picked up a ukulele and tried to play it. I was amazed to find how tender the ends of my fingers felt. The calluses had disappeared.

We could say metaphorically, that extreme extroverts possess a *cerebral callus* that allows them to function in situations that would be extremely difficult (if not impossible) for an extreme introvert. For example, extreme extroverts can usually handle the crowded environments and high levels of sound often associated with assembly lines. They can survive as war correspondents or as traders in the Wall Street *pit*.

Another example would be politicians on the campaign trail. They must greet and mingle with thousands of potential voters. They never know what the press will report about them next. If they agree to a debate, it's anybody's guess what their opponents might say—on national television, no less! Who but an extrovert could enter such a competition and survive?

Because of this cerebral callus, extreme extroverts are at higher risk than introverts to adapt away from natural brain lead in order to fit in and achieve success. In other words, they can usually do whatever it takes, even when doing so exacts a high personal toll. Their E:I ratio can, at least for a time, override brain lead. Researcher Roy King of Stanford University reports that dopamine has been found in higher levels in the brains of extroverts (as compared to introverts), which may help to account for some of the differences.

Extremely extroverted infants may stop crying only when they're passed back and forth among fifteen different individuals. Extremely extroverted children who lack sufficient brain stimulation may rock back and forth, drum fingers against the table, or even bang their heads on the wall or a chair.

In general, extroverts:

- Seek stimulation in order to wake themselves up because the brain possesses lower-than-average levels of alertness

- Are outer-directed, constantly interacting with the external environment

- May be participative and highly competitive, especially if they also possess a prioritizing brain lead

- Are viewed by introverts as restless, noisy, argumentative, and even hyperactive

- May be at higher risk for delinquency because they are often easily bored and are continually searching for something exciting

EXTREME INTROVERTS

Extreme introverts, about fifteen percent of the population, are believed to be born with a brain that innately requires very little stimulation to keep it alert and interested. We can say that their brain is too wide-awake; that the opening on their metaphoric camera lens is very large. Their higher-than-average level of alertness pushes them to seek lower-than-average levels of stimulation in order to avoid being overwhelmed. Because the brain is so super alert, it needs to periodically take a break in order to process the vast amounts of information it takes in. This tendency to back off from stimulation, to be more inner-directed, facilitates their continued quest for mastery, understanding, and comfort. Introverts may enjoy relating to others very much—as much as do extreme extroverts—but they don't so consistently put themselves *where the action is*. They do not need other people and activities to keep their brain stimulated in the way in which extroverts do. In fact, extreme introverts may, at times, be viewed as rude because all they want is to be left alone.

George was a young high-school graduate who engaged in selling children's home-library books, door-to-door, hoping to earn a major portion of his future college tuition. He painstakingly applied himself to the task and worked long hours. Sales were slow. George was near exhaustion and burnout. It was so difficult for him to face rejection, especially that meted out before he was even able to progress beyond the threshold of a home with children who would benefit from his product. Fortunately, he was able to procure a job as an equipment operator in highway construction. He worked twelve-hour days but the job seemed

like play. In fact, he liked construction so well that he gave up his plans for college.

Several years later, George discovered that introverts and door-to-door sales aren't really that compatible, no matter what the age of the marketer or the name of the product. This knowledge helped George to realize that his lack of success as a salesperson was due neither to a lack of purpose, nor to some basic defect in his character. Laughingly he told a good friend, "Now I realize that I provided both roads and room for the extroverts—so they could sell the books!"

Extremely introverted infants may stop crying only when they are put down and allowed to lie quietly instead of being rocked. An extremely introverted child may periodically go off to play or rest in solitude. Highly introverted adults may try to moderate the level of stimulation to which their brain is exposed in a variety of ways. They may spend time reading, or exercising alone. They may limit their interaction with others to small groups, or may take vacations in locations that are off the beaten track. Extreme introverts usually prefer working independently or in small teams (e.g., doing research or writing books). They prefer low volumes of sound as in libraries, backroom offices, and research labs.

In general, introverts:

- Back-off from stimulation in order to prevent overloading their already super-alert brain

- Are inner-directed, constantly processing the large amounts of data they take in

- Prefer to avoid competition

- May be viewed by extroverts as quiet, observers, wallflowers, or bookworms

- May feel like *misfits* in our society

- May be at higher risk for depression because of their tendency to process information internally, and because society does not generally reward introversion.

BALANCED EXTROVERSION/INTROVERSION

As mentioned earlier, the majority of individuals are neither extremely extroverted nor extremely introverted. They can handle most office-type situations, prefer moderate amounts of sound in the environment, and can excel at a variety of jobs including some sales positions.

When individuals don't understand what they need, how they operate, or the differences between an extremely alert brain and one that requires great amounts of stimulation, they can seriously misunderstand behaviors in themselves and in others. Their relationships will definitely be impacted.

I often refer to the dog/cat analogy in this context. We wouldn't think of expecting a cat to bark or a dog to meow. We routinely, however, expect human beings to exhibit behaviors outside their innate giftedness. Not only that, we tend to put pressure on others to conform to our expectations—in subtle, and sometimes not so subtle, ways.

SUMMARY OF EXTROVERSION/INTROVERSION EXTREMES

Extremely Extroverted Brain	**Extremely Introverted Brain**
• Possesses ↓ than average levels of alertness (camera has small *lens*)	• Possesses ↑ than average levels of alertness (camera has large *lens*)

Extreme Extroverts	**Extreme Introverts**
• Are usually outer-directed	• Are usually inner-directed
• Continually interact with the environment to obtain the stimulation they need to feel vibrantly alive	• To avoid overload, periodically back off from stimulation in order to process the huge amounts of data absorbed
• Are able to perform in situations that would be difficult (if not impossible) for a more introverted brain	• Are able to retreat *inwardly* almost automatically to evaluate the data in their search for insight
• May be very competitive as competition provides more stimulation	• May avoid competition whenever possible

• May be viewed by others as:
  - noisy
  - hyperactive
  - participative
	• May be viewed by others as:
	  - very quiet
	  - wallflowers or as readers
	  - observers

• Tend to become easily bored	• May feel like *misfits*
• Are at higher risk for delinquency	• Are at higher risk for depression

SOCIETAL REWARDS

In Europe during the Middle Ages, introversion was generally valued over extroversion. Individuals who were highly introverted often entered one of the religious orders. This was especially true if they also possessed a harmonizing brain lead. It was considered a high honor to be in this category. Away from the bustle of materialism, introverts found solitude. Some also found validation for their abilities to study, nurture, and write. Others found that such an environment was conducive to developing a spiritual connection with a Higher Power.

Gradually, as the shift toward industrialization occurred, extroversion came to be more highly valued, rewarded, and encouraged. In our present culture, extroversion has been rewarded to the point of devaluing introversion. This is unfortunate, because both types of brain-alertness levels represent natural phenomena that occur in normal distribution patterns.

> If the human brain were so simple that we could understand it, we would be so simple that we couldn't. —Pugh

The labels simply describe the personally unique ways in which different individuals respond to their environments and/or seek radically different environments. Individual E:I ratios help us to understand why some people hate to be alone, and why others crave alone time. If only we would let them be! If only we would learn to accept and validate individuals as they innately are!

Societal conditioning especially impacts children. Extremely introverted children are often pushed toward competition, and may even be punished for a perceived lack of participation. Extremely extroverted children are often punished and/or medicated with Ritalin (a brain stimulant) in an effort to dampen their stimulation-seeking behaviors. A recent news report indicated that in America Ritalin is prescribed five times more often than in any other nation. For many of these children, a more extroverted and whole-brained-learning environment could be a better long-term solution.

TWO SIDES OF ONE COIN

Benziger's research indicates that many individuals regularly use the skills of at least one thinking style in addition to that of their cerebral lead. Depending upon whether they are utilizing lead skills or auxiliary skills, they may exhibit their extroversion/introversion ratios differently. Think of it as two sides

of one coin. High extroverts tend to exhibit their extroversion (by relating outwardly to others and to the environment) when actuating brain-lead. When using their auxiliary thinking style, however, they tend to move toward the introverted portion of their E:I ratio. That is, they exhibit behaviors that appear more introverted.

High introverts tend to exhibit their introversion (by processing internally) when actuating brain-lead functions. When using their auxiliary thinking style, however, they tend to move toward the extroverted portion of their E:I ratio, relating outwardly to others and to the environment.

If their auxiliary thinking style is more highly valued by society, they may build strong competencies in that rewarded style—so much so that they may actually be viewed as naturally gifted in its functions. Excessive or prolonged utilization of nonlead thinking styles is referred to as *adaption*. The ensuing increased metabolic-energy expenditure can lead to burnout and midlife crisis. (Refer to Chapter Seven.)

Because high introverts in our culture are not rewarded for their innate giftedness, they may experience prolonged anxiety. They may even try to exhibit extroverted behavior and exhaust themselves in the process. Chronic anxiety can also be triggered by other situa-

tions (e.g., abuse, catastrophic/chronic illness, or unresolved grief). Recognized or unrecognized, it can have an unfortunate effect upon our lives.

Individuals (both children and adults) who are considered to be *highly emotional* may be struggling to hold onto their brain lead in the face of opposition, or are excessively adapting in order to succeed—and their brains know it. They often experience chronic anxiety because they are working hard at tasks that do not match their innate aptitudes, or are working in environments that don't match their individual E:I ratios, or sensory preference.

The brain may respond to chronic anxiety (usually two years or more) by gravitating toward protective alertness—what I refer to as situational introversion. This accounts for the change in our usual manner of relating to others when we are going through very stressful times. With resolution of the problems, when we are able to return to a level of safety and comfort, the brain will usually shift back to its innate E:I ratio.

Here is a general rule of thumb: Avoid making any major lifestyle changes for at least twelve months after experiencing major stress (e.g., death of a partner, bankruptcy, divorce). Studies have found that individuals who remarry within twelve months of the death or divorce of a spouse are at significantly increased risk of separating within five years.

Perhaps one of the contributors to this potential risk is the shift toward protective alertness that can occur in the presence of chronic anxiety. With resolution of the anxiety, when the brain returns to its natural extroversion/introversion ratio, these individuals may be uncomfortable with their earlier choices.

PROTECTIVE ALERTNESS SUMMARY

The brain may respond to chronic anxiety (usually two years duration or longer) by gravitating toward protective alertness (situational introversion)

FACTORS THAT
CAN CONTRIBUTE
TO CHRONIC ANXIETY:

- Abuse
- Catastrophic events
- Chronic stress
- Crisis
- Dysfunctional environment
- Excessive adaption
- Severe illness

When the chronic anxiety is resolved and the brain perceives a return to comfort and safety, it can readjust to its innate E:I ratio

TALK THE TALK

Several years ago, I was invited to speak at an AA meeting. After my presentation, one of the participants thanked me for giving him some *new words*. He explained that the more he was able to verbalize recovery concepts—*talk the talk* he called it—the less stress he experienced, the better others seemed to understand what he was trying to accomplish, and the more successful he was in attaining his goals. I borrowed that concept and have found it to be truly helpful.

In childhood, I did not feel accepted or rewarded for skills congruent with my preferences as an auditory, highly-introverted visualizer. I felt much more accepted and rewarded for skills congruent with an extroverted harmonizer. Consequently, for more years than I care to count, I often overextended myself. The additional energy expenditure contributed, no doubt, to a slightly suppressed immune system. Case in point. I was diagnosed with bronchopneumonia four Christmas seasons in a row. Back then I didn't get the connection, however. Talk about a slow learner!

As I discovered my innate preferences, I gradually began to choose with much greater care the situations in which I voluntarily placed myself. Almost immediately, my energy level increased and my illness episodes decreased. I learned to set healthy bona fide boundaries (well, I'm still learning). And I started *talking the talk*—articulating brain function information in my conversation with others.

One of the first times I applied this strategy was with a caller who wanted permission to place my name on the ballot for a county office. The very thought nearly made me nauseous. Rather than trying to make some feeble-sounding excuse, I chose to *talk the talk*:

Caller: The committee voted unanimously that you are just the person for this position; we're sure you'll win the election.

Me: Thank you for the vote of confidence. However, my extroversion/introversion ratio is incompatible with an election campaign. Just thinking of the energy it would require absolutely wipes me out. Therefore, I'm unable to acquiesce to your request.

Caller: Absolute silence.

Me: Hello? Are you still there?

Caller: I'm not sure I understand everything you've said, but I'll forward your reply to the committee. Bye.

Me: Help us all! It really worked. No argument at all! Chuckle, chuckle. Now I can get back to work on my next presentation. Speaking at a packed workshop—that's something my brain really enjoys!

Who wants to be where the action is?

INNATE PREFERENCES AND CAREER EXAMPLES

A whole host of factors influences not only the selection of a career, but also the level to which required skills (competencies) are honed. These factors can include brain lead, gender, sensory preference, expectations, our degree of self-esteem, available resources, what is *popular* at the time, and who our role models or mentors are. In addition, individuals with a similar brain lead might choose to express their giftedness in very different settings because of differing extroversion/introversion ratios and/or sensory preference.

Although overall success can usually be enhanced through a whole-brained approach, most careers require proficiency in a certain set of skills that usually derive from only one or two thinking styles. This can help to explain why tri-brainers sometimes have difficulty not only selecting a career, but being satisfied with it over time.

Following are some examples of career matches:

- **Prioritizers** (quarter-brainers) often gravitate toward scientific research, or professions such as banking, public administration, and engineering. They become business leaders, mathematicians, certified public accountants, auditors, financial vice presidents, chairs of corporate boards, members of hospital/community boards, military generals, physicians, and auto mechanics. Trying to diagnose illness in a human body or to figure out malfunction in an engine requires a similar type of inductive/deductive reasoning. Extroverts gravitate toward leadership and hard-ball negotiation; introverts toward research.

- **Prioritizers-organizers** (half-brainers), sometimes referred to as left-brainers, might gravitate toward law, dentistry, medicine, electrical engineering, operations management, intensive-care nursing, and machine operation.

- **Organizers** (quarter-brainers) might choose administration, middle management, or assembly-line positions. They can be found as librarians, computer wizards, school administrators, operating-room scrub techs, dental hygienists, bookkeepers, and clerks of all kinds. They can be excellent line supervisors, and excel at any job that requires structuring and careful attention to detail. High extroverts might gravitate toward assembly lines or toward mechanics (working with or repairing machines). Introverts would likely prefer uninterrupted work such as managing data in a library/office, bookkeeping, or the stocking of supplies.

- **Organizers-harmonizers** (half-brainers) might choose to be waiters, chefs, secretaries, school teachers, therapists, head nurses, supervisors, receptionists, probation officers, and neighborhood police. Extroverts might choose to work in large, bustling corporations or for politicians—especially during a campaign. High introverts would naturally gravitate toward quieter work environments.

- **Harmonizers** (quarter-brainers) often gravitate toward some form of counseling, teaching, home economics, or nursing (e.g., medical-surgical). They might become chaplains or pediatricians. Extroverts might become school teachers, staff development specialists, or public relations directors. Introverts might choose a career in music, acting, or interior decorating.

- **Harmonizers-visualizers** (half-brainers), sometimes referred to as right-brainers, might become home health nurses, exotic dancers, painters, or poets. If extroverted, they might enjoy marketing, organizational development, or public relations. If introverted, they might gravitate toward a career in music, acting, interpretive dancing, or interior designing and decorating.

- **Visualizers** (quarter-brainers) are often drawn to careers that allow them to use their troubleshooting skills. Geologists, psychiatrists, emergency-department physicians, and urologists fit into this category, as do the mad scientist and the dreamer. High extroverts often gravitate to highly-challenging endeavors (e.g., putting out oil-well fires, entrepreneurial ventures, commissioned sales). High introverts might lean toward computer programming, philosophy, psychiatry, creative writing, artistic endeavors, musical composition, or interior designing.

- **Visualizers-prioritizers** (half-brainers) might gravitate to architecture, chemical engineering, building contracting, orthodontia, or surgery. If extroverted, they might join a SWAT team, or become fire fighters or business leaders. If introverted, they might become artists, investigative journalists, creative writers, poets, economists, or research scientists.

When we can select a career that matches our innate aptitudes, we are usually happier, healthier, and more successful. To facilitate a desirable career match, our environment must provide appropriate competency-learning opportunities, contain appropriate tools/accessories, and must reward us for using our natural aptitudes. Nonetheless, we, individually, need to take responsibility for seeking the knowledge, opportunity, support, and nurturing that can help us to match our career to our innate giftedness.

The chiefest point of happiness is that individuals are willing to be themselves.
—Erasmus

BRAIN BUILDERS

Points to Ponder

- The golden opportunity you are seeking is in yourself. —Marden

- Two key concepts I have learned in this section:

  _____

  _____

- Two facts I've learned about myself while studying this section:

  _____

  _____

- One way in which I am now applying this information:

  _____

  _____

- Metaphorically speaking, extroverts possess a cerebral _____
  that allows them to function in situations that would be extremely difficult
  for introverts.

- Introverts generally back off from _____ in order to prevent overloading their already superalert brain.

- Individuals labeled highly _____ may be struggling to
  hold onto their innate giftedness in the face of opposition.

- **T F** Extroversion/introversion describe the brain's alertness level.

- **T F** Introverts may feel like _misfits_ in our society.

- **T F** Chronic anxiety may push one's brain toward extroversion.

Brain Teasers

1.	2.	3.	4.
/READING/	CRYING IKML	ECNALG	O T T F F S S __

Creativity Corner

APPROACH TO SPIRITUALITY/WORSHIP ACTIVITIES

PRIORITIZERS

- Systematic

- Drawn toward:

- hierarchic worship
- doctrinal study
- preaching/proof texting
- public prayer
- power of office
- developing conscience
- managing willpower

VISUALIZERS

- Unconventional

- Drawn toward:

- independent worship
- individual study
- stories, drama, plays
- meditation
- new music and liturgy
- imagination/conjecture
- innovation

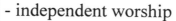

ORGANIZERS

- Traditional

- Drawn toward:

- conservative worship
- attending church
- group study
- following rules/routines
- memorizing scripture
- reading holy books
- maintaining status quo

HARMONIZERS

- Relational

- Drawn toward:

- collegial worship
- group retreats
- spirituality
- private prayer
- music/drama
- potlucks
- nurturing/connection

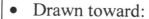

Chapter Four
Whole-brained Worship

One afternoon, little three-year-old Jeni came running into the house and found her mother visiting with the new neighbor lady. The lady was introduced to Jeni, and, trying to be friendly, asked, "What were you doing outside all by yourself?" Blonde, bubbly, imaginative Jeni quickly replied, "I've been playing in heaven. A big swan gave me a ride on the River of Life."

The neighbor lady, who was not religiously inclined, asked with a twinkle in her eye, "If you were riding a swan on the River of Life, whatever that is, why aren't your shoes wet?" Jeni paused for a moment, looked down at her feet, and replied, "I wanted to talk to Jesus, so the swan took me over to the bank. It fluffed its feathers and dried off my shoes."

After the neighbor went home, Jeni's mother spanked the little girl and put her to bed without any supper—for lying. Mother obviously didn't realize that the ability to distinguish between imaginary scenes and actual happenings is a function of the frontal lobes of the brain, not yet mature in a child of Jeni's age.

Little Jeni was a fast learner. Several weeks later, the neighbor lady came over to visit again. When Jeni bounced into the house, the lady greeted her pleasantly and asked, "Does that swan still take you for rides, Jeni?"

Jeni hung her head and softly replied, "Nope, I don't go there anymore." She had stopped using the power of imagination—at least to think about playing in heaven. Jeni had begun the socialization process that most of us go through as children, a socialization that generally rewards functions of the left hemisphere over those of the right. This process can push us toward adaption and can reduce our options, at least temporarily.

BIBLICAL EXAMPLES

As I study brain function, I believe it is not only possible, but also signally desirable, to develop a personal relationship with a Higher Power from the perspective of our own individual uniqueness, while being open to expanding our interactive awareness from the perspective of the other three thinking styles, as well. (I call my Higher Power God, but recognize that others may use different labels.)

The great commandment admonishes us to love the Lord with all our heart, soul, and mind (Matthew 22:37; Mark 12:30). Many of us haven't taken time to really ponder what this means. We can strive for connection with our Higher Power, personally and corporately, with all our mind. Our relative comfort level with specific worship activities, along with our approach to affiliation with religion and to a spiritual connection with a Higher Power, are rooted in a myriad of determinants. These factors range from gender differences to socialization experiences, and include perceptions and preferences based on brain lead, sensory preference, and extroversion/introversion ratios, just to name a few. We can worship from the position of our own innate uniqueness; we can learn to honor, and even appreciate, the worship styles preferred by others.

The parable of the talents (Matthew 25) makes it clear that each one of us has at least one outstanding aptitude. Unfortunately, we sometimes get caught in the trap of comparing our talents to those of others. We may even worry about whether what we have is good enough to be shared. Paul makes it very clear that if the willingness is there, the gift is acceptable according to what one has (2 Corinthians 8:12). If the environment is nurturing, and we are encouraged to develop a particular aptitude congruent with our brain lead, we may exhibit that talent. Otherwise, we may *bury* it until later in life. Grandma Moses possessed an aptitude for painting; yet she didn't really develop and express that talent until her late seventies. It is never too late to begin! As with worship, we can offer our talents to God from the position of our own innate giftedness; we can learn to honor and appreciate the differing gifts offered by others.

Learning more about the way in which the brain functions has changed the way I relate to descriptions of historical events, especially biblical events. As a PK (preacher's kid), I grew up hearing many stories from the best-selling book of all time. At some level I believed that the Bible characters had once been alive; but basically they were one-dimensional personalities. No longer. Against this emerging backdrop of relevant research (and especially since our travels in Jordan, Israel, and Egypt) these same characters have sprung to life. They now exist for me in three-dimensional living color. I try to imagine the probable thinking style, sensory preference, and extroversion/introversion ratio of each one.

I actually view stories of Christ's life differently, as well. Recorded history suggests that not only was Christ whole-brained, but that He also practiced a pattern of nurturing communication that incorporated the three main sensory systems. No doubt, He must have been balanced in terms of extroversion/introversion, as well. There are descriptions of His mingling with the multitudes, and also of withdrawing to a quiet place for prayer and meditation. He was the ultimate example of a whole-brained speaker; one who could attract and hold the attention of one individual, or an entire multitude. The Apostle Mark (4:34) reports that Christ always used parables when addressing the multicultural audiences that flocked to hear Him speak.

Not too long ago, a friend phoned to say, "I've been studying the Bible from the perspective of brain function. Have you noted the three-part prescription for whole-brained spirituality?" I hadn't, and was delighted with the reference. Here is a brief summary of the passage (1 Thessalonians 5:16-18):

First, we are admonished to rejoice always. We are not promised that we will like everything that happens to us; life can be very turbulent like the surface of the ocean in a storm. Beneath the turbulence, however, far below the surface there is a calm stillness. Just so, we can develop a deep inner joy and a contentment that is not based on circumstances.

Second, we are encouraged to pray continually, to open our hearts to God, to be in that attitude of connectedness at all times. Remember the bumper sticker that read, "There's nothing that God and I can't handle together." What a great description of being associated with the ultimate source of energy and wisdom!

Third, we are challenged to give thanks in all circumstances. This doesn't mean we necessarily give thanks for everything that happens to us, but we can always find something to be thankful for in all situations.

WHOLE-BRAINED SPIRITUALITY

Rejoice always

Pray continually

Give thanks in all circumstances

Sometimes, individuals affiliated with established religion are a bit skeptical, if not downright fearful, about exploring brain-function information. They occasionally ask, "Is it biblical?" Absolutely. The Bible is filled with stories of individuals who exhibited behaviors based on either their innate giftedness or weakness.

Recently, I received a letter from a radio listener asking why there were *four* gospels, instead of one or three or ten. (I should know?) I think there are four because all four thinking styles needed to be represented. Each author appeals to readers with a similar preference. Try reading each gospel in the light of brain-function information. Which one seems easiest for you to understand? Notice the similarities and the differences. Here is how I identify writer preferences:

WHICH GOSPEL IS YOUR FAVORITE?

A physician

- Recorded facts after a thorough investigation
- Used a variety of medical terms
- Traced Christ's ancestry back to Adam

The first gospel writer

- Wrote innovatively with dramatic vitality
- Emphasized the unusual (miracles, signs, wonders)
- Presented Christ as a Man of *action*

A tax collector

- Wrote a historical narrative
- Reported several sermons in their entirety
- Presented Christ as a *Teacher*

The beloved apostle

- Wrote of connection, and faith in the gospel
- Emphasized the coming of the *Comforter*
- Presented Christ as the *Word* of God

To get you started exploring brain-function from a biblical perspective, I've included some scriptural references that correlate each thinking style to examples of worship activities, selected Bible characters, and common religious controversies. Watch for examples in other inspirational writings, as well.

ORGANIZING PREFERENCE

Skills that derive from the organizing preference help us to:

- Be on guard. Acts 20:30-31

- Follow traditions and worship routines. Luke 22: 17-19; Psalm 55:17. Daniel continued his custom of praying three times a day in spite of orders to the contrary. Daniel 6:10

- Follow the rules. Hebrews 13:17; Mark 12:17; 2 Timothy 2:5

- Listen to sermons, readings, and to the voice of God. 1 Samuel 3:10; Exodus 19:8; Matthew 13:23; Isaiah 39:5. Often, we get so busy asking God for things that we fail to

listen in return. In most cases, we will hear God's voice only if we listen for it. You may have heard the anecdote about two men who were walking along a crowded sidewalk in the center of a busy city. Suddenly one turned to the other and exclaimed, "Listen to the lovely sound of that cricket." A zoologist, he had trained himself to listen for the voices of nature. The other man couldn't hear the cricket, and wondered aloud how in the world his friend could detect the sound of a cricket amid the din all around them. Rather than explaining verbally, the zoologist took a coin from his pocket and dropped it on the sidewalk. Immediately, several individuals began searching for the coin. "You see," he proffered, "people hear what they're interested in."

- Pay attention to detail. Mary and Joseph didn't pay enough attention to detail, and temporarily lost track of their Son on a trip to Jerusalem. Luke 2:43-46

- Remember the words of the Lord. 1 Corinthians 15:2; Isaiah 46: 8-9

- Serve others in a fitting manner. Luke 22:26. Martha honed organizational skills into a fine art. John 12:2. So did Phoebe. Romans 16:1-2.

- Read the Bible and other instructional books. 2 Timothy 2:15; Romans 15:4. Organizers tend to read the Bible to discover *how to* live right; to identify the rules that need to be followed. They may also read to discover what happened in history, and are the most likely to memorize names and dates associated with biblical history.

HARMONIZING PREFERENCE

Skills that derive from the harmonizing preference help us to:

- Accept God's gift of salvation. John 3:16

- Ask for God's gifts and give gifts in return. Matthew 6:3-15; Psalm 96:8-9

- Assemble together to worship. Psalm 122:1; Hebrews 10:25

- Clap our hands with joy. Psalm 47:1

- Encourage one another. Hebrews 10:25; Luke 22:32; 1 Thessalonians 5:11

- Engage in private prayer and communication with our Higher Power. Matthew 6:5-14; Colossians 4:2-4; James 5:13; Luke 6:12; Luke 9:28; John 17:1-26

- Exhibit gracious speech. Colossians 4:6; Proverbs 25:11

- Feel our feelings. Hebrews 4:15; Philippians 4:4; Philemon 1:7; Ephesians 4:26

- Give thanks. Colossians 1:12; Colossians 3: 15-17; 1 Thessalonians 5:16-18

- Inform/help others. 2 Kings 5:2-4; Mark 5:19; Matthew 6:1-4; 1 Timothy 6:18. Harmonizers tend to read the Scriptures to connect with the Bible characters through the stories; to discover what happened to each of the individuals and to learn from their recorded experiences; to develop a spiritual experience with a Higher Power.

- Love one another and exhibit appropriate touch. 1 Thessalonians 5:26. 1 John 3:23; I John 4:7-19; 1 Thessalonians 4:9-10; Colossians 3:13-14; 1 Peter 4:8

- Play musical instruments and sing songs. Psalm 98:5-6; Psalm 1:2-3; 81:1; 98:4; 1 Corinthians. 14:15

- Praise. Isaiah 42:11; Psalm 103:1-2; Psalm 100; Psalm 66:1; Psalm 95:1. Although most *audible* speech is generated by Broca's Area in the left frontal lobe, *affective* speech (exclamations such as Amen, Praise the Lord, Hallelujah) springs from the right temporal lobe.

Once upon a time, there was an elderly church member who frequently punctuated services with his loud *Amens* and *Hallelujahs*. The local church elder, who was particularly tired of hearing these exclamations, decided one weekend to read a scientific exposition about the ocean. He was certain the article contained nothing that could possibly occasion any spontaneous eruption of praise during the reading. Imagine his consternation when, before very long, the good brother let go with several very loud *Amens*. The elder stopped reading and asked, "What prompted that outburst?" "Why brother," the member exclaimed, "God promises to bury my sins in the depths of the sea, and you just read that it's seven miles deep in places. I'm thankful that so much water covers my sins!"

The good Samaritan nurtured and cared for the wounded traveler on the road to Jericho (Luke 10:33-36). By the way, my husband and I recently had the privilege of traveling the Jericho Road. The touring bus was eight feet wide; the road about seven! With all the curves and rugged terrain, it wasn't difficult to imagine robbers in hiding, waiting to attack weary travelers.

With her gift of hospitality, Lydia made her home available not only as a lodging place for itinerant missionaries, but also as a meeting place (Acts 16:12-15, 40). The wise woman of Tekoa put her acting skills to excellent advantage (2 Samuel 14:1-20). Sarah's tendency to comply, along with Abraham's fear and deceptiveness, caused problems for both of them. (Genesis 12:10-20).

In terms of music, the song of Miriam has been referred to as one of the oldest and most splendid anthems in the world (Exodus 15:20-21). Mary's song is recorded in Luke 1:46-55; Hannah's spiritual lyric in 1 Samuel 2:1-10. David sang and played the harp in an effort to lift King Saul from his depression (1 Samuel 16:23). David also danced with joy before the Lord (2 Samuel 6:14).

VISUALIZING PREFERENCE

Skills that derive from the visualizing preference help us to:

- Be artistically creative. Exodus 31:1-11

- Create innovation in worship (sing to the Lord a new song). Psalm 144:9; Isaiah 42:10

- Cultivate a cheerful heart and a positive mind-set. Proverbs 17:22; Philippians 4:8

- Express emotions through tears. John 11:35

- Give up worry and anxiety. Luke 12:22-30, 34)

- Imagine! Imagination is a first cousin to meditation. This skill allows us to form a picture in the mind about something that is not present at the moment or has not yet occurred. 1 Corinthians 2:27 tells us that no eye has seen, no ear has heard, no mind has yet conceived what God has prepared for those who love Him; but God has revealed it to us by His Spirit, and we can imagine what it will be like. We rarely expend the time, money, and energy to take a vacation (e.g., to Disneyland) except that we have first imagined doing so. Similarly, long before the baby is born, most couples have spent time imagining what it will be like to add a new member to their family. Likewise, we can use our imagination to think about spiritual things, to help us point our lives in a desirable direction, and to assist us in exhibiting behaviors that will enhance our own environment as well as the environments of others.

- Meditate. Psalm 46:10; Psalm 1:2; Psalm 19:14; Psalm 143:5; Ecclesiastes 7:25; Philippians 4:8; Joshua 1:8; Luke 12:34. Mary, the mother of Jesus, exhibited the skill of meditation. She treasured the experiences associated with her special son and pondered them in her heart. Some people are frightened of meditation because they don't understand it. It basically involves choosing a particular topic upon which one wishes to ponder. Incidentally, there are some who advocate forms of meditation that encourage us to clear the mind of all conscious thought. Doing so is dicey, as the mind was not designed to be devoid of thought. It will think about something. Trying to clear the mind of all thought can place us at risk for having it flooded with thoughts on which we may not want to dwell.

- Pay attention to the journey on the way to the goal. Matthew 7:12

- Relax and rest. Matthew 11:28-29. During part of His sojourn on this planet, Christ practiced the art of carpentry. A large portion of His business likely involved the creation of yokes for use with teams of oxen. No doubt those yokes were finely crafted with skill and balanced precision. I like to think that the oxen fortunate enough to benefit from such fine craftsmanship were more comfortable and could work with less fatigue.

- Utilize parables, stories, drama, and pageants. Matthew 13:34; Mark 4:34. Visualizers tend to read the Bible to dig out the new ideas contained therein; to discover what life might be like in the future; to brainstorm new options for living. They may be somewhat reticent to discuss their future vision with others, however, especially if their musings have been *shot down* in the past. Many times we gain a new perspective when we experience ideas or concepts presented either as a pageant or in drama format. The ideas and concepts *come alive*, as it were, and definitely appeal to the right side of the brain.

Jochabed developed an innovative plan to save baby Moses (Exodus 2:1-10; Hebrews 11:23). Rahab risked her own life by ingeniously hiding the two spies among flax stalks on her roof (Joshua 2; Matthew 1:5-16; Hebrews 11:31).

Lot's wife, on the other hand, didn't want to leave the routines, traditions, possessions, and city to which she was accustomed (Genesis 19:15-26; Luke 17:32). The woman of Bahurim displayed innovative problem solving (2 Samuel 17:17-19). Abigail's sense of vision marked her as a truly great woman (1 Samuel 25:2-42).

PRIORITIZING PREFERENCE

Skills that derive from the prioritizing preference provide us with the ability to:

- Develop conscience. Hebrews 13:18; 1 Timothy 1:5

- Exhibit self-control and manage willpower. Titus 2:1-7; 2 Peter 3:14; Mark 14, 36

- Forsake evil. Job 28:28

- Learn to delegate. Exodus 18:17-26; Acts 6:3

- Make decisions and set/pursue goals. Philippians 3:14; . Isaiah 7:15-16; Joshua 24:15

- Pray. 2 Chronicles 6:12-42; 1 Corinthians 14:15

- Preach and discuss spiritual truths. Isaiah 1:18; 2 Timothy 2:14, 23. The skill of verbal fencing must be moderated by the advice that Paul gives us in Titus 3:9. He reminds us to avoid foolish controversies, arguments, and quarrels because these are unprofitable and useless.

- Respect and honor God. Matthew 4:10; Luke 4:8

- Study doctrine. Isaiah 28:10,13; 2 Timothy 2:15; 3:15-16. Prioritizers tend to read the Bible to discover doctrine and to identify proof texts that can be used to support theology. They might select, as a goal, reading the Bible through in a year and make the commitment to read whatever portion is necessary on a daily basis to realize that goal.

- Test information and maintain sound doctrine. Titus 2:1; 1 Thessalonians 5:21

The Apostle Paul reasoned with King Agrippa (Acts 26). King Solomon wisely decided between the petitions of the two women who both claimed the same child (1 Kings 3:27). Deborah, judge of Israel, helped the people of her nation to live in peace for over forty years. She is credited with possessing the gift of prophecy (Judges 4-5). Queen Vashti carefully weighed the king's request for her to appear before his assembled banquet guests—and declined (Esther 1:12). Two Hebrew midwives, Shiphrah and Puah, courageously made the decision not to destroy the baby boys as Pharaoh had commanded (Exodus 1:17). Priscilla, along with her husband, Aquila, explained the way of God to Apollos, correcting his doctrinal errors (Acts 18:26).

Ananias and Sapphira died as a result of their unwise decisions (Acts 5:1-11). Queen Athaliah, the daughter of Jezebel, ruthlessly killed nearly all of the royal seed of the house of Judah in her search for power and control (2 Chronicles 22:20). Herodias solved one of her *problems* by calculating that her daughter's beauty would interest Herod. It did, but the premature death of John the Baptist was one of the dire consequences (Matthew 14 and Mark 6). The five foolish virgins lost track of time and delayed preparation until it was too late (Matthew 25:1-7). Miriam was unwilling to accept hierarchy, and was stricken with leprosy for a time (Numbers 12:1).

WHOLE-BRAINED WORSHIP

Whole-brained worship includes activities that appeal to all thinking styles; activities that promote respect, devotion, the learning of spiritual information, and that also add life, fervor, and collegiality to the service. We each need to think about our own life, and about the types of worship activities with which we are comfortable. Picture a set of balances. Group left-brained worship activities on one side and right-brained worship activities on the other. Are the scales balanced? They need to be.

Strive for balance

BECOME AS LITTLE CHILDREN

As a girl, I enjoyed attending camp meeting every year with my parents. It was so exciting! There were tents and picnics; musical performances, pageants, stories, and crafts; all manner of wonderful things for a child to do. There was usually a parade with visiting missionaries dressed up in colorful and unusual costumes from faraway lands. I loved it, and dreamed of the day when I could travel to parts unknown and see the sights for myself.

Once, a storyteller began his presentation in the *big tent* by saying, "I brought a gift with me from Indonesia. I'll give it to the first person who comes up here to receive it." I wanted that gift, but my early training, as well as my innate introversion, did not allow me the freedom to hop out of my chair and take him up on his offer. Interestingly enough, no one else moved, either. The speaker repeated the offer. Suddenly, there was a stir near the back, and a child about six years old emerged into the aisle. Hands outstretched, she walked confidently up to the front and received the proffered gift. I recall feeling very ambivalent at the time; happy because the little girl had received the gift; unhappy because I wasn't extroverted enough to go up front and get it myself (although I, as yet, had no such labels in my vocabulary).

Children, especially those who are raised in nurturing environments, often exhibit many delightful traits. One of these is the relative ease with which they ask for and receive gifts. Another is the confidence with which they trust the adults in their lives to give them the gifts that have been promised. They sometimes continue to trust even when there is nothing in their surrounding environment that would encourage them to do so. They approach life with a freshness born out of interest and a willingness to learn—an approach that looks at life, initially at least, without rigid and preconceived notions. Because their delicate brains are less differentiated, they can easily become proficient in any language. In addition, unless they have been taught differently, little children are often more open to accepting the differences of others. Perhaps this is why Jesus brought a little child to His disciples and admonished them to become like little children (Matthew 18:3, 30). As adults, many of us need to exhibit more understanding, more tolerance, and a greater willingness to risk learning to do things in a new way.

CONTROVERSIES

Controversies have been with us since the first humans set foot on the planet. The blame is often laid upon male/female differences. Certainly misunderstandings related to gender do play a part. Beyond that, however, and perhaps even more applicable is the fact that many controversies arise because of thinking style differences. Some of the controversies that abounded in biblical times no doubt hinged upon thinking style differences:

FOUR THINKING STYLES AND BIBLE TIMES

Zealots— a fanatical sect with the goal of repelling Roman domination	**Essenes—** a monastic brotherhood who lived in seclusion, and prepared the Dead-Sea Scrolls
Pharisees— a group who, in an effort to do things correctly, emphasized strict observance of rites, oral traditions, and ceremonies	**Sadducees—** a group whose dislike of conflict led to compromise which eventually resulted in the loss of truth and hope

Controversies within the religious community are often a reflection of the individual differences (e.g., brain lead, extroversion/introversion ratio, sensory preference) of clergy and parishioners. For example: the justification/sanctification debate, the traditional versus celebration services dilemma, the hierarchy/collegiality emphasis, the goal versus experience approach to life, and even the argument related to the pluses or minuses of hypnotism. The contentious discussions, triggered by differing perspectives, can be compared to the *foolish arguments* that the Apostle Paul admonishes us to avoid (Titus 3:9).

Let's briefly look at each of these controversies.

Hypnosis or Not

There have been countless arguments about the pros and cons of hypnosis. In terms of brain function, no one seems to know exactly how hypnotism works; it just seems to work for some individuals. The ability to become hypnotized, or to engage in self-hypnosis, is believed to be a function of the right side of the brain. In other words, in order for hypnosis to occur, the logical, analytical functions of the left hemisphere need to be placed in *neutral*.

Studies show that approximately ten percent of the population are easily and deeply hypnotizable. These individuals are usually above average in intelligence, very creative in terms of thinking styles, have a vivid imagination, and possess high capabilities for both concentration, and absorption in fantasy.

At the opposite end of the spectrum, approximately ten percent of the population are not easily hypnotizable. The eighty percent in between are capable of experiencing various degrees of hypnosis if they choose to do so. There does not seem to be any gender difference in terms of susceptibility to hypnotism; children, however, are more easily hypnotized than adults.

Proponents of hypnotism say that a person really doesn't give up actual control of the mind to the hypnotist; that the most the practitioner can do is to provide suggestions for future behaviors. There is some evidence, however, that the practice of repeated hypnotic experiences can influence the mind to become more susceptible to hypnosis. Since control over one's own mind is of paramount importance to one's unique being, many therapists believe there are more advantageous ways to modify behavior.

Justification/Sanctification

Differences in brain lead and societal conditioning undoubtedly contribute to the justification/sanctification debate that takes place in some religious environments. The word *justified* means to be released from the guilt of sin and to be accepted as righteous, as good and worthy. John 3:16 illustrates that concept; whoever believes can have everlasting life. The only way to become justified is to accept God's freewill gift of salvation—to say, "Thank you, Lord, for dying in my place and releasing me from the guilt of sin. Thank you for covering me with Your righteousness." Justification calls for a demonstration of childlike faith that can reach out and accept a gift. Sometimes called *salvation by grace*, justification can be represented by the symbol of a cross.

Sanctification, on the other hand, can be defined as learning to live on a daily basis without making a practice of sinning. The decision-making and organizational skills, governed by the left side of the brain, enable us to embrace sanctification. Learning to make consistently positive and desirable daily choices is the work of a lifetime. The Ten Commandments are an example of a set of principles that can help to guide our decision-making in the left hemisphere.

Individuals who prefer a right-brained thinking style may easily accept God's gift of

grace, and be puzzled by others who seem unable to open their hearts to receive it. They may place less importance on the process of sanctification, however, and may even label left-brained thinkers as *legalists*. On the other hand, individuals who use a left-brained thinking style may be very desirous of developing a lifestyle that role-models true Christianity but are liable to gloss over the concept of salvation by grace. They are often somewhat suspicious of those who go around talking about *grace*. Sometimes they overemphasize *doing;* or exhibit judgmental, critical attitudes that crush the spirits of sensitive individuals; or they even make comments such as, "Cheap grace, who wants it?" The truth of the matter: it's difficult to get very far along the road of living lives that forsake evil unless we have received God's gift of unmerited favor first.

SANCTIFICATION/JUSTIFICATION DEBATE

Left Brain   Right Brain

SANCTIFICATION

Learning to live without making
a practice of sinning . . .

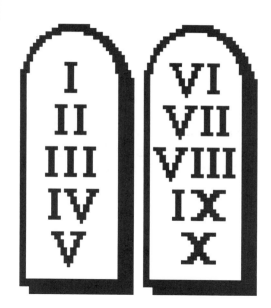

JUSTIFICATION

Being released from the guilt of sin
and being accepted as righteous . . .

LAW

OBEDIENCE

GRACE

TRUST

Traditional Versus Celebration Services

Several years ago, I overheard an argument taking place in the foyer of a large church. One individual declared seriously, "Celebration churches are of the devil. I wouldn't be caught dead visiting one, and I'll do everything possible to keep those activities from creeping into my church!"

The other lamented, "But many of our young people have stopped attending church regularly. Perhaps if we featured some drama presentations during services and included more of the songs young people enjoy they would start attending again. What can be the harm if it brings them back to church?"

Both individuals were undoubtedly speaking from their own innate brain lead. One could conclude that each was comfortable with worship activities that derive from only one portion of the brain. And the controversy continues.

Traditional churches promote the inclusion of primarily left-brained activities in their services. They lean toward:

- an emphasis on reverence and conservatism
- traditional music with primarily organ/piano accompaniment
- lecture-style preaching
- structured class discussions

Individuals with a lead in one of the right-cerebral thinking styles are not attracted to, and are often downright bored, in such environments. They may begin attending but will likely not hang in for the long haul, preferring to either gravitate to a service environment that more closely matches their preferences or *worship* out in nature (e.g., seaside, forest, or mountains).

Celebration churches, on the other hand, prefer to include a preponderance of right-brained activities in their services. They lean toward:

- an emphasis on innovation and connection
- skits and drama
- spontaneous expression of praise
- music using a variety of instruments

Individuals with a lead in one of the left-cerebral thinking styles are often very uncomfortable in such a setting. Should they stumble into a celebration service they would probably leave fairly quickly, or, if they lasted through the service, choose not to return.

Why not encourage the development of right-brained churches and left-brained churches? Because each contains a portion of desirable worship activities and each misses the big picture. The ideal is to develop whole-brained services where all attendees, regardless of brain lead, can find some activities that match their preferences and get to practice developing skills in those that match the other three styles.

TRADITIONAL VERSUS CELEBRATION SERVICES SUMMARY

Left Brain   Right Brain

Goal Versus Journey

In general, the left hemisphere and the male brain overall are somewhat goal oriented. This single-mindedness can be most useful in getting a particular job done; it can also cause hurt feelings and divisiveness during the process. The Bible indicates that God

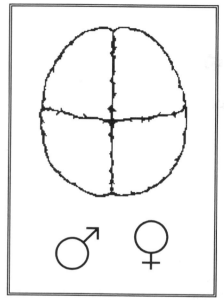

has goals. According to 2 Peter 3:9, one of those goals is that everyone should be saved. We all need to set some goals in life. Education, career, relationship development, travel, preparation for retirement and so on.

The right side of the brain and the female brain overall are more interested in the experience, or the *journey,* as some refer to it. What happens on the way to the goal is as important as, or more important than, reaching the goal itself. There is more emphasis on making sure everyone agrees, and has a good time with the project. This type of emphasis helps smooth the path with consensus, but it can sometimes delay the realization of a particular goal.

In childhood, many of us learned to quote the golden rule*: do unto others as you would have them do unto you* (Luke 6:31). This gem speaks to an emphasis on the journey—to life experiences on the way to the goal. God wants us to pay attention to more than goal completion; to develop a balanced lifestyle that includes nurturing, connection, contemplation, and relaxation.

I never think of this concept without recalling my childhood. When I was a little girl, ice cream cones were few and far between. Therefore, when we did experience that treat—usually on a vacation trip—it was a memorable occasion. Sometimes after eating lunch while Dad was driving (and if you don't think that was a challenge you haven't ridden with my Dad), he would briefly detour into a Dairy Queen and purchase a soft-ice-cream cone for each one of us. (Remember those? I think they cost all of a dime back then.) Cone in hand, being very careful not to get any drippings on the car upholstery, my brother and I would drag the pleasurable experience out as long as possible. Believe me, it was never a race to see who would finish their cone first!

Goal setting and achievement plus enjoying the journey on the way to the goal. Both perspectives are needed. When we don't understand this ideal, we can find ourselves more comfortable with half the picture while pointing fingers of misunderstanding at those who are comfortable with the other half.

70

Hierarchy Versus Collegiality

The left hemisphere and the male brain overall are more attuned to hierarchy. Consequently, most men (and some women who have a lead in one of the left-cerebral thinking styles) are very comfortable with hierarchy. Most of us are familiar with a typical hierarchic organizational chart that can be pictured somewhat like an isosceles triangle with the apex up at the top and the two long sides flowing down to the base.

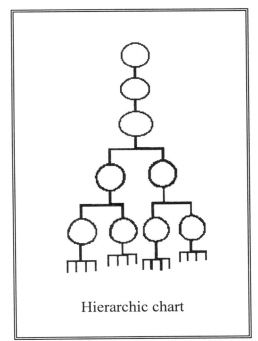

Hierarchic chart

There are definite benefits of hierarchy. Indeed, principles of hierarchy enable complex organizations, including churches, to exist with some semblance of order. In the Old Testament, we find the story of Jethro, priest of Midian, who taught his son-in-law to appoint officials over thousands, hundreds, fifties, and tens (Exodus 18:16-26). Those suggestions lightened the load of Moses considerably. As recorded in the New Testament, the early church chose seven individuals to supervise the daily distribution of food to the widows. That innovation, recorded in Acts 6:2, freed the apostles to preach and to teach.

Hierarchy also plays a part in enjoining respect and reverence for the Deity. Moses was commanded to take off his shoes because the ground on which he stood was holy (Exodus 3:5; Acts 7:33). Too much hierarchy, however, can have a negative influence. Through multiple layers of administration, it is very easy for the top layers to lose track of what is happening further down on the organizational chart. Conversely, individuals at the lower levels don't understand the why and the wherefore of decisions made by top administration.

The right hemisphere and the female brain overall are more attuned to collegiality. Consequently, most women (and some men who have a lead in one of the right-cerebral thinking styles) emphasize collegiality. I picture a collegial organizational chart as one that resembles a wagon wheel in design. The director's position resides in the hub and the spokes lead out to the various departments or employees. Each department has equal access to the director.

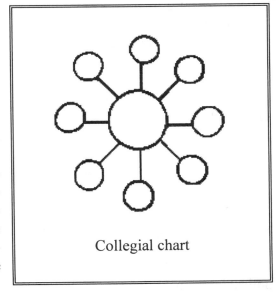

Collegial chart

Collegiality also provides other benefits. Theoretically, at least, minimal layering and direct access reduce some of the miscommunication that is often typical of hierarchic organizational structure. In a spiritual sense, the closer individuals get to God, the closer they get to each other. No wonder the Bible enjoins collegiality. It promotes warm, equalitarian, nurturing relationships such as the one reported in the fifth chapter of Genesis. Enoch walked and talked with God as with a friend and enjoyed this relationship on earth for over three hundred years. Lazarus was spoken of as a man whom Jesus loved (John 11:5). The souls of David and Jonathan were *knit* together (1 Samuel 18:1).

All collegiality and no hierarchy, however, wouldn't make for a very efficient organization. Some religious denominations use a hierarchic model for organizational structure and a collegial model for the *priesthood* of each believer. Before my father died in 1990, we sometimes discussed ways in which to reduce hierarchy within organized religion. Reducing layers of personnel could result in sufficient savings to provide both a male and a female pastor in most churches. Because of differences between the male brain and female brain, same-gender pastoral counseling (and preaching) would be ideal.

We had some lively discussions, my Dad and I. They usually ended with his smiling and reminding me that changes in organizational style usually are most effective when they begin at the grassroots level.

The Blind Men and the Elephant

These foregoing controversies remind me of a poem my mother made me memorize in childhood. Written by John Saxe, it's the story of six blind men who went to visit an elephant. Each touched a different part of the animal's body and came to a definite conclusion about its appearance. One thought it much like a rope, another like a wall, another like a tree, still another like a fan, and so on. Perhaps because memorization was so difficult for me and required so much effort, the poem's message was indelibly imprinted on my mind.

I have always enjoyed the last few lines and think of them every time I hear about controversies related to religion (or to any other entity, for that matter). They presented a moral as applicable today as it ever was. These men of Indostan disputed loud and long. Each one of them clung to his own opinion. Interestingly enough, each one was partly correct and each one was also wrong.

This poetic moral is certainly applicable to many of the controversies that plague today's churches.

Pastor Bob (not his real name) unwittingly found himself in the middle of one of them. He told me the story while attending one of my brain seminars. It seems that he had become accustomed to delivering his sermons as close to his congregation as possible. Bible in hand, wearing a lavaliere microphone, he sometimes even walked right down into the congregation. He was genuinely interested in nurturing and encouraging his flock, and in helping each to develop a personal relationship with God.

Pastor Bob eventually accepted a call to a large church in another state. It so happened that the pulpit at his new assignment was immense. Its intricate carving was lovely to behold, but it dominated the rostrum. Bob not only felt somewhat dwarfed by the pulpit, but totally separated from his congregation, as well. Before very long he enlisted the help of a couple of deacons who moved the imposing pulpit to one side of the platform. Alas, the pastor was unprepared for the *storm* of protest that ensued after the next service.

Pastor Bob was accosted by a group of long-time members. Joe actually looked stressed as he said, "The pulpit has been in the center of the platform for years and years, ever since I was a little duffer!" Derek asked pointedly, "Who gave you permission to move the pulpit?" Some voiced the opinion that Pastor Bob's innovation was a welcome change, but they were definitely in the minority. Still others didn't have a strong opinion either way, but were decidedly uncomfortable with the conflict. In an effort to promote harmony, they expressed some agreement with each opinion in turn, and eventually went home from church with splitting headaches.

The chair called a meeting of the church board to "get this problem resolved." Three hours of heated discussion followed, and the *don't move the pulpit* contingent prevailed. The following week, Pastor Bob arrived at church to find the pulpit back in its original position and firmly attached to the platform. The atmosphere was strained, to say the least.

Knowing that he really enjoyed preaching *eye to eye*, I asked Pastor Bob how he planned to solve this dilemma. "I think I'll leave the pulpit just where it is," he said. "That will honor the perspective of the left brainers. I'll preach in front of the pulpit once in awhile, though," he added thoughtfully. "Maybe even as often as once a month. That will give the right brainers some variety, meet my preference for connection, and," there was a twinkle in his eye, "give everyone the opportunity to practice adjusting to a bit of change."

Mark Twain would have enjoyed Pastor's Bob's solution. Twain's philosophy was that it isn't best for all to think alike. Indeed, a difference of opinion has created the stimulus for many useful inventions. In fact, a difference of opinion resulted in simplifying the multitudinous *rules* set out for the Gentile believers, as well as the creation of a second missionary team (Acts 15). Accepting the fact that four thinking styles exist can definitely help us to avoid some of the foolish arguments that the Apostle Paul cautions us against.

CEREBRAL COMPETENCIES

Over the past few years there have been profoundly interesting findings by scientists involved in brain research on several continents. Evidence of this has shown up in magazines such as *Time* and *Newsweek,* both of which have recently featured articles related to brain-function research. One of the techniques being used to explore brain function is called positron emission tomography, or PET Scan for short. This research modality enables researchers to visualize the brain during cognition.

Briefly, food comes to the neurons in the form of glucose which is brought to the brain through the blood stream. The more active the brain cells, the more glucose they need to carry out their activities.

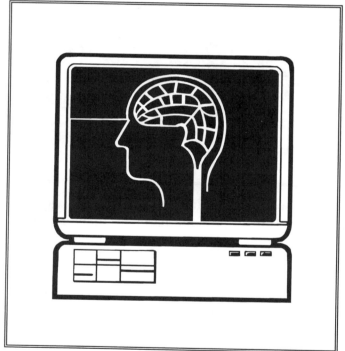

For study purposes, a small amount of radioactive glucose is injected into the subject's blood stream. A special camera, surrounding the subject's head, relays information to a computer that generates a map of the brain's metabolic rate in each section.

In one study, an individual, without any special musical training, was asked to listen to symphonic music (music without words), and neuron activity was recorded. Increased activity was shown in the right temporal lobe. This was the beginning of the understanding that innate musical ability is associated with the harmonizing thinking style.

Subsequently, the procedure was repeated with a trained musician. As before, there was increased activity in the right temporal lobe involved in the processing of nonspeech sounds. There was also increased activity in the left temporal lobe involved with the form of music (e.g., building blocks such as chord structure, time signature, and measure divisions). There was increased activity in the left frontal lobe in which the musical experience was being analyzed. The right frontal lobe was also engaged wherein the musician was actually visualizing a page of music and the instruments themselves as he identified them by their sound. In other words, portions of all four cerebral sections of the trained musician's brain were engaged.

PET Scans have shown that, with training, human beings can become *whole-brained* with respect to music. Therefore, I believe it would be beneficial for everyone to experience some type of musical training. One does not need to pursue public performance to benefit from this discipline. The resulting whole-brained competencies could certainly be utilized in other aspects of life. In other words, once we are whole-brained in one field, it may be much easier to subsequently become whole-brained in another. It is never too late to begin!

Imagine what could happen in our worship lives if a variety of activities, that represented all four thinking styles, were honored and included? Doing so just might refreshingly change religion and religious services for all time!

PET SCAN DEPICTION

NONMUSICIAN	TRAINED MUSICIAN

BRAIN SUSPENDERS

Our cerebrum is susceptible to the influence of, what I label, *brain suspenders*. Some of you may already have pictured old fashioned suspenders, the kind grandpa used to hold up his trousers, or the colorful types that are in vogue today (used more for looks than for function, no doubt). I'm not talking about that type of suspenders. I'm referring to certain substances and activities that can temporarily interfere with a variety of cerebral functions (e.g., reasoning, judgment).

Brain suspenders can be positive or negative, beneficial or harmful. For example, exercising (e.g., walking, swimming, cycling) after a hard day at the office can temporarily *suspend* some left-hemisphere functions because that side of the brain quickly becomes bored with monotonous movement and a paucity of intellectual stimulation. The right hemisphere is thus allowed to take over and foster relaxation. Singing is another suspender that can help to shift an individual's focus to the right hemisphere.

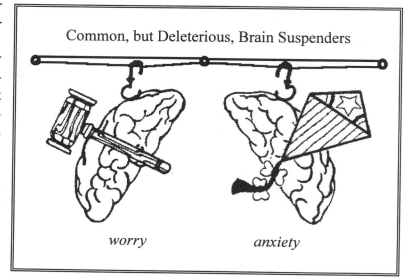

Common, but Deleterious, Brain Suspenders

worry   *anxiety*

Unfortunately, many denominations have *religicized* brain suspenders. That is, they have prohibited certain activities and substances under the rules of the church. When members are simply told to avoid brain suspenders and do not understand how these activities affect brain function, they tend to associate them primarily with denominational regulations. Should the members become disenchanted with something, or someone, associated with the church, they may try to make a *statement* by adding undesirable brain-suspender activities to their lifestyle— little realizing they are shooting themselves in the foot.

Here are several more examples of suspenders:

- Extreme stress tends to interfere with functions in both frontal lobes (e.g., brainstorming options, making logical decisions).

- Extreme grief can suspend functions in both frontal lobes (e.g., decrease certain types of artistic creativity). This can be especially devastating for individuals who make their living by painting, writing, or composing music.

- Deprivation of sleep can interfere with functions throughout the cerebrum and, over time, can lead to a variety of aberrant behaviors (e.g., violence). Prolonged sleep loss can also hinder memory recall.

- Starvation can suppress left-cerebral activity and increase right-cerebral activity. For example, extreme hunger might override the conscientious objections an individual might ordinarily have to stealing food.

- Alcohol can slow the rate at which impulses move along the nerve pathways. It can dull both the decision-making skills in the left hemisphere and the motor-visual skills in the right hemisphere. It also affects the RAS (reticular activating system) in the brain stem, thus decreasing alertness. Under the influence of alcohol, individuals often make less-than-optimum decisions—decisions that they may later heartily regret.

- Cocaine causes an outpouring of certain neurotransmitters within the brain. One of these, dopamine, can induce a feeling of euphoria. However, cocaine can also block the neuroreceptors from storing and reusing these chemicals. This deficiency can eventually result in an intense craving for more of the drug. Some of the thinking abilities of the brain can also be temporarily suppressed.

- Flashing disco lights can suspend activities in both frontal lobes. When a combination of suspender activities (e.g., dancing, flashing disco lights, alcohol or other drugs) is present, the effects can be compounded.

- Worry can engage the prioritizing mode as we rehearse events that took place in the past, events we wish had not happened. The organizing mode can whip itself into a frenzy and *worry itself sick* over some small, almost insignificant mistake. Anxiety can tie up the visualizing mode when we imagine undesirable events that might take place in the future, or when we fear desired events may never materialize. Being overly anxious about preserving harmony can keep the harmonizing mode *on edge,* thereby impacting relationships negatively. With cerebral function tied up by worry and anxiety, we may have very little energy to use in the present—to say nothing of the sabotage to our spiritual life.

I am reminded of the story of two monks who were traveling by foot one lovely spring morning. They came upon a river, swollen with melting snow, surging above its banks. In fact, the only crossing for miles in either direction was under two feet of water. A young woman stood by the footbridge, her body language portraying *I'm frightened, help, help!* Without a word, the first monk scooped her up in his arms and held her high as he struggled across the submerged bridge. He set her down safely on the far bank, and the two monks continued on their journey. They walked in silence until sunset, when the vows of their order allowed them to speak. "How could you pick up that woman?" sputtered the second monk, his eyes blazing with anger. "You know very well that we are absolutely prohibited from thinking about women, let alone touching them. You sullied your honor, and are a disgrace to the whole order." He shook his fist angrily at his partner.

"My brother," replied the first monk kindly, "I put that woman down on the river bank at sunrise. You are the one who has been carrying her around all day."

The habits of worry and anxiety are brain suspenders that program us for failure. Unless we make conscious choices to spring free from these traps, the mind can hold onto situations, creating suffering and anger long after the initial incident has passed—and it can create imaginary situations of astronomical proportions.

In large measure, we do tend to act out whatever our minds imagine; whatever we envision happening; whatever we think about. We need to follow the example of the first monk and set down our burdens (worry and anxiety) so that they do not occupy our minds throughout the day, or even throughout life.

In his book, *A Reader's Notebook,* Kennedy tabulates this information about worry:

- Forty percent of what most people worry about will never happen

- Thirty percent has already happened in the past and cannot be changed

- Twelve percent involves others' criticism of us (often untrue and spoken by individuals who have self-esteem problems)

- Ten percent concerns our health, which only tends to get worse as we worry

- Only eight percent is about real problems of life—those about which we can do something.

Based on these statistics we can give up at least ninety-two percent of our worrisome thoughts. Someone has said that worrying is the interest paid on a debt you may not owe. What a waste of mental energy! No wonder the Bible is so clear about the need to avoid worry and anxiety. Philippians 4:6 admonishes us not be anxious about anything. Matthew 6:25, 34 tells us not to worry or be anxious about tomorrow. Fortunately, we do possess the ability to learn new patterns of thinking.

ACCOLADES FOR A WOMAN OF WISDOM

Some have read the description of a *noble woman* in Proverbs 31 and felt discouraged by the sheer magnitude of its expectations. From a whole-brained perspective, however, it seems much less daunting. This passage essentially describes a woman who has developed whole-brained competencies, and knows when and how to use them.

Here are some of her characteristics:

Using the ***organizing*** functions, she:

- Is able to develop routines (operates a spinning wheel, sews and sells garments)

- Plans ahead (watches over the affairs of her household and is prepared for adversities)

- Is efficient (knows how to purchase the best, even if she has to obtain supplies from afar)

- Knows how to organize (provides food for her family and portions for her servant girls)

- Is trustworthy (close family members have full confidence in her)

- Is industrious (works hard with eager hands)

- Maintains traditions (keeps the lamp burning all night, as was the custom in well-ordered Eastern homes)

Using the ***harmonizing*** functions, she:

- Teaches others (kindly instruction is on her tongue)

- Is generous (extends her arms to the poor and needy)

- Enjoys beauty and color (she and her family are clothed in scarlet and purple)

- Nurtures and encourages others, helping them to grow personally (husband is respected in public)

- Is loved, valued, and appreciated by others (husband praises her and children call her blessed)

- Has developed a personal relationship with a Higher Power, the quality of which is reflected in her other relationships (fears the Lord)

Using the *visualizing* functions, she:

- Is an entrepreneur (able to secure unique goods)

- Has a sense of humor (can laugh at the days to come)

- Is energetic and visionary (does not eat the bread of idleness)

- Knows how to take care of herself (her arms are strong)

- Has a healthy self-esteem (exemplifies virtues by her works)

- Is artistic (clothes herself in high quality and aesthetically-designed garments)

Using the *prioritizing* functions, she:

- Makes decisions (buys a field)

- Knows how to investigate and evaluate (considers)

- Possesses and knows how to use power (girded with strength)

- Manages money (plants a vineyard out of her earnings; her trading is profitable)

- Has bona fide personal boundaries (clothed with dignity)

- Communicates intelligently (speaks with wisdom)

SUMMARY

We all tend to exhibit our innate giftedness differently; and yet how necessary all of these approaches are to the functional operation of the world community. With cerebral biochemical predisposition, to say nothing of gender, extroversion/introversion, and sensory preference, there are bound to be variations in thinking style. Unfortunately, there are individuals (even entire groups) who find it almost impossible to accept those *who march to a different drummer*. The Apostle Paul wrote, "Make my joy complete by being like-minded, having the same love, being one in spirit and purpose" (Philippians 2:1-2). Paul doesn't say we are to be clones or robots. We are to be like-minded in spirit, purpose, and love; to move in the same direction. In a whole-brained worship environment, individuality is not threatening to anyone. When differences are accepted, honored, and utilized, they enrich the entire congregation.

Admonition presented in the Gospel of John, contains a message for today's world. You may want to study the passage in several different versions:

- *Yet a time is coming, and has now come, when the true worshipers will worship God in spirit and in truth for they are the kind of worshipers that God seeks—John 4:23-24*

- *Those who worship God must do it out of their very being, their spirits, their true selves, in adoration—John 4:23-24 (TM)*

When we include worship activities that represent only one or two of the four cerebral thinking styles, our worship will be unbalanced, and our spiritual life can be impoverished. What a wonderful goal for us individually—to trust and obey, to relate to our Higher Power in spirit and truth, to worship in wholeness and balance.

BRAIN BUILDERS

Points to Ponder

- We are what we think about all day long. —Emerson
- To be wronged is nothing unless you continue to remember it. —Confucius

- Two key concepts I have learned in this section:

  _____

  _____

- Two facts I've discovered about myself while studying this section:

  _____

  _____

- One way in which I am now applying this information:

  _____

  _____

- Imagination is a first cousin to _____.

- Traditional churches promote the inclusion of primarily _____ brained activities in their services.

- In general, the right side of the brain, and the _____ brain overall, are more interested in the experience or journey.

- In large measure we tend to act out whatever our minds _____.

- **T F** Worry and anxiety are common, but deleterious, brain suspenders.

- **T F** As children, many of us go through a socialization process that generally emphasizes left-cerebral functions.

- **T F** Controversies rarely involve a difference in thinking styles.

Brain Teasers

1.	2.	3.	4.
MIND ↑	CYCLE CYCLE CYCLE	MIND MATTER	YOU/JUST/ME

Creativity Corner

*Sure, I'd like to go out with you—but first I need
to know your brain lead, E:I ratio, and sensory preference . . .*

Chapter Five
Whole-brained Nurturing

One evening, a family decided to go out for dinner at their favorite restaurant. They were shown to a table that overlooked the bay and within minutes the waitress arrived to take their order. She began with the father and asked each member in turn what they wanted to eat. Finally reaching the youngest member of the family, the waitress asked, "And what would you like to eat, young lady?"

"A burger and fries," the little girl answered politely.

"Bring her lasagna," said the mother. The waitress wrote something down on her order form.

"Would you like something to drink?" she continued. After a few seconds of reflection the child answered, "I'd like a 7-UP."

"Bring her lasagna and milk," the mother said firmly.

In due time, the waitress returned with the food. To the delight of the little girl, and the consternation of the mother, the waitress placed a burger, fries, and 7-UP in front of the littlest member of the family. In a voice that carried throughout the restaurant, the child fairly shouted, "Mommie, that lady thinks I'm real!"

I don't know how smart the actions of the waitress were in light of a possible tip, but the child certainly felt validated. We all like to feel real; and most of us want other people to feel that way, also. The secret, of course, lies in learning how to apply this concept to everyday life—to conscientiously practice *whole-brained nurturing*.

Although many men, individually, have become adept at nurturing, society in general has delegated this task to women. Unfortunately, in many cases, they have primarily concentrated their nurturing efforts on men and children to the exclusion, at times, of themselves and other women. Fortunately, we can all learn the necessary skills.

THE SENSORY SYSTEMS

Unless sensorially impaired in some manner, we all possess the ability to use all three sensory systems: visual (seeing), auditory (hearing), and kinesthetic (touching, smelling, and tasting). Within the posterior lobes of the cerebrum, the two occipital lobes house the visual system; the two temporal lobes, the auditory system; the two parietal lobes, the kinesthetic system. The sensory systems were designed to work together—each offering the specialized skills it possesses. Together, they are capable of creating an integrated whole, especially as we make an effort to become whole-brained.

Just as most of us possess an innate biochemical preference for processing information in one of the thinking styles, just as some of us favor the right hand over the left, most individuals have a sensory-system preference. In other words, one system tends to dominate. It is as if our brains actually respond to some types of stimuli faster than to others. Some individuals respond more quickly to visual stimuli. Others react more quickly to auditory stimuli, and still others prefer kinesthetic cues. We prefer using one of these systems over the other two, rely on it more consistently, and learn more quickly when information is presented to us in our preference. We may, however, and often do, switch to one of the other systems in specific situations.

For example, Elizabeth is primarily auditory; but she definitely needs her visual system when she sight-reads a musical selection. David is primarily kinesthetic; but he taps into his auditory system when he needs to distinguish between clarity of tones in his electronic business. Alleen is primarily visual; but enjoys using her kinesthesia whenever her cat jumps into her lap and wants to snuggle.

Large-sample studies suggest that sensory-system preference is distributed proportionately throughout the population. Visuals predominate.

SENSORY PREFERENCES

60% Visuals	20% Auditories	20% Kinesthetics

We often mistakenly assume that others make decisions in the same way we do. Not so. Suppose I ask, "Are you comfortable right now?" Those of you who are visual will likely internally picture what you look like when you're in a comfortable position and compare that with your present state. Those of you who are primarily auditory will likely hold a short conversation with yourself. You may even hear sounds in your head that you associate with comfort and that will help you to determine whether or not you are comfortable at the moment. You who are kinesthetics will probably evaluate the relative sensations within your body in order to decide whether or not you are comfortable. In the process you may shift your position somewhat, wiggle around, and even stretch.

As an aside, should we lose the ability to use one of our sensory systems, most of us could quickly refine our ability to perceive information through the other two. I have often been amazed to observe how extensively and accurately human beings can hone auditory and kinesthetic senses following an accident that temporarily or permanently affected the visual sense; or can hone the visual sense when the auditory system is damaged.

Surveys suggest that individuals exhibit certain characteristics, based on their own preference for relating to others through one of the sensory systems—visual, auditory, or kinesthetic. Here are some general characteristics common to each group. Look for yourself in one of the groups. You may recognize some of your friends in the same group—others in a different group.

VISUALS

Individuals with a visual preference generate internal pictures of everything they see, hear, and feel. That is, they translate words, thoughts, and ideas into visual images. They often carry photographs of the people they love. They are not usually considered to be overly emotional, but they tend to gesture a great deal with their arms and hands during conversation. It's as if they are trying to *draw* pictures in the air.

Visuals often select careers that allow them to use their visual preference. They can be found as:

- artists
- fire fighters
- airline pilots
- sharp-shooters
- photographers
- television producers
- motion-picture directors

Visuals often have a high-pitched voice. They tend to breathe shallowly, high in their chests. When asked a question, they may even hold their breaths while searching for the appropriate cerebral picture from which to formulate their response. Their facial skin may pale slightly. Their speech is usually rapid, concise, and to-the-point. Because they are trying to keep up with the visual images as they flash across their internal movie screens, their words may burst out in quick volleys— like corn popping in the microwave

Some researchers believe that visuals may be more prone to migraines. The theory being that, by means of a splitting headache, their bodies are trying to get their attention and to inform them about something that needs to be addressed or avoided. Unfortunately, many of us have not learned to readily identify and interpret the cues our bodies send us. We often try to mask signals (such as headaches) rather than investigating the underlying cause.

Visuals naturally use words related to the way things *look*. Their speech patterns tend to be sprinkled with words and expressions associated with sight, and they lean toward the use of visual metaphors.

Examples include:

- That's a horse of a different color
- She talked until she was blue in the face
- That looks like liquid sunshine
- That looks okay to me
- How does it look to you?
- That's a shade off-color
- I see what you mean
- From my point of view
- Picture this
- When I look at it that way
- That's not clear to me
- You need to see a different perspective
- The light just went on
- That's a bright idea

In terms of romance and marriage, the brains of visuals register a perception of being understood, appreciated, loved, and nurtured when they receive positive visual stimuli. This doesn't mean that they cannot respond to auditory and kinesthetic stimuli. The visual system will respond faster and more intensely to visual stimuli.

Characteristics of the visual child

Most children like to look at things. The visual child, however, will be the one who is jumping up and down saying, "Let me see, let me see, let me see!" Visual children are concerned about how they look. Paul simply would not leave the house for school unless he looked right. His clothes had to be neat, clean, and in style. Nancy wouldn't leave her bedroom, even when visitors, whom she enjoyed seeing, arrived—because her hair didn't look

> How can I know what I think until I see what I say? —Wallas

right. She thought the beauty parlor had frizzed it unmercifully. Her little brother Eric didn't help the situation a great deal when he casually remarked, "Doesn't look much different to me, Nance." Eric was not a visual!

Visual children love stories that are illustrated, and may want to be close to the reader so they won't miss seeing any of the pictures. They like to look at you when you are talking with them; and they want you to look at them, too—right in the eye if they feel comfortable. They can be very sensitive to facial expressions, and may burst into tears if the look on your face indicates anger or displeasure.

Visual children are often concerned about the appearance of the food on their plates. Nellie insists on keeping everything separate so that the different foods don't *run together* and change color. She will not eat mashed potatoes and beets at the same time—unless they

are in separate dishes so that the potatoes stay white. Donald can never bring himself to eat canned spinach because he says it looks like *frog slime*. Neither Nellie nor Donald will try tasting something new if it doesn't look just right.

Visual children like pets that are interesting to look at. They will want their pets to look pretty, and may put a ribbon around the cat's neck, or paint the dog's toenails pink. They often enjoy watching fish swim around the tank, rats playing endlessly on the circular treadmill, or a parakeet kissing itself in the mirror attached to the side of its cage.

Visual children are sensitive to things they see in the environment. They will be concerned about the colors of their pencils or books—wanting them to look attractive. They may not want to play with toys that are battered, scratched, or torn. They may become very frightened by shadows cast across the wall by the harvest moon. They may have nightmares because of violent or emotional images they saw on television. They like to learn by seeing what needs to be done rather than by just being told what to do.

AUDITORIES

Approximately one in five individuals has an auditory preference. Auditories translate words, thoughts, and ideas into sounds and often enjoy conversing with others. Since they primarily relate to the world through hearing, they can easily be distracted by loud or annoying sounds.

Unlike visuals, who frequently hold their breaths, auditories usually breathe regularly and rhythmically using the diaphragm or the whole chest. Auditories do not gesture with their arms as much as do visuals, however. When listening intently, they may cup an ear or cock the head slightly. Auditories tend to release tension by deeply exhaling and sighing. There is something very relaxing about hearing the sound of air flowing out of one's lungs.

Auditories are usually very selective about the words they use because words are important to them. They are conscious of their voice tones, which are often quite resonant. The rhythm of their speech is measured and even. Their words usually flow out like a gently running stream.

Their speech patterns tend to contain words and expressions that are associated with sound, and their conversations are often sprinkled with metaphors that relate to sound. Examples include:

- His voice grated like gravel on a tin roof
- Her laughter sounded like tinkling bells
- That proposal sounds like a jackpot
- It was as irritating as a dripping faucet
- That sounds okay to me
- How does that sound to you?
- That's as clear as a bell
- Can we talk?
- I hear what you mean
- I'll keep my ear to the ground
- That doesn't ring true
- That clicks with me

Auditories can be found in professions that allow them to express themselves through sound. They can be found in the fields of music, counseling, therapy, linguistics, broadcasting, and public speaking. In terms of romance and marriage, the brains of auditories register a perception of being understood, appreciated, loved, and nurtured when they receive positive auditory stimuli.

Characteristics of the auditory child

Auditory children like to hold conversations. Tina was just as likely as not to strike up a conversation with a complete stranger—and could ask no end of questions in the process. If no one answered her questions, she answered them herself. When there was no one available to talk to, she would talk to herself, to her toys, and to her dog Kipper—out loud. Many auditory children do.

Speaking of pets, auditories often prefer pets that make noises: dogs, cats, and birds rather than fish, rabbits, or hamsters. They can become very irritated by the raucous sounds of a parrot or the endless barking of the neighbor's dog, however.

Auditory children often like to eat foods that make sounds: dry cereals that snap, crackle and pop; chips that crunch when they chew down on them. Sometimes they avoid certain foods because of the sounds associated with them. Ned would not stay at the table whenever his family had a crayfish feed—he didn't like the sounds of their sucking the crayfish heads. Tilly was very aware of the sounds of other people eating. She would cover her ears whenever her brother slurped his soup.

Auditory children are often sensitive to voice tones and may burst into tears when spoken to loudly or harshly. They can also be frightened by certain environmental sounds such as the loud crack of thunder in a storm. They may be unable to fall asleep when rain is dripping from the eves, or when the shade is banging against the window in the wind.

KINESTHETICS

Twenty percent of the population have a kinesthetic preference. These individuals translate words, thoughts, and ideas into bodily sensations. Not into feelings in the sense that they are interpreting emotions, but into a physical sense of aesthesia. When they are thinking kinesthetically, their facial skin may flush. Kinesthetics tend to breathe deeply, low in the abdomen, which gives them pleasant, low-pitched voices. They often speak more slowly than do either auditories or visuals.

Kinesthetics tend to use metaphors that are associated with touch and physical sensations. Their speech patterns often include words and expressions related to taste, touch, or smell.

Examples include:

- Spare me from the jolting headlines
- The storm of protest was nipped in the bud
- Another day older and deeper in debt
- He exercised at a snail's pace
- Get a load of that
- Get a whiff of that
- That's an intense idea
- That doesn't feel just right
- I have a gut feeling
- I don't have a handle on that yet
- That fits into my plans
- I'm trying to get in touch with that

Kinesthetics are often attracted to occupations that allow them to utilize their kinesthesia. They can be found as athletes, woodworkers, surgeons, mechanics, potters, and counselors. In terms of romance and marriage, their brains register a perception of being understood, appreciated, loved, and nurtured when they receive positive kinesthetic stimuli.

Characteristics of the kinesthetic child

Kinesthetic children care less about how things look or sound, and more about how they feel. They can spend hours trying on clothes until they find something that feels good against their skin. They can experience difficulty falling asleep because the bed sheets do not feel smooth or because the covers make them too hot or too cold. The little fairy-tale princess, who couldn't sleep because of a tiny pea under a whole stack of mattresses, was undoubtedly kinesthetic.

Kinesthetic children are concerned with the way food feels in their mouths. They may refuse to eat foods such as canned spinach or boiled okra because they feel *slimy*. They may avoid carrot sticks or hard crackers because these foods feel rough. They may enjoy cool smooth foods such as ice cream and watermelon on a hot day; hot chocolate on a cold day.

Kinesthetic children are sensitive about the way in which they are touched—or not touched. It is not so much how you look at them that matters, or the tone of your voice; it is important how you touch them. They can often tell by a touch if an individual is impatient, frustrated, or angry with them. Conversely, they can tell by a touch how much they are

loved and cared about. Because they love to touch others and to be touched, they may be at higher risk for having their sexual boundaries violated. They are extremely sensitive to corporal punishment; to being hit, spanked, slapped, kicked, or jerked around roughly.

Kinesthetic children enjoy pets that feel good to the touch. They like to hold and stroke cats, dogs, and hamsters; and often are very sensitive and intuitive with animals. They like projects that they can touch, too. Rather than just seeing something or hearing about it, they want to feel it. They often prefer to learn by doing. They are the children who say, "It's my turn to hold that," or "I can't reach that and I want to know how it feels."

PERSONAL SENSORY PREFERENCE

While most people do have an overall sensory preference, they rarely use one system exclusively. A person may be primarily visual, but have an auditory preference in terms of romance. A person may be primarily auditory, but have a visual preference in terms of responding to advertising. The Sensory Preference Assessment (next page) can help you to identify your preference. You may make copies of the assessment for your personal use.

Instructions:

- Read each question and ask yourself, "Does this apply to me at least 51% of the time?" If the answer is yes, place a check mark beside that item.

- When you have finished answering all the questions, add up the check marks in each column and write in the total.

The column with the highest score usually represents one's overall preference for relating to others and the environment. One's second and third preferences usually follow in descending order. Sometimes an individual will have two identical scores. One of these will usually indicate innate preference; the other, skills that have been developed in order to relate to a significant other who has that preference.

What about individuals who have three identical scores? Who knows? Perhaps they don't know themselves very well and need to get in touch with who they innately are. It may be that they have had to hone skills in all three systems in order to relate successfully with a variety of individuals in their environment.

Share the checklist with your partner, children, best friends, associates . . . Sit down and talk with them about your need to feel nurtured. Ask them what makes them feel real. (Even without using the checklist, some individuals know themselves well enough to tell you what their preference is.) When you know someone's preference you can tailor your nurturing to quickly make them feel real. When you don't know, you need to nurture them in a whole-brained style—do all three. Everyone will be pleased with the benefits that can accrue to partners, friends, parents, and children.

If one of your scores is very low, pay attention, and take appropriate action. One possible reason is that you were not encouraged to develop skills in that sensory system. Another is, that you have experienced some abuse in that sensory system and, consequently, have adapted away from it or have *shut* it off to some degree. If so, you will need to identify, address, and heal the woundedness.

SENSORY PREFERENCE ASSESSMENT

© Arlene Taylor PhD in collaboration with Katherine Benziger PhD
and with acknowledgment of work by Donald J. Moine PhD

❑ I like my living space to look attractive	❑ I especially appreciate musical programs/concerts	❑ I have been labeled a *gourmet*
❑ I enjoy looking at and using maps	❑ I keep abreast of current events through radio news rather than through the newspapers	❑ I prefer pets that I can touch or cuddle
❑ I learn much about people from their appearance	❑ I would rather listen to a cassette tape than read a book	❑ My furniture must feel comfortable
❑ I can easily assemble toys and models when I have a picture or diagram to follow	❑ Individuals sometimes say I talk too much	❑ I prefer my home to be *climate controlled*
❑ I avoid wearing clothing that is mismatched in color or design	❑ I learn much about people from the tone of their voices	❑ When blindfolded, I am able to recognize objects by touch
❑ My appearance is very important to me	❑ I talk to my pets as to a friend	❑ I maintain membership at a gymnasium or health club
❑ Art exhibits appeal to me	❑ I am considered chatty and personable	❑ Frequent changes in body position help to keep me relaxed
❑ When I take notes, I tend to draw/doodle in the margins	❑ I enjoy verbal discussion	❑ I'd rather participate in sports than observe others
❑ I enjoy drawing/coloring/ painting	❑ I use rhyming words to help me remember names, labels, or pertinent facts	❑ I enjoy physical exercise (e.g., walking, dancing, cycling)
❑ I like to daydream	❑ I enjoy singing, alone or in a group/choir	❑ I enjoy touching and hugging my friends
❑ I study for exams by summarizing the main points	❑ Talk shows and interview programs appeal to me	❑ I enjoy soaking in the tub and/or taking a hot shower
❑ I like to watch television, movies and videos	❑ I am an attentive listener	❑ I readily learned the *touch typing* system
❑ I prefer books and magazines that contain colorful pictures and illustrations	❑ I enjoy prolonged telephone conversations	❑ I like to receive/give massages
❑ I like to observe people	❑ Strange noises (e.g., rattles) in my automobile annoy me	❑ I learn much about people from their handshakes
❑ I like to keep my car washed and waxed	❑ Jingles and acronyms help me recall facts	❑ Most of the time I have good coordination
❑ I enjoy looking at photo albums	❑ I study for exams by repeating my notes aloud	❑ Space and comfort are important considerations when I purchase a car
❑ Mirrors are important fixtures in my home	❑ I enjoy listening to records/ tapes/CDs	❑ I purchase certain items of clothing because the texture of the material feels right
❑ To me, beauty is as important as is functionality	❑ I dislike the sound of jangling keys or a dripping faucet	❑ I often tap my toes to music
❑ Innovative billboards capture my attention	❑ I frequently talk to myself	❑ I enjoy being outdoors
❑ When selecting an abode, I prefer a home with a view	❑ I repeat new words to myself to help fix them in memory	❑ I enjoy making things with my hands (e.g., crafts, woodwork, crocheting, knitting)
❑ I often use expressions such as, *I see what you mean. That looks like a great idea.*	❑ I often use expressions such as, *I hear you. That sounds like a great idea.*	❑ I often use expressions such as, *My gut says. My sense is.*
Visual Score = _____ /21	Auditory Score = _____ /21	Kinesthetic Score = _____ /21

PRACTICAL APPLICATIONS

We can use sensory-system information to help others quickly feel comfortable and understood. When you meet an individual for the first time, listen to the type of words used and *mirror* that style. Suppose someone says, "I think that's a bright idea. Your presentation looks very clear to me." Those words suggest a visual preference. If you reply with auditory (I'm glad it sounds good) or kinesthetic (I'm glad you have a handle on the concept) assertions, you may come across as if hailing from a different planet. Try replying in kind: "I'm glad you see . . ." And so on. Using this strategy can often help avoid misunderstanding and conflict. For example:

- Imagine you're presenting a business proposal and an individual interrupts you to say, "I don't see (visual) how this will help me." You might reply, "I respect your view. If you'll allow me to show you the rest of my presentation, however, I believe you'll see how this will benefit you."

- Suppose the client says, "This doesn't sound (auditory) right to me." You could respond with, "I agree that this may not sound very clear as yet, but if you will listen a bit longer you'll hear how this can be of benefit to you."

- If the individual says, "I can't seem to get a handle (kinesthetic) on what you are saying," you could answer, "I can appreciate your wanting to get a grasp on this state-of-the-art concept. I believe I can put this all together so you can recognize how this idea fits in with your plans."

In general, individuals tend to perceive that they're understood when communication patterns at least acknowledge their sensory-system preference. Conversing with them in words that mirror their preferent style will usually help them to feel comfortable. It will help them to feel *real*. In fact, nurturing others in a whole-brained style is useful in almost any situation. Perhaps you are serving as a greeter for a particular program, a social event, or an organizational meeting. As individuals arrive, offer them nurturing in all three styles. It can make a tremendous difference in the perception they have of your club, school, church or organization.

- Offer visual nurturing (look them right in the eye and smile)
- Provide auditory nurturing (say, "I'm happy you've chosen to be here.")
- Give them kinesthetic nurturing (shake their hand or touch them on the arm/shoulder)

George is a real-estate agent. When others in sales are moaning and groaning, he regularly manages to connect buyers with sellers. Why is George successful? Because he understands the sensory systems. Initially he asks prospective buyers to describe exactly what they want in a home. He watches their body language, listens for the types of words and phrases they use, and tries to sense their motivation. Then he tries to match his offerings to their primary nurturing style. He also describes features of the property to them using their sensory preference. If he is tapping into the visual system, he may tell them that the house possesses eye appeal; that there are windows everywhere so they can see outdoors; that there is much craftsmanship from the carving on the doors to the trim over the portico.

If he is tapping into the auditory mode, he will talk about the house being soundly constructed; that there is plenty of insulation to block out undesirable sounds; or that the rustling of leaves on the full-grown trees surrounding the property, or the babbling of the brook nearby, can provide restful sounds from nature for them to enjoy.

If he is tapping into the kinesthetic mode, he will draw their attention to the fine finishing detail and the plushness of the carpets. He may suggest that they touch the wood on the railing to feel how smooth it is. He may remind them that the way in which the kitchen window is positioned allows the warmth of the sun to permeate the room. He may talk about the potential for sitting on the wide patio in order to soak up the perfume from the wild flowers that are growing in the lot next door, or how they will enjoy the raspberries that are growing on bushes near the fence.

When George can't be sure which of the three nurturing styles is most appropriate, he includes all three in his presentation. Some of his colleagues poke fun at the scientific way in which he approaches sales. They say he is using manipulation. George says that he just understands human nature. He never tries to sell people a home they do not want—he just tries to present options to them in a language that they can understand and relate to quickly. And people love to buy from George. They recognize that he speaks their language—even if they can't explain how he does it.

Victoria uses a similar approach when working with patients who need to change their lifestyle in order to regain their health. When encouraging smokers to quit, she helps auditories to understand how nice it will be not to hear themselves wheezing and gasping for air whenever they climb stairs or exercise. She reminds visuals how nice it will be to avoid nicotine stains and burn-holes. She suggests that kinesthetics will enjoy enhanced tasting ability to say nothing of sweeter breath.

When she is presenting information about dietary changes, she explains to visuals how a healthier diet and an exercise program can help them to look better to themselves and to others. How they can regain a glow to their skin, tighten up flabby muscles, and see a spring return to their step. She reminds auditories how pleasant it will be to hear other people tell them how much healthier they appear. She helps kinesthetics realize how much better they will feel on the new program. Their clothes will soon fit better, they may sleep more soundly, and will likely experience a resurgence of energy. Within three weeks, their taste buds can readjust (e.g., low-fat, low-salt, low-sugar foods). Victoria has discovered that, in general, human beings are much more willing to accept change and to invest the time and energy that it takes to foster personal growth when she communicates with them in their sensory preference.

When we make a presentation before an audience, we need to keep in mind average distribution ratios (sixty percent visual, twenty percent auditory, twenty percent kinesthetic) and be alert for ways in which our presentations can include auditory, visual, and kinesthetic cues. As much as possible, presentations need to offer something for everyone and involve all four cerebral thinking styles. We can include stories, word pictures, tangible objects, and a combination of multimedia that engage all three sensory systems.

Sometimes an individual doesn't seem to *fit* in a particular classroom or even in a particular family. This can simply be due to a mismatch in brain lead, sensory preference, or extroversion/introversion ratio. In classrooms, for example, much of the information is presented visually and auditorily. In this type of environment, the kinesthetic may have difficulty learning and may even be regarded as being learning disabled. It would be ideal if all classrooms were set up to cover all bases.

Suppose I asked you to tell me how you would pronounce the puzzle spelled: CHO PHO USE. Some of you would be able to respond after running the *sounds* of the letters together. Some of you would have to write those nine letters out and study them *visually*. Some of you would *sense* the answer. In other words, based on individual differences, there are a variety of ways to arrive at the pronunciation *chop house*.

Interestingly enough, researchers have found that when people are raised in a dysfunctional or abusive environment, they may try to partially shut down one of these three sensory systems. For whatever reason, when individuals avoid using one of the senses, they may fail to develop competencies in that area and, later on in life, may experience what our culture refers to as hallucinations. Studies of patients in mental institutions have shown that if they have shut off the auditory sense, they may have auditory hallucinations—hear voices coming from strange places. If they have shut off the visual sense, they may have visual hallucinations—see things floating around in the air. If they have repressed their kinesthesia they may have kinesthetic hallucinations—feel bugs crawling all over them.

Let's say, that a child is regularly spanked or beaten and after each experience he is told how much he is loved. The child may be unable to make sense of the mixed messages—the physical pain and the words of love are not compatible. Consequently, based on the child's own preference, he may begin to shut out either kinesthetic or auditory stimuli, or both. Unfortunately, what is repressed becomes obsessed; and what is obsessed ends up being expressed later on—often in rather dysfunctional behaviors.

Actually, all of us probably hallucinate in one way or another about something or other during our lifetimes. That is, we may imagine certain sights, sounds, or smells that are not actually present. Or we may perceive something differently from what it really is. The reason some people are in mental institutions may simply be that some hallucinations are deemed less socially acceptable, or potentially more hazardous than others.

MY PARTNER CHANGED AFTER MARRIAGE

During courtship, partners tend to relate to each other through all three sensory systems. This can apply to any type of courtship, from searching for a life partner to pursuing a business partnership, although we'll primarily deal with family situations here.

When two individuals are attracted to each other and begin the courtship ritual, they automatically activate whole-brained nurturing. The partners tend to relate to each other through all three sensory systems—regardless of personal preference—as they try to woo and impress each other. They actually *talk* and listen. They express affection verbally. They are particular in their appearance and take pains to show their prospective partners a good

time. They look at each other in that special way and tell their partners how much they like the way they look. They touch their partners; they hug, kiss, and caress them. I call this the three "T"s of courtship: take, talk, touch. As a result, their special friends receive nurturing in all three styles and tend to reciprocate. Being on the receiving end of this type of nurturing can make an individual want to spend the rest of his/her life with the nurturer.

Can whole-brained nurturing last? Can it continue after marriage? Often it doesn't; but it can if we understand the sensory systems and utilize them appropriately. Let's say that Joe meets Sue and they begin dating. After several months of whole-brained nurturing, Joe pops the question and they become engaged. Each believes the other is the perfect partner. Who wouldn't after receiving whole-brained nurturing? Joe and Sue get married—and that's often when the trouble starts. Why?

First, we don't begin acting out our subconsciously absorbed expectations and perceptions about roles in marriage until after we sign on the dotted line. This means that individuals often do change after marriage. That's why living together is never a trial marriage—it's simply living together. (Marriage involves much more than cohabitation.) We never really get to know the other person as a husband or wife until we actually get married. This helps to account for stories we've all heard about couples who lived together fairly successfully (sometimes for years), finally decided to get married, and then were divorced within months—each partner vehemently claiming the other really changed after the wedding ceremony. Changed? The truth is, they probably both did.

Second, unless partners happen to have the same nurturing preference style, or understand whole-brained nurturing and consciously continue their courtship routines in all three areas, they will gradually tend to revert to each one's preferred personal strategy. In other words, most of us tend to express ourselves in the manner in which we would prefer to receive nurturing unless we make a conscious choice to do differently.

When two individuals happen to have the same primary sensory preference, there isn't as great a disparity between the before and after marriage validation. When they have different primary strategies, they are more likely to get caught up in the "my partner really changed after we got married" phenomenon or the "he/she doesn't love me any more" posture. The *visual* person may dress and groom carefully and take the partner places, but may not articulate *love words* as frequently, nor meet the partner's skin-hunger needs. The *auditory* person may talk of love, but neglect to look at the other person in that special way, fail to groom carefully, overlook the planning of outings, and neglect to touch or hug enough. The kinesthetic person may be good at touching the partner, but may neglect attentions that would appeal to a visual or an auditory person. When the preferred nurturing styles are not understood, and when partners are not nurtured in a whole-brained manner, both partners may eventually begin to feel very unloved. Let's take several examples.

- Sam is visual and Sheila is auditory. After their marriage, he takes her places, buys her things, and sends her flowers—that's his way of showing love. One day she says to him, "I don't think you love me any more." Sam is more than nonplussed. "Good grief," he says, "Look at everything I have bought for you and the trips we have taken." "I know," Sheila replies, "but you never tell me you love me." "I love you, already," he shouts—and cannot imagine what is wrong with the woman he married. Of course, being an auditory, Sheila is sensitive to tone of voice and misses the intended message because of the shouting.

- Ted is kinesthetic and Nell is visual. They have been married about three years. Ted comes home from work and wants to be comfortable so he kicks off his shoes, throws the mail on the table, takes a cold soda from the refrigerator, grabs the paper, and sprawls out on the couch. He throws each page of the paper on the floor when he has finished reading it. The empty can ends up on the floor, too. Nell arrives home a few minutes later, sees the disarray in the family room that she so neatly cleaned just that morning, and complains. "Ted, just look at this place—it is a mess. Your stuff is always scattered everywhere! I got up early this morning to straighten the place up before going to work. If you cared about me at all . . ." Ted, of course, feels that Nell is not giving him permission to be comfortable in his own home. Nell now sees *red,* and because his stuff is strewn all around the house she concludes that he doesn't respect her—and perhaps doesn't even love her anymore.

- John is kinesthetic and Toni is auditory. John comes home from work, walks in the door, doesn't say anything to his wife, just walks up to her and puts his arms around her. The years go by. The same pattern continues. One day Toni says, "Get away from me. Don't touch me. All you ever want to do is grab me and mess up my hair and clothes. You don't love me any more; all you want is sex!" "Don't love you any more?" John asks in a bewildered tone of voice. "No, you don't love me any more. You don't even talk to me before you grab me!" It's easy to guess the direction in which this relationship is headed.

- David is visual and Anabel is kinesthetic. He takes her places, gives her gifts, and sends her flowers—that's his way of showing love. Anabel, remember, is kinesthetic. She

likes to feel comfortable. In addition, she loves food and is a sensational cook. Two years after they are married she has gained sixty pounds and David rarely sees her in anything but sweats. Her husband says to her one day, "I don't think we have much of a relationship any more." "Why ever not?" Anabel asks. "I cook the kind of foods you like. In fact, I've made pie for dinner nearly every day since we've been married!" "I know," he replies. "But, look at you!" Anabel starts to cry and says that if David really loved her what she looked like wouldn't matter. In a perfect world that might be true. The truth is that Anabel's kinesthetic nurturing will not meet David's visual needs in a way that will quickly register in his brain that he is loved. Both of them need to start nurturing each other in a whole-brained style—in a hurry.

Scenarios such as these regularly occur between partners everywhere. Multiply that by what happens between parent and child, teacher and pupil, boss and employee, as well as minister and congregation. Not a pretty picture.

NURTURING STRATEGIES

What can we do to provide *visual nurturing* to others?

- Look at them and smile
- Give them flowers
- Dress and groom ourselves carefully
- Maintain a visually-pleasing environment

Some people misunderstand biblical admonitions regarding humility. In an attempt to appear humble and to look *natural,* they sometimes present a very drab, exceedingly plain, and even somewhat unkempt appearance. They (albeit unwittingly) offend the visual sense of others. True humility means that we give God credit for who we are—and not only do our best, but look our best as well.

Recall Christ's model. At the crucifixion, the Roman soldiers cast lots for His beautiful garment because it was of such fine quality that they hated to rend it. It is better to have a few, well-chosen, quality garments that are pleasing to the visual sense than an entire closetful of poorly chosen ones that do little to enhance one's appearance.

What things can we do to provide others with *auditory nurturing?*

- Talk to them in carefully modulated tones of voice
- Listen to them
- Take them to a concert of their choice
- Avoid unpleasant or irritating sounds in the living environment

Again, recall Christ's model. He talked with people, told them stories, and listened to them. His voice wooed the people who heard it, and even when He pointed out their errors, the listeners could hear gentle tones of concerned love underlying the words.

How can we provide *kinesthetic nurturing* to others?

- Shake hands and touch them appropriately
- Provide comfortable chairs
- Be sensitive to climate control and odors in the living environment
- Take them to dinner at their favorite restaurant

Sadly enough, appropriate human touch, though known to be a highly effective avenue for nurturing, is often neglected. It would be well to consider the example Christ set when on this earth. Children sat on His lap. Mary Magdelene used her flowing hair to wipe her tears from His feet. If people had not been accustomed to touching Christ, and being touched in return, there would have been no need for His postresurrection admonition, "Don't touch me yet."

All human beings have *skin-hunger* needs. This is especially true for kinesthetics. Parents need to touch their children appropriately. This can be particularly critical during adolescence. Hugs are worth a mint! As adults, we need to take responsibility for getting our skin-hunger needs met appropriately, as well. Individuals who have unmet skin-hunger needs, are at risk for losing control with the first person who touches them with kindness.

Some sociologists have suggested this accounts for many of the unwed pregnancies that occur in our world today. It is important that all individuals differentiate between physical and sexual touch, because those who don't know the difference, may try to meet their skin-hunger needs through sexual activity. Consider the risks.

BRUISING OTHERS

We can bruise (wound) others, as well; accidentally or intentionally. When bruising occurs in one's sensory preference, the physical/emotional pain experienced can be especially damaging. What might bruise *visuals?*

- Frowning at them or not looking at them at all
- Appearing unkempt or wearing sloppy apparel
- Combining colors that do not harmonize
- A living environment that's dirty, messy, or visually uninviting

What might bruise *auditories?*

- Giving them the *silent* treatment
- Speaking in harsh or very loud voice tones
- Subjecting them to irritating sounds
- A living environment that is auditorily irritating (e.g., traffic, loud radio/TV)

What might bruise *kinesthetics?*

- Touching them roughly, unkindly, or not at all
- Violating physical boundaries (e.g., invading personal body space, hitting, slapping, shoving, pinching, pulling hair, and spanking). Note: corporal punishment can be especially devastating to a kinesthetic
- Violating sexual boundaries (hidden, overt, or vicarious)
- A living environment that is uncomfortable

There are some gender generalizations that can apply to situations of abuse. In brief, males may bruise others physically when they are unable or unwilling to dissipate their frustration through an intellectually-developed emotional outlet, through an exercise program, or through verbal processing. Physically, a man can bruise a woman or child easily. Males have fewer nerve endings to register pain, so they may not realize the extent to which they are inflicting physical pain upon others.

Males are more likely to batter children physically while women are more likely to neglect them. There is some indication that boundary violations, especially physical, sexual, and spiritual, may occur more frequently in homes that are rigidly and excessively religious.

Women are more likely to batter others emotionally rather than physically. Emotional bruising can occur when a woman misinterprets a male's signals. Thinking that a little feedback means he is finally beginning to express his emotions, she pushes him to *open up* in the way to which she is accustomed. The male often feels manipulated or even emotionally damaged. Males can also experience emotional bruising when a woman expresses a massive amount of negative emotional energy, because men generally take longer to return to *normal* after an emotional confrontation. In such situations, women also experience stress, but their bodies tend to dissipate it faster, and return to normal sooner.

A LEARNED SKILL

Is there any hope? Absolutely. A good place to start is to identify our own sensory preference. Awareness is a powerful tool. Once we understand this modus operandi, we can be our own agent of change. Remember that we tend to nurture others in our primary preference unless we choose to do otherwise. Can we learn how to nurture in a whole-brained

Is there any hope?

style? Again the answer is an unqualified yes. To some degree at least, our ability to perceive sensory system stimuli is learned. Therefore, we can learn a new way. If most of our present skills fall into one system, we can begin developing skills in the other two systems. Learning something new does not detract from what we already know. It simply builds on our skills and enhances our potential for success in giving and receiving nurturing.

Learning the art of whole-brained nurturing is a little bit like following a recipe. Have you ever eaten something that you absolutely loved and later asked to have the recipe? I certainly have. A recipe is simply a plan that tells you what to do and how to do it in order to achieve a certain outcome. In the process of using the recipe, we sometimes even add a twist of our own in order to achieve a personalized outcome. Usually, the more we use the recipe, the easier it becomes and the more certain we are of the outcome.

Understanding the sensory systems is like following a recipe. We can always add a twist of our own. And while we wouldn't change our sensory preference any more than we would natural brain lead, we can develop nurturing competencies in all three systems. The more we practice, the easier it becomes for us to use the skills, and the more certain we can be of achieving the desired outcome—helping others feel *real*.

I often challenge professionals in private practice to evaluate their office waiting room for components of all three modalities. Is there *something for everyone* regardless of their sensory preference? Does it matter how we look, how we sound, how we act, how the environment is set up? Absolutely. Every day we have the opportunity of improving the comfort level of others, or of diminishing it. Why make the effort? Because human beings tend to stay where they are comfortable.

We need not be limited by our sensory preference. We can learn to recognize and appreciate the gifts of nurturing that others offer to us whether they are presented in our preference or not. The ideal is to be able to use all three systems at any given time. There may be situations when we are more aware of one over the other, but the ability to give and receive nurturing in all three styles allows us the option to shift among them as necessary, to be creative and combine them in any number of strategies.

We can change our strategy, alter our behaviors—especially with children—to increase the likelihood of achieving our desired outcome. We can adjust our facial expressions; change our tone of voice; alter our body language. There are endless possibilities. It really takes very little effort to help others to feel real.

Here are five easy steps to whole-brained nurturing:

1 We must make a choice to learn about the sensory systems: visual, auditory, and kinesthetic. Awareness is the first step. We can only implement what we know. Practical application of the information we learn can help to make others feel *real* and enhance our relationships beyond measure.

2 We must develop competencies in all three sensory systems and then practice, practice, practice, practice, practice—until the behaviors become almost second nature. In general, we can expect morale levels to rise in direct proportion to the amount of whole-brained nurturing available in any given setting.

3 We must find creative ways in which to use these three nurturing systems. They can be used in interactions between partners, parents and children, teachers and students, ministers and congregations, as well as employers and employees. They serve equally well at work or at play.

4 We must offer whole-brained nurturing to others. When our preferences match, it's easier to nurture each other in a way that helps to promote a sense of love and acceptance. When styles differ, one or both individuals may eventually perceive a lack of nurturing—unless each makes a special effort to offer appropriate nurturing.

5 We must learn to recognize and graciously accept the attempts of others to nurture us, whether or not it matches our preference. Not only does this ability enrich our own lives immeasurably; it also allows us to validate the nurturing efforts of others—a practice that, in and of itself, is a form of nurturing.

Happy climbing!

We were doing just fine until we learned to talk....

BRAIN BUILDERS

Points to Ponder

- I have striven not to laugh at human actions, not to weep at them, nor to hate them, but to understand them. —Sponza

- Two key concepts I have learned in this section:

  _____

  _____

- Two facts I've discovered about myself while studying this section:

  _____

  _____

- One way in which I am now applying this information:

  _____

  _____

- The three main sensory systems are the _____,
  _____, and _____.

- When we don't know an individual's specific sensory _____,
  we need to relate to him/her using all three sensory systems.

- **T** **F** Abuse can be especially damaging when it involves our sensory preference.

- **T** **F** Partners do not really change after marriage.

- **T** **F** It is important to make a conscious effort to nurture our loved ones in their sensory preference.

- **T** **F** Human beings tend to stay where they are comfortable.

Brain Teasers

1.	2.	3.	4.
BRAIN	WORLD ↓↓↓↓	D A N C E A C N N C A E C N A D	BADLY DRAWN

Creativity Corner

Innate Characteristics Influence Learning Styles

♦ **Brain lead**—an innate biochemical preference for processing information in one of the four thinking styles—what information we take in

♦ **Sensory preference**—visual, auditory, or kinesthetic—how we take information in

♦ **Extroversion/Introversion ratio**—the brain's level of alertness—context in which we function most effectively

♦ **Gender**—male/female differences in brain structure and function—opportunities and societal expectations for our gender

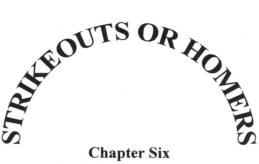

Chapter Six
Whole-brained Learning

The ability of the human brain to store and recall information is one of the most remarkable phenomena in the universe. The distinguishing characteristics of human beings—language, knowledge, culture, inventions—are the result of this extraordinary aptitude. Although learning has been defined as the act of gaining knowledge or skill, it has been suggested that in adulthood, many of us act from a basis of attitudes and beliefs that were absorbed by the age of five. Fulghum's bestseller, *All I Really Need To Know I Learned In Kindergarten*, addresses this perspective, albeit somewhat tongue-in-cheek. The truth is we are learning all the time, at least to some degree.

The ultimate goal would be to understand learning in terms of brain function so that the process of education (both studying and teaching) would be not only appealing and stimulating, but also appropriate and practical. The first stratagem would be to identify our own learning style and to select opportunities that match it. That wouldn't prevent us from consciously striving to assimilate knowledge in a nonpreferent style when the need arises.

Individual learning style results from the interaction of a complex constellation of factors—and differs because human beings differ. Four significant factors are:

♦ Brain lead—an innate biochemical preference for processing information in one of the four thinking styles—what information we take in

♦ Sensory preference—visual, auditory, or kinesthetic—how we take information in

♦ Extroversion/Introversion ratio—the brain's level of alertness—context in which we function most effectively

♦ Gender—male/female differences in brain structure and function—opportunities and societal expectations for our gender

Unfortunately, all factors have not always been considered when planning learning environments. For example, the majority of school systems set up their programs to match the *average* person (whatever that is), treat all students pretty much the same, and primarily emphasize one thinking style. This approach really works well for approximately one quarter of the population. The other three quarters are often left to flounder. Some studies show that many high-school dropouts tend to be students with a preference for using one of the right-hemisphere thinking styles. In addition, many adolescents, in locked mental-health units, are believed to be right-brainers who were unable to conform to society's left-brained expectations. Moreover, most schools present information in a manner that is virtually unchanged from that introduced decades ago, when it was decided to adopt an assembly-line approach. We are at least a decade *behind* in this the decade of the brain. It's time we joined the information revolution and began to work *with* the brain instead of around or against it.

Encouragingly, there are individual parents, teachers, coaches, and even schools who are apprised of the latest brain-research database as it applies to the classroom. I saw a cartoon the other day showing a child arguing with a guru about the ideal way to spell the word spell. The letters SPEL were written across the chalkboard with the caption, "The schools of the future will be child-oriented." What would it mean for a school to be child-oriented? It would mean a school system with a whole-brained emphasis. One in which:

✺ Teachers understood their own individual preferences, strengths, and weaknesses

✺ Students understood their own preferences, were allowed to excel within them, and were given nonthreatening opportunities to develop nonpreferent skills

✺ Teachers evidenced a mind-set that not only allowed for individual preferences but encouraged and rewarded them. Each child was valued for *being* as well as for *doing*

✺ Teachers accommodated and addressed their students':

   ❑ brain lead
   ❑ extroversion/introversion ratio
   ❑ sensory preference
   ❑ gender

✺ The educational program provided the appropriate environment, accessories, and opportunities for each child to develop competencies throughout the brain, in preferred as well as nonpreferred thinking styles

✺ The curriculum addressed all four thinking styles not only in terms of content and presentation but in terms of examinations

Impossible goals? I don't think so. In such an educational environment there would definitely be fewer discipline problems, fewer failures/drop-outs, and fewer incidents of burnout. Both teachers and students would perceive that they are understood and accepted as they innately are. Communication and creativity would blossom. Morale would soar. And, of course, the greatest attainment would be enhanced academic outcomes.

MYELINATION

Axons of many of the neurons in both the brain and the peripheral nervous system

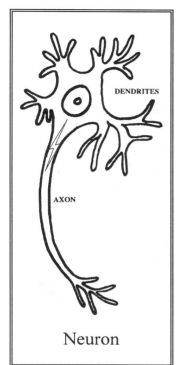

Neuron

are coated with a multilayered covering called a myelin sheath. It serves as a type of electrical insulation that is needed for the rapid conduction of nerve impulses. In the peripheral nervous system, myelination begins during fetal development and continues during the first year of life. In the brain, it is believed to take much longer. In fact, the amount of myelin increases from birth to maturity. This means that responses to stimuli become more rapid and coordinated as we grow from childhood to adulthood. Until certain axons are myelinated, we aren't able to control some voluntary functions (e.g., bowel and bladder evacuation); nor are we able to perfect cognitive control over muscle groups related to fine eye-hand coordination.

To recap, the brains of human beings take a long time to mature. In general, the sensory areas of the brain mature during early childhood. The limbic system matures by puberty. The frontal lobes continue to mature into late adolescence. The prefrontal portions may not become mature in some individuals until the age of twenty or twenty-one. We sometimes forget about this progressive maturation and expect our children (including teenagers) to act in seasoned ways with which their developing brain is not yet compatible. Teenagers, and sometimes even young adults, so called, aren't working with a *full deck!*

IDENTIFYING BRAIN LEAD IN CHILDREN

Brain lead is usually evident from about the age of two if the environment has provided for, and has not interfered with, a child's natural development. We can often identify their preference by watching for characteristics typically exhibited:

Organizing Thinking Style

Prioritizers	Visualizers
Organizers	Harmonizers

Children with an organizing lead need routines and limits. They often ask questions such as, "Am I doing this right?" or "Is it time?" They usually follow the rules, try to be good team players, and like to keep things in order. They don't like others to move their belongings. They tend to remember the *word*s to a song. Like most children, they enjoy stories; but will usually prefer factual stories. They may ask you to read the same story to them repeatedly.

In general, children with an organizing lead:

- prefer small motor activities that involve handling/manipulating bounded shapes
- show stress when asked to *change* (e.g., when the schedule is unexpectedly varied or the lunchbox menu is different)
- don't venture out by themselves
- exhibit separation anxiety, especially when expected to move into a new situation such as enrolling in day-care or starting school
- want repetition, predictability, familiarity, and stability
- prefer routines and are bothered by interruptions
- need added time to adjust to change

In the classroom, organizers:

- are often labeled as well-behaved children
- are likely to do whatever the teacher expects
- don't *know* the environment and don't see the big picture easily
- often exhibit anxiety when change is required
- need *time* to learn, to incorporate new information into an existing body of knowledge, or to insert a new step into an already-mastered routine
- see school as *the way life is* and try to fit in
- easily master subjects such as reading, spelling, writing (printing or cursive), bookkeeping, civics, history, and typing
- prefer true-or-false test questions and like predictability in terms of examinations (can experience extreme stress if a *surprise quiz* is announced)

Human history becomes more and more a race between education and catastrophe. —Wells

- often gravitate toward reading *how-to* books, as well as stories about athletic heroes and favorite historical figures
- are talented in following detailed procedures, repetitive tasks, operating machines, routine self-care
- are limited in drama, novelty, inspiration, and imaginative forecasting/trending

Desirable environments/accessories for organizers include:

- organized space
- neutral or subdued colors
- filing cabinets with appropriate files and labels
- a computer with which to track information
- a dictionary, a calendar, and a *to do* list
- a selection of *how to* books
- a desk set that contains divided portions for pencils, pens, erasers, and paper clips
- martial music

Ways to validate organizers:

- teach procedures sequentially, using at least three steps for each
- develop, state, and enforce appropriate regulations (rules provide them with predictability and security)
- discuss pros and cons of needed change with the child
- introduce concept of change with a preface such as, "You and I are going to *load* a new procedure" or "You can add this step to the routine you are already using"
- acknowledge the discomfort associated with change and help the child to adjust
- compliment the child for:

  - an ability to follow directions accurately
  - completing assignments on time
  - keeping belongings organized
  - memorizing facts, figures, and names
  - spelling words accurately
  - printing/writing neatly

Harmonizing Thinking Style

Children with a harmonizing lead need interpersonal connection. They usually make friends easily and encourage everyone to participate. They aren't particularly adept at details. If allowed to work on a detailed project with a friend, so they can connect and communicate with each other during the learning process, they will likely do the *detail* much more accurately.

Prioritizers	Visualizers
Organizers	**Harmonizers**

113

In general, children with a harmonizing lead:

- like to dress and undress, to change clothes and play dress-up endlessly
- enjoy singing, rhythmic music, and movement (e.g., ballet)
- are sensitive to nonspeech sounds (e.g., cries and shouts)
- like nature sounds such as pounding surf, falling rain, singing birds
- like to collect souvenirs—provided there is a connection with a pleasant experience
- separate easily if they can transfer to another person (e.g., mother to teacher)
- want to touch everything and like to be touched
- like to be with others and may dislike being alone
- seek facial and eye contact
- enjoy pets and stuffed toys that can be held
- talk, talk, talk, talk, talk

In the classroom, harmonizers:

- are often seen as *pleasers*
- have difficulty saying *no*
- stay close to the teacher
- enjoy giving gifts
- need to talk, play, and work with others in order to learn
- see school as a chance to associate with friends, and view studying as incidental
- enjoy drama, languages, interior decorating, home economics, counseling, and music
- aren't *wild* about test questions of any kind (prefer practical questions and situations that allow them to exhibit, demonstrate, role-model, or portray the answers)
- usually enjoy poetry, nonfictional animal stories, and stories about people
- are talented in hosting, spiritual experiences, dressing, and connecting
- are limited in logical or unpopular decision making, hardball negotiations, and cost-benefit analysis

Desirable environments/accessories for harmonizers include:

- upbeat, colorful space
- photos of family members and close friends
- decorations that include items such as plants, pine cones, candles, and stuffed animals
- a computer for personal use
- a chair with a cozy afghan or blanket
- inspirational books and pictures
- smiley stickers and colorful crayons
- sounds of nature
- musical instruments
- rhythmical melodic music

Ways to validate harmonizers:

- allow harmonizers opportunities to help plan and give a party; to make and give a gift
- give everyone time to talk about the rules and make sure they apply to everyone equally
- support them in decision making
- verbalize comments such as, "If you need help making a choice, I'm here to help you"
- provide playing time and dress-up costumes
- afford plenty of touch affirmation
- compliment the child for:

  - an ability to verbalize feelings
  - observing and acknowledging the feelings of others
  - smiles and hugs
  - harmonizing sounds, colors, clothes
  - being a peacemaker

Visualizing Thinking Style

Children with a visualizing lead tend to enjoy innovation, and troubleshooting. In fact, they may go searching for problems to solve; and if none exist, they might make one up. They can arrive at answers in an abstract intuitive way, but often cannot tell you how they arrived at the answers. They take in copious data second for second and can almost lose touch with reality as they generate ideas. They *get the picture* quickly and then tend to get bored as the teacher finishes going through all the sequential steps so often emphasized in most curricula.

Prioritizers	**Visualizers**
Organizers	Harmonizers

In general, children with a visualizing lead:

- prefer to be active; enjoy outdoor activities (often accompanied with noises/gestures)
- can sit still for hours, however, if their interest is piqued
- can be leaders, but can also wander off if something else catches their interest
- can separate fairly easily and are not afraid in new situations; can be daring and even reckless (may leap before they look)
- enjoy using metaphors (e.g., it's raining cats and dogs, it's raining violets)
- prefer to have clothes, books, and assignments in stacks where they can see them
- enjoy *pretend* stories and ask many *why* and *what-if* questions
- enjoy drawing, especially caricatures, and often cover the entire page
- dislike rules and routines and may drop out of the traditional school system
- often start multiple projects, skip from one to another, and may not finish any

In the classroom, visualizers:

- are often seen as the *geniuses* although they may not perform or fulfill expectations
- may have oodles of incomplete projects
- usually have difficulty in writing and spelling
- may have trouble with self-care as in brushing the teeth, tying shoelaces
- may be considered dyslexic due to a reduced ability to perform organizing functions
- may exhibit symptoms of stress when required to conform to rules and regulations
- need to be able to *move* around in order to learn
- tend to see school as a situation that is barely tolerable and often *drop out*
- often excel at subjects such as chemistry, physics, geometry, trigonometry, philosophy, creative writing including poetry/essays, as well as artistic endeavors such as drawing, painting, and sculpting
- can handle exam questions that ask for an essay (especially if it can be prepared on a computer rather than in longhand), lines of poetry, a musical composition, or an art project
- tend to like books on science fiction, adventure, fantasy, philosophy, art and poetry; may read several books at the same time just for variety
- are talented in exploring the unknown, finding new solutions (inventions), visioning, mimicry, and inspiration
- are limited in routine self-care, detailed procedures, sequenced details (spelling), and accuracy in addition

Desirable environments/accessories for visualizers include:

- airy unstructured space
- flat *stacking* surfaces
- a computer to assist with innovative creativity
- geometric models
- 3-D puzzles
- a reading corner with a wide range of topics
- large sheets of paper, pencils, erasers, and markers
- caricatures and cartoons
- pillows on the floor
- a bulletin board with pins
- jazz and baroque music

Ways to validate visualizers:

- create an affirmative atmosphere for daydreaming and imagining (remind visualizers that some of the world's most creative individuals are daydreamers)
- understand that to them rules represent an unnecessary evil; set and enforce a minimum number of rules and explain why they are necessary; be willing to adjust rules/regulations
- encourage exploration, variety, spontaneity, and individuality
- compliment the child for:

  - imaginative choices
  - artistic creativity
  - exhibiting a sense of humor
  - innovative problem solving

Prioritizing Thinking Style

Prioritizers	Visualizers
Organizers	Harmonizers

Children with a prioritizing lead tend to be verbal, logical, and conceptual. They want to make decisions and like to direct others. They are usually careful and somewhat cautious.

These children test almost everything to the limit. They may look self-assured in new situations but are slow to warm up to strangers in separation situations. They can focus their attention on a problem until it is solved to their satisfaction.

In general, children with a prioritizing lead:

- prefer large-muscle activities
- like to use tools of all kinds and try to gain the most effect with the least effort
- tend to arrive at answers by evaluating pros and cons
- can become impatient when things do not go their way
- enjoy taking things apart to *see how they work*
- like to set the rules and tell others what to do
- tend to argue and debate
- are competitive and like to win

In the classroom, prioritizers:

- are usually quite precise
- need to *reason* in order to learn
- are seen as leaders, are articulate, and may even intimidate the teacher
- are viewed as *bright,* and appear to *know more* than the other students
- see school as a *game* that must be won in order to be successful (may underachieve, just doing enough to get by)
- often easily master subjects such as arithmetic, algebra, calculus, statistics, auto-mechanics, electronics, engineering, public speaking, and research science
- like to read scientific books and research journals; also like stories about leaders
- prefer tests with multiple-choice questions but can handle essay questions or verbal presentations
- are talented in goal setting/achievement, strategy development, precision, and inductive/deductive reasoning
- are limited in foreign languages, spiritual experiences, nurturing, dressing (color, fabric, and style harmony)

Desirable environments/accessories for prioritizers include:

- uncluttered space
- colors: black, white, gray, and navy
- machines and mechanical tools
- a computer for research projects
- scales, gavel, calculator
- charts containing numbers and percentages
- framed awards
- abstract photographs of arrows
- a list of goals and objectives
- a five-year plan
- structured background music (e.g., Bach)

118

Ways to validate prioritizers:

- allow prioritizers to create debating games and participate in them
- say things such as, "It's helpful to have a strong logical argument for what you want to accomplish"
- understand that they have a tendency to want to make decisions (whenever possible, try to let them participate in setting the rules; provide opportunities for making decisions from a selection of previously established options)
- positively reinforce their attempts at critical analysis
- compliment the child for:

>   - an ability to reason logically
>   - making decisions
>   - setting and achieving goals
>   - investigating and experimenting

TIME-OUT FOR DIVERSION

Not long ago, several friends and I were discussing individual differences related to brain lead, extroversion/introversion, and sensory preference. Someone asked when we would have dinner, and that led to the topic of food and how cooks might approach food preparation from the position of their innate giftedness. Extroverts might want everybody crowded into the kitchen with them, while introverts might prefer cooking alone or with just one other individual present. Kinesthetics would likely *taste* everything periodically. Visuals would likely be very aware of presentation. Auditories might talk to themselves, or even to the food. Brain lead? One of the group presented his perception of how each thinking style might approach making quick potpie. While exaggerated, it was so entertaining that I've decided to share it with you. Here's the basic recipe as he presented it, along with his specific instructions matched to each of the four thinking styles. Enjoy!

QUICK POTPIE

1 medium carrot
1 onion
1 1/2 cups cooked lentils, beans, or peas
3 medium potatoes
1 1/2 tbs. low-fat margarine
3 tbs. browned flour
1/4 tsp. sage
1 tsp. dehydrated chives
1 low-fat pie crust (whole wheat flour)

BRAINWORKS—SUCCESS SMARTS UNLIMITED

Instructions for organizers

We know you want to do this right so here are some steps for you to follow:

1. Assemble needed bounded shapes: mixing bowl, deep Pyrex pie plate, saucepan, Teflon frying pan, wooden mixing spoon, encyclopedia (volume S), tape measure, measuring cup, measuring spoons, and timer.

2. Check *sage* in the encyclopedia to make sure it's safe and approved.

3. Measure carrot and potato to be sure they are medium sized (medium carrot = 6 inches in length; medium potato = 7 1/2 inches in circumference).

4. Cut carrot into long slender pieces. Place carrot and chopped onion, two cups of water, and half a teaspoon of salt into saucepan. Bring to a boil. Set the timer for ten minutes and boil for ten minutes. Add diced potatoes, a cup of cold water, and bring to a boil.

5. Turn on the oven to 350 degrees F. so it will reach desired temperature by step six.

6. (a) In Teflon frying pan, melt margarine. Stir browned flour and sage into melted margarine. Add six tablespoons of hot liquid from saucepan and stir until smooth.
   (b) Pour gravy over vegetables. Cook two more minutes or until wooden spoon easily mashes a cube of potato.

7. Place lentils and contents of saucepan into mixing bowl and shake together. Pour into Pyrex pie plate.

8. Cover with pie crust and bake at 350 degrees F. until browned. Set timer for ten minutes and pay attention.

9. Be sure family is already seated at dining table. Remove potpie from oven, cut into six sections, and serve piping hot.

10. You will want to clean and reorganize the kitchen as soon as dinner is finished.

Instructions for harmonizers

☺ We know that you are capable of pleasingly blending almost anything (colors, sounds, as well as foods). Be sure to remember to use celery root or rutabaga instead of onions. (It's your partner that hates onions with a passion, right?)

☺ Your friends are bringing the salad? Great! After all, it's the connection with family and friends that's really important to you.

120

☺ Why not invite a couple of friends over early? All of you can put the quick potpie together, each one doing some of the tasting and some of the work.

☺ Remember to add the extensions so that everyone can eat together at one table.

☺ You always set such a pleasing table! It's exactly one year since your son got his driver's license back, so make sure there's one candle on the cake.

Instructions for visualizers

You've been making potpie without a recipe since your grandmother turned the kitchen over to you when you were nine years old. (She wanted to take up oil painting.) You'll only need a couple of pointers:

♦ You might prefer to substitute a parsnip, or even a yam, for one of the potatoes
♦ If it's the weekend and your guests don't mind, throw in a few cloves of garlic

By the way, since you are so innovative and the oven will already be fired up, you may as well make a batch of hot rolls, too. If the pot pie turns out especially yummy, you might want to jot down today's creative additions. In fact, in light of your derring-do attitude, we wouldn't be surprised if by this time next year you've published your own cookbook and/or opened your own restaurant.

Instructions for prioritizers

1. Decide whether or not you even want quick potpie for dinner

2. Before beginning, review and evaluate:

   • the apparatus needed (the fewer the utensils dirtied the better)
   • the procedure; a lot of effort could be saved—step 6 (a) on page 120 —by simply using a package of instant gravy
   • the recipe itself (e.g., the goal is to have enough food for family as well as company and some leftovers to freeze for later—so multiply the recipe two and a half times)

3. Approach this project logically. Decide exactly what time you need to begin preparation in order to have dinner ready at 6 PM sharp. Prioritize activities to make the best use of your time.

4. You may want to delegate part, or all, of the preparation to someone else. If so, make sure the cook knows how to follow directions, especially steps #5, #6 (b), and #7 in the organizing section.

IDENTIFICATION OF BRAIN LEAD IN CHILDREN

Some parents have told me that, while the BTSA helped them figure out their own brain lead, they just can't figure out their child's. (A BTSA for children is under development.) I suggest they try giving the child a variety of experiences that cover the gamut of the four thinking styles, all the while being very careful to avoid prejudicing the child for or against certain tasks through verbal or nonverbal cues (often based on parental preferences, likes, and dislikes). Arrange for the child to spend time with friends who have a brain lead not present in the home. Observe the child and his/her exhibition of emotionality, procrastination, ease of learning, and level of competence in a variety of tasks. You may discover that procrastination or emotionality is much more pronounced with certain individuals, in certain environments, and in the presence of certain tasks. These observations can give you clues to your child's innate brain lead.

Females with a prioritizing lead, males with a harmonizing lead, and children of either gender with a visualizing lead, are at higher risk for adaption. (Refer to Chapter Seven.) Such individuals may exhibit emotionality, may be physically sick much of the time, and may eventually be headed for a midlife crisis.

Pay attention to their sensory preferences as well as their extroversion/introversion levels. Introverts are more likely to feel like *misfits*. They may try to become extroverted, or adapt to whatever thinking style is honored within the family.

It is also important to consider position in the family as well as differences in expectations. For example, parents typically expect eldest and only children to be organized, on time, predictable, responsible, dependable, successful, and outgoing. That means that these

children tend to be socialized to succeed—but often do so at the high price of excessive adaption. As the first born, I used to joke that my parents *practiced* on me. Furthermore, I was held to a code of behavior, deemed appropriate for a female, that was very different from the expectations for my brother when he arrived on the scene three and a half years later. These family dynamics certainly influenced my move toward adaption.

LEARNING DISABILITIES

Our perception of learning disabilities is often tied to expectations within the particular environment. Certainly, learning disabilities would be viewed quite differently in a whole-brained educational system. Dyslexia, for example. There are many differing viewpoints concerning dyslexia, although there is some consensus that many highly creative people, such as Van Gogh, were dyslexic. While some individuals described as dyslexic may have some structural or physiological problems within the cerebrum, others may merely have a strong natural visualizing lead and, consequently, find it very difficult to develop skills that derive from the diagonal organizing thinking style.

If dyslexic children could experience a whole-brained learning environment, some educators hypothesize that much of their dyslexia would vanish. Often, however, these children are placed in a traditional learning environment where they are pressured to perform, primarily using their weakest functions. It is no surprise that they are generally somewhat unsuccessful. It is no wonder that many develop *learning/test-taking anxieties*.

Some teachers have asked their dyslexic students to envision their responses prior to talking or writing about them, with very positive results. Others have had success in helping these youngsters learn to absorb information through their sensory system of preference. Sometimes this means helping them to learn to visualize a problem, a process, or a solution. Sometimes it means helping them to translate visual and auditory information into a kinesthetic format; to connect information to concepts they already know and enjoy applying.

Children labeled as hyperactive may have a *glitch* somewhere within the central nervous system. According to current research data, mothers who smoke during pregnancy have an increased chance of birthing a child who exhibits hyperactive behavior, since the developing fetal brain is especially sensitive to nicotine. Sometimes, however, hyperactivity may be a reactive-behavior pattern—engaged in by extreme extroverts who are seeking brain stimulation in order to feel comfortably alert.

When you couple extreme extroversion with a visualizing mode, you have a child who needs, and who regularly seeks, a great deal of stimulation. When this behavior pattern occurs in a highly regulated environment with a minimal amount of stimulation (the average elementary/high-school classroom), the child will, by contrast, appear extremely hyperactive. The drug Ritalin is not necessarily the only answer (refer to societal rewards in Chapter Three). Often, when these children are mentored by a highly creative adult, or are allowed to spend time out-of-doors in nature, their level of hyperactivity diminishes.

TEMPERAMENT CORRELATIONS

Individuals invariably ask about *temperament* and brain lead. Eugene Brewer chose this topic for his doctoral project. He assessed one hundred school teachers (fifty males and fifty females) and identified the following correlations:

- Choleric - prioritizers
- Phlegmatic - organizers
- Melancholy - harmonizers
- Sanguine - visualizers

> My mind to me a kingdom is;
> Such present joys therein I find,
> That it excels all other bliss
> That earth affords or grows by kind.
> —Dyer

Yes, our brain's characteristics show in everything we think and do. Some may believe there isn't much incentive for becoming excited about the decade of the brain. What do you think? What will you do?

INTELLIGENCES

> In youth we learn; in age we understand.
> —von Ebner-Eschenbach

Researchers now recognize that there are different types of intelligence: such as mathematical, linguistic, artistic, musical, and emotional, to name several. We can increase our level of intelligence by developing competencies in all of the intellectual skills; recognizing that we can usually achieve higher levels of competence in those that match our innate giftedness. While we may not choose to try to develop all of them equally, we can become well-rounded by consciously choosing to provide our brains with an enriched environment through some degree of exposure to all of them.

I heard a radio program recently in which the host interviewed several individuals from the state department of education. According to these educators, the State of California plans to reincorporate the study of phonics into the existing whole-language approach. This certainly sounds like a whole-brained proposal that can't help but benefit more students.

One way in which we can foster the development of *intelligences* is to include a wider variety of application techniques. Here are a few examples:

- mathematical intelligence can be honed by tackling problem-rich questions or real-life situations that require exploration, rather than only the generation of correct answers based on memorized facts

- linguistic intelligence can be enhanced by practice in public speaking, telling stories, debating, journaling, and through writing poetry/short stories. Foreign-language study is great at any age; the sooner the better

- artistic intelligence can be fostered through engaging in any manner of artistic endeavor whether that be building a kite, learning the skill of photography, computer graphics, carving/sculpting, painting, or a whole host of other activities

- musical intelligence can be stimulated by learning to play an instrument, by joining a choir, taking a music-appreciation course, attending a variety of musical programs, and by composing/arranging music. Don Campbell, author of *Introduction to the Musical Brain,* believes that using the whole body to learn opens the channels between mind and body. We can combine music with other learning tasks. For example, instead of only writing the letters of the alphabet, we can try singing them or performing them to music

- emotional intelligence can be fostered by learning the difference between emotions and feelings, by learning to manage moods, by developing social skills such as active listening, and by honing assertiveness and optimism. (Refer to Chapter Nine.)

Whatever you choose to do, remember that intelligence is not static. Through our choices, we definitely play a role in determining our individual levels and whether or not they rise or fall. In a similar way, as parents and educators we hold in our hands the key to helping our children achieve higher levels of intelligence. All are capable of *homers.* As my stepsons so often said, that's *totally awesome!*

I will work

in my

own way,

according to

the light that

is in me.

—Childs

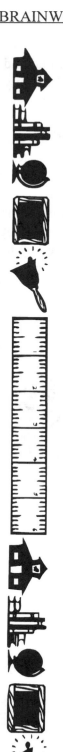

BRAIN BUILDERS

Points to Ponder

- Every one has something to learn and something to teach. —Anonymous

- Two key concepts I have learned in this section:

  _____

  _____

- Two facts I've discovered about myself while studying this section:

  _____

  _____

- One way in which I am now applying this information:

  _____

  _____

- The ultimate goal for education would be to understand
  _____ in terms of brain function.

- Four significant factors that influence one's learning style:
  1. _____   2. _____

  3. _____   4. _____

- A whole-brained learning environment would recognize and honor one's
  innate _____.

- **T F** Learning disabilities would likely look quite different in a whole-brained learning environment.

- **T F** Emotional intelligence may be even more important than I.Q.

- **T F** One's brain has matured by the age of puberty.

Brain Teasers

1.	2.	3.	4.
GROUND	4 5 7 11 19 ___	0 BS MS PhD	$\dfrac{\quad F \ M}{A \ M \ J}$

5.	6.	7.	8.
HILL	BACK	? RAINRAINRAIN	U N I O N N O I N O N N O I N U

Creativity Corner

ADAPTION

The use of nonpreferred cerebral functions can require the expenditure of up to one hundred times more metabolic energy second for second.

Excessive/prolonged adaption can lead to:

↑ Fatigue   ↓ Emotional tone
↑ Frustration   ↓ Concentration
↑ Illness/injury   ↓ Competency
↑ Procrastination   ↓ Self-esteem
↑ Risk of burnout   ↓ Thriving
↑ Risk of midlife crisis   ↓ Success

Chapter Seven
Pluses and Minuses of Adaption

Reporters ask questions. That's their job. A radio program recently reported a survey of responses from individuals who were challenged, "In one sentence, tell me who you are." There were a variety of interesting, if not always enlightening, responses including:

- Today I'm not sure!
- John (or Jane) Doe
- A mother of five
- You tell me
- Talk to me next week
- An engineer; a tired engineer
- It's none of your business! (*Granted, but this is part of a research project.*)
- Why do you want to know? (*Curious.*)
- Busy and don't have time for questions (*Wouldn't think of asking any.*)
- How much time do you have to spare?

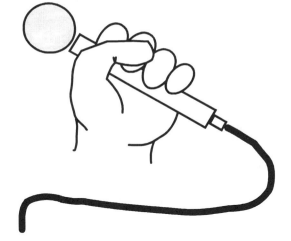

In reality, it's not possible to provide a complete answer in one sentence. The question makes for great conversation, however, when a group of individuals interested in—and somewhat versed in—brain function get together. Imagine throwing out the question, "Who are you?" in such a setting:

- Who, me? I'm a high extrovert. That, plus a harmonizing brain lead, and an auditory preference, means I'll probably be one of the last to leave this networking session. And the potluck is always great!

- I'm an introverted auditory with a visualizing brain lead. I'll probably be one of the first to leave. By the way, the story you told at the last meeting had me chuckling for days!

- I'm visual with a balanced E:I ratio and a prioritizing brain lead. I'm here because I'm hoping to meet a couple of individuals that can help my company function more effectively.

- I'm an extremely introverted kinesthetic with an organizing brain lead. I'm pleased to know that these meetings are scheduled on the first Monday of each month and are held at the same place. It's great that they always start on time!

Some individuals hate labels, but others readily use them to describe the way in which their brain functions best. Regardless, having some of this info in hand can help us to allow for diversity in thought and action. Most of us wouldn't think of expecting a hippo to run like a deer, to say nothing of hopping like a rabbit. We often don't offer the same courtesy to human beings, however, or we tolerate differences from a position of benign superciliousness. Perhaps the greatest gift we can give each other is twofold: to be ourselves—to honor and respect our uniqueness—and to genuinely respect and honor that of others. This gift usually helps life to flow much more smoothly. Here are some examples of career matches and mismatches:

- For as far back as he can remember, Bill wanted to be a teacher. When other little boys were talking about becoming doctors, dentists, and firefighters, Bill was creating *play school* in the backyard. He corralled his friends for students—along with the cat and the neighbor's dog. There had never been a male school teacher in Bill's lineage, but, fortunately, his family supported his desire. Twenty-five years later, in spite of all the hype about how difficult it is to discipline young people, Bill still loves teaching.

- Eric had always been creatively artistic. He loved to draw, paint, and sculpt. His father, however, was a military man and insisted that Eric follow in his footsteps. He was sent away to a military boarding academy. Even though he hated it, Eric studied hard and made an effort to fit in, but his grades were not up to par. The dean suggested that Eric take a week off to visit his family and discuss his future. At home, Eric begged to be allowed to study art. His father would not hear of it. No son of his was going to attend a sissy art school. Two weeks later, back at the military academy, Eric committed suicide.

- Jill's parents found her, at the age of four, taking apart the electric typewriter. Typical for a child with a prioritizing lead, she was trying to see how it worked. Her parents put a lock on the study door, so Jill started taking her dolls apart. While still in grade-school, she announced that she planned to become a scientist. When it was time to go to college, however, Jill reluctantly enrolled in home economics because that was her mother's profession. Two years later, Jill disappeared. Her parents searched for her without success. Ten years later, friends of theirs noticed an article in a research journal. Jill and two colleagues had just published the results of their brilliant research on viral identification. The family was reunited—after suffering ten years of needless alienation.

- Secretly, Jane felt very different from her girlfriends. In fact, she began to believe that she was below average in intelligence. Familial expectations did not allow her to take medicine, which was what she yearned to do. Instead, she enrolled in nursing school because that was acceptable to her family. Twenty years later, burned-out, depressed, and discouraged, Jane learned about brain lead and decided to reown hers. Taking a job with a law firm, she was able to use her nursing background in healthcare-law research. Jane learned that she actually had an extremely high IQ; a fact which improved her self-esteem and motivated her to enroll in evening classes. Eventually, Jane hopes to join the firm as an attorney specializing in medical malpractice.

- Because of familial expectations, Ted became a CPA. After several years, he developed migraines and other stress-related illnesses and experienced a midlife crisis. Through counseling, he realized that he had adapted away from his natural harmonizing lead in order to fit in with his family's expectations. To reown his brain lead, Ted left accounting and joined the staff at a large counseling clinic. He now teaches clients practical strategies for managing their money. Not only does he love his job, but his health is steadily improving, as well. In fact, his migraines are a thing of the past.

Of course, I'm exhausted. Racing isn't my thing . . .

EXCESSIVE ADAPTION AND MIDLIFE CRISIS

A competency can basically be defined as a skill that has been honed through practice. We can develop competencies within our brain lead as well as without. A simple way to observe competency differences is to sign your name holding a pen in your lead hand. Next, place the pen in your nonlead hand and sign your name. Most people will notice a difference, not only in the ease of writing, but in the legibility between the two signatures. If we choose to do so, we, through practice, certainly can increase our writing competency in our nonlead hand—although our comfort level may never be quite as high as it is when using our lead hand.

The term adaption refers to the development and use of competencies extrinsic to brain lead. We all adapt from time to time. It allows us more options in life and can enable us to be more successful. There is a difference, however, between *temporary* adaption and *excessive/prolonged* adaption—habitually identifying and *leading* with, an auxiliary thinking style.

There is an exorbitantly high price tag on excessive/prolonged adaption. It drains our energy. Engaging in tasks that primarily utilize skills outside innate brain lead can consume up to one hundred times more metabolic energy second for second. Over time, this greater expenditure of energy can lead to a variety of problems such as increased fatigue, frustration, illness, injury, procrastination, risk of burnout and midlife crisis as well as diminished emotional tone, concentration, competency, self-esteem, thriving, and success.

Some researchers believe that those who are at greatest risk for experiencing a midlife crisis are individuals who have spent years denying a brain lead and using nonlead competencies almost exclusively in order to succeed. This phenomenon, adaption, may actually be much more common than at first believed. The higher the level of extroversion, the more likely an individual is to adapt and also to suffer from a health problem during a midlife crisis.

I suppose it's a bit late for that ounce of prevention . . .

Here are a few examples of tasks that, depending on one's innate brain lead, could represent either desirable temporary adaption or undesirable excessive/prolonged adaption:

Temporary adaption	Excessive/prolonged adaption
• Balance the checkbook monthly • Write a short article for the newspaper • Play tennis at the annual picnic • Favor a friend with a listening ear	• Become an accountant • Try to earn your living as a writer • Become a tennis pro • Open a counseling office

Reasons for excessive/prolonged adaption include:

- Mismatch between innate giftedness and expectations of family/church/school/society
- Shamed for giftedness or rewarded for weaker functions
- Mimicking a loved family member; disowning characteristics of a disliked member
- Being the eldest or only child
- Lack of opportunities to develop and use giftedness
- Search for personal identity (as in being one of identical twins)
- Abuse (first-hand or vicarious)

COMPETENCY DEVELOPMENT

According to Webster's, the word thriving means to have oneself in hand, to flourish, and to grow. One illustration provided is that trees *thrive* in good soil. Thriving is as advanced beyond surviving as the ocean is removed from the tiny prairie pond. In order to thrive we need to: be in an environment that promotes our ability to be who we innately are; develop, use, and be rewarded for using our innate giftedness.

In order to increase our levels of self-esteem and to achieve immediate success, we can strive to:

- Match our career with innate giftedness

- Develop hobbies that use innate giftedness

- Spend time with friends who have similar preferences

- Select an accomplished role model with a similar brain lead whose life demonstrates a healthy development and use of innate giftedness

As already mentioned, our self-esteem increases when we select activities that match our lead because these activities can be accomplished with the most ease, the least energy output, and the most reward. Does this mean that we should develop competencies in the area of brain lead only? Absolutely not. Imagine selecting a house in which to live and then never stepping out of it. We would miss a great deal in life if we confined all of our activities to that one environment.

Conversely, imagine traveling all of the time and continually living *out of a suitcase*. How we would long for a home base! Applying this metaphor to the cerebrum, the ideal is to have a home base (our innate brain lead) in which we feel absolutely comfortable,

and in which we spend the majority of our time. We would, however, travel to the other three bases from time to time to gain a more global perspective, to learn new options, and to discover new ways of accomplishing tasks.

To obtain a better sense of this concept of competencies, sign your name five times on a sheet of paper, exactly as you write it on your checks. How long did it take you to do that? Compare that with the length of time that same task took when you were first learning to write? Many times longer than it did just now, I'll bet.

Now trying signing your name using your opposite hand. How long did it take you? If you wanted to develop writing competency in this hand you could do so. It would take time, though. Competencies are simply skills that have been developed as the result of repeated usage, skills honed through practice. We are all born with innate abilities but we develop competencies within those abilities only by investing time and energy in practice.

In one sense, whole-brained living means that we identify our natural brain lead, develop competencies in that area first and then work on developing skills throughout the cerebrum. Once you have identified your brain lead, define the competencies that you have developed within that lead. If you have largely ignored your innate aptitudes, select an activity that derives from your lead and develop skill in that activity. Remember that we learn more easily and with less energy output when we are working within our brain lead because of the reduced resistance in the synaptic gap.

If you have already developed competencies in your brain lead, branch out. Metaphorically spread your wings and begin to develop skills in a nonlead thinking style. To accomplish this, deliberately involve yourself in a variety of activities that depend upon the functions within that style. However, try to schedule no more than two hours of practice on any given day and, whenever possible, follow each practice session with an activity that matches your natural lead. Resist the temptation to quit. Give yourself plenty of time in which to succeed, and develop a tolerant, supportive attitude toward yourself during the process.

Finding accomplished role models or mentors, individuals who are gifted in the thinking style we want to develop, can be of great help. We need to get to know them; to find out how they approach solving problems and making decisions; to try to see things from the perspective of their brain lead. We can learn about their interests, values, and skills. We can practice seeing the world through their eyes.

For example, when we want to develop prioritizing skills, we need to look for role models who possess skills in decision-making, negotiating, financial analysis, technological research, and in using tools of all kinds.

When we want to develop organizing competencies, we need to find mentors who demonstrate skills in holding to deadlines and schedules, in performing routine or procedural tasks accurately (whether operational or administrative), and in proofreading.

In order to develop harmonizing skills, we need to seek out those who exhibit skills in the realm of music, who are encouraging and nurturing, who have a flair for interior decorating, and who like to write personal notes and letters.

When we want to develop visualizing competencies, we need to associate with individuals who are imaginative, and who exhibit skills in creative problem solving, in designing, in making changes, in seeing the big picture, in identifying trends/patterns, and in taking healthy risks.

EXAMPLES OF COMPETENCY-BUILDING ACTIVITIES

Prioritizing Thinking Style	Visualizing Thinking Style
• Join a debate club • Give a speech • Read and abstract information • Participate in a research project	• Draw, paint, sculpt, carve, design • Write poems, stories, songs • Assemble 3-D puzzles • Travel
Organizing Thinking Style	**Harmonizing Thinking Style**
• Read and outline information • Make/follow lists; balance checkbook • Join a club/team • Sight-read music	• Join a choir; play an instrument by ear • Take a drama class • Play games for fun • Participate in peer counseling

COLLABORATION

Undoubtedly, it would be ideal if all of us could *instantly* become whole-brained. Unfortunately, such an expectation is not realistic because it takes time to develop competencies. In addition, not everyone is willing to invest the energy in that process nor is it always practical. Whole-brained living can also mean that we team up with the brains of others in order to achieve an exponentially greater outcome. Our overall success and competency in life can be enhanced through collaboration with those who have strengths to complement our weaknesses.

To enhance our long-term potential for thriving we need to:

- Find a mentor to help us develop competencies in our nonlead thinking styles

- Select a coach with a complementary brain lead to advise us

- Partner with a complementary brain lead—value, listen, learn from his/her strengths

- Sandwich nonpreferred activities between lead activities to minimize procrastination

Many of us have already utilized collaboration in our lives. For example, Jeannie is a visualizer. She doesn't want to devote the time it would take to develop the organizing skills required to balance her checkbook. Consequently, she *trades* with Sue for whom balancing a checkbook is like falling off a log. Once a month, Sue balances Jeannie's checkbook; Jeannie trades her a weekly loaf of homemade bread. They're both delighted with this arrangement.

Patty's son was showing every sign of becoming a talented violinist. He needed someone to spend an evening each week accompanying him on the piano. Patty arranged for one of her husband's pianist

> I use not only all the brains I have but all I can borrow. — Woodrow Wilson

friends to practice with her son once a week. In exchange, she spent one evening a week baby-sitting so he and his wife could have a night out. They, too, are pleased with their trade.

Although Grandma Mary was physically quite healthy, she often forgot where she was. Consequently, her nephew and his wife, with whom she lived, began to feel very *tied down*. They didn't want to place her in a nursing home, but they needed to give themselves some scheduling flexibility. So they located two high-school students who were interested in painting. You see, Mary had been an art teacher and a watercolor artist. They set up an easel in the spare room so the students could paint and keep an eye on Mary at the same time. She loved to sit in the room with the students and talk about art. She gave them excellent suggestions. The students quickly grew to love her, and looked forward to their weekly visits. Another whole-brained solution for a potentially thorny problem.

EXERCISE, NUTRITION, AND EATING PATTERNS

According to Blair Justice, author of *Who Gets Sick,* we can give our bodies *love* through exercise and good nutrition. In addition, our customary eating patterns play a more significant role than many suppose. Let's briefly review these three factors.

1 Is there a link between exercise and brain function? Yes. Physical exercise can help both the brain and the body in a variety of different ways. Indeed, some have referred to physical exercise as a problem-solving tactic. Researchers are beginning to explore and understand the synergism that can exist between exercise and a creative approach to solving problems. Albert Einstein and Charles Dickens reportedly took walks in order to produce flashes of insight, or to discover creative solutions to problems.

Here are some ways in which exercise can benefit the brain:

- **Improves oxygen transport**.

A regular supply of blood containing the necessary oxygen (transported by red blood cells) is vitally important to the brain. In order to function properly, it needs twenty percent of all the oxygen we take in through our lungs; a full fifth! Exercise enhances blood flow as well as oxygen intake (deep breathing). Many individuals are in the habit of breathing shallowly. We need to take many deep breaths of fresh air every day using the abdominal muscles so that all parts of the lungs are expanded.

- **Carries glucose and other nutrients**

In order to *think,* the neurons require food. This food comes to them in the form of glucose via the blood stream. Exercise enhances circulation. Thus, depending upon what nutrients the blood contains, exercise can enhance our alertness and improve our ability to process information. Recent studies at the University of Illinois have found that exercise can increase the number of blood vessels to the brain, thus bringing increased nourishment. Increased nourishment contributes to an improved ability to think.

- **Helps to clean the brain**

Physical exercise has been called an *antioxidant* for the brain. Exercise, especially the type that utilizes the large muscle groups of the body, speeds up the heart rate and increases the circulation of the blood. This action not only helps to prevent the accumulation of metabolic wastes in the brain, but also to eliminate those that have accumulated.

- **Stimulates the release of endorphins**

Aerobic exercise (also *moving* experiences such as attending a superb musical concert, the beauty of a glorious sunset, viewing exquisite works of art) is believed to stimulate the release of endorphins, the body's natural morphine. Endorphins help to increase feelings of well-being. They are associated with relief of pain, and with turning on a placebo response (as when individuals strongly believe that a certain procedure/pill/coping skill will reduce their discomfort).

- **Helps with stress management**

Exercise has been found to buffer the effects of stress. In one study, high-stress managers, who combined psychological hardiness (defined as possessing a sense of control, challenge, and commitment) with exercise, and a social support system, remained healthier. Their chances of suffering a severe illness in the near future were less than one in ten. For high-stress managers without these components, the severe-illness probability was more than nine chances in ten. Exercise has been found to increase one's sense of control, and to elevate the level of norepinephrine, a neurotransmitter that can become depleted in depression.

- **Increases resistance to illness**

Regular exercise can increase our resistance to both mental and physical illness. It is one of the factors believed to be an essential addition to effective coping strategies. And, everything begins in the brain—dis-ease as well as effective coping skills. Regular exercise can also promote healing as well as reduce levels of depression and anxiety. Increased work satisfaction and fewer sick-leave days are two benefits that can accrue to participants in aerobic fitness programs. According to recent research, individuals who exercise are less likely to get cancer. In three different studies researchers discovered that:

> - Active people were more cancer-free than moderate exercisers
> - Former college athletes have a lower lifetime-occurrence rate of cancer than their nonathletic peers
> - Nonathletes had almost double the risk of breast cancer and over double the risk of reproductive-system cancer as did former athletes.

- **Improves one's body image**

Most people who exercise have a healthier body image. This may be, in part, because a fit body usually looks better and functions more efficiently. Because these benefits contribute to our feeling better about ourselves, our personal sense of self-worth can be boosted.

2 Psychoneuroimmunology (PNI) suggests that the brain/body connection can be influenced by the foods we ingest. Neurons require glucose to fuel their activity. Calories found in natural fruits, vegetables, and complex carbohydrates are preferable sources of glucose. They have been referred to as clean-burning energy. Highly refined foods on the other hand, especially fats and sugars, are believed to negatively impact brain function. They can *clog* the mind and decrease mental alertness. They can also contribute to a whole smorgasbord of health problems that, in turn, impact brain function.

Physicians such as Dean Ornish, John McDougall, and Nathan Pritikin have become well-known for their emphasis on the relation of nutrition to brain and body health. Typically, the same types of foods that are believed to enhance immune-system function also enhance brain function:

Here are some general guidelines:

- **Additives**

Avoid food additives: especially monosodium glutamate (MSG) and any others ending in *"ate"*; artificial colors, flavors, and/or preservatives; paraffin or pesticides.

- **Beverages**

Use herb teas without caffeine (e.g., chamomile, mint); freshly squeezed or frozen fruit and vegetable juices.
Avoid alcohol; cocoa; coffee; artificially flavored, colored, or sweetened drinks and beverages; canned juices; nondairy creamers.

- **Dairy Products**

Use sparingly, if at all; *nonfat* dairy products such as yogurt, cottage cheese, milk, buttermilk, cream cheese/other uncolored cheeses. Gradually try to reduce intake.
Avoid all saturated fats (solid at room temperature); ice cream and toppings, colored cheeses.

- **Eggs**

Use sparingly, if at all; poached, boiled, or baked eggs—mainly egg whites.
Avoid egg yolks and fried eggs.

- **Fish/Sea food**

Use sparingly, if at all; boiled or baked fresh white-fleshed fish. Be alert to problems with mercury or other contaminants.
Avoid all deep-fried fish.

- **Fruit**

Use fresh or frozen, preferably unsweetened, stewed, dried (preferably unsulfured).
Avoid canned and sweetened fruit.

- **Grains**

Use whole-grain breads/muffins whenever possible (e.g., rye, wheat, oats, buckwheat, barley, millet, corn, brown rice); unsweetened whole-grain cereals; whole seeds (e.g., flax, sesame, sunflower).
Avoid products made from refined white flour; most crackers; snack foods; white rice; most processed cereals.

- **Meats**

Use sparingly, if at all; try to gradually reduce intake.
Avoid all red-meat products.

- **Nuts/seeds**

Use in moderation fresh, raw, or lightly roasted (unsalted) nuts and seeds. Soaking raw nuts or seeds in water for a day or two starts the germination process and makes them not only more nutritious, but easier to digest.
Avoid roasted and/or salted nuts (especially peanuts which may contain aflotoxins).

- **Oils/fats**

Use sparingly cold-pressed oils (e.g., olive).
Avoid shortening; refined fats and oils (saturated or unsaturated); hydrogenated margarine or other spreads; use of oils or fats in cooking, frying, and baking.

- **Seasonings**

Use salt sparingly. Include herbs such as: garlic, onion, rosemary, parsley, marjoram, thyme, cayenne.
Avoid black pepper and the excessive use of *hot* spices.

- **Soups**

Use soup made from *scratch*. Aim for low-salt and fat-free. Include vegetables, legumes, and grains such as barley, millet, and brown rice.
Avoid canned and creamed soups; commercial bouillon; fat stock.

- **Sweets**

Use sparingly pure unfiltered honey, unsulfured molasses, and pure maple syrup.
Avoid refined sugars (white, brown, turbinado, powdered), chocolate, candy, syrups, and artificial sweeteners.

- **Vegetables**

Use fresh or frozen vegetables; (raw, baked, steamed, or stir-fried without oil)
Avoid canned vegetables; corn and potato chips; deep-fried vegetables in any form.

3 Our eating patterns can significantly impact our brain/body connection. We need to pay attention to how our body works most effectively. There may be some foods that, when eaten together, cause gas, bloating, or indigestion. Some individuals are allergic to specific foods or to chemicals within the foods. For example, some artificial sweeteners have been associated with migraine headaches. The allergic response can be mildly irritating, interfere moderately with one's disposition, or be totally life-threatening.

Remember that intense emotions such as anger, fear, and sadness can interfere with digestion. Any effort to make the environment at mealtime pleasant, and even interesting, is an investment in longevity and improved brain/body function. Avoid rushing through a meal or making mealtime a time for resolving arguments.

You may want to evaluate your own eating patterns in the light of the following factors:

- **Amount of food**

Laboratory studies show that rats live longer when their food intake is slightly reduced from normal. Moderate overeating shortens their lifespan. As human beings, we need to eat the right amount of food—not too little, not too much. Many Americans *overeat*. Overeating often pulls blood to the digestive system from other parts of the body, including the brain. This can temporarily contribute to decreased alertness. Some health professionals advocate the use of appropriate *juice fasts* for one evening meal each week, or for a whole day each month. A juice fast can help the body to rid itself of toxic wastes. (Be sure to consult a health professional/physician before developing any type of fasting program.)

- **Bingeing**

Binge eating may release endorphins that provide a temporary feeling of well-being. This can be especially true when one primarily indulges in candy, pastries, high-carbohydrate snacks, and high-fat fast foods. The effect is short-lived, however, and the long-term problems (e.g., weight gain, yo-yo dieting, purging) can be quite devastating.

- **Eating schedule**

For most people, the digestive system functions most effectively when it receives food on a regular schedule, two or three times a day. Eating too frequently or going too long between meals can disrupt body function. Certainly, the habit of munching between meals can negatively affect the digestive system. Many of us recall the fable about the little girl whose task mistress kept adding cream to the churn. It certainly affected the little girl's progress. At the end of an entire day of churning, she was exhausted and there still wasn't any butter! The constant addition of food to the stomach disrupts digestion. If fermentation sets in, the gamut of problems may range from halitosis to painful headaches, or worse.

- **Brain chemistry**

Inside the body, certain substances such as caffeine and alcohol can cause alteration in brain chemistry. For example:

- Caffeine mimics the effect of amphetamines and can stimulate the release of dopamine

- Alcohol can deplete stores of dopamine and can slow the speed of information transfer

Changes in brain chemistry have also been linked to the food eaten at the last meal. For example, for some individuals, chocolate is associated with changes in mood. Some foods are believed to stimulate alertness and mental acuity (e.g., natural proteins) while others promote calmness (e.g., high carbohydrate foods such as pasta).

- **Fluid intake**

Dehydration is disastrous to brain tissue. Very few individuals drink too much water; many are believed to be dehydrated. An insufficient intake of water on a daily basis is known to increase bodily free-radical production which can damage brain tissue, as well as hasten the onset of symptoms of aging. For the majority of us, drinking for *thirst* only will result in inadequate intake of water. Unless our water intake must be limited due to an existing medical condition, we need to drink at least eight glasses of water each and every day. There are times when we may need to drink more than eight (e.g., hot weather, strenuous exercise, hard physical labor, pregnancy). Remember that drinking fruit juices and other beverages is not the same as drinking water. No digestive action is required for water. When we drink pure water, we get the liquid the brain needs but don't activate the digestive system as would happen when ingesting juices.

- **Supplements**

We need vitamins, minerals, enzymes, and a whole host of micronutrients on a daily basis. These can be found in wholesome, unrefined foods; but it can be difficult to take in sufficient amounts each day with today's frenetic schedules. Many people report improved brain function when they take a food supplement. (A cold-processed synergistically balanced herbal formula, based on the green superfoods, works best for me.) It is important to avoid megadoses of one particular micronutrient in order to prevent an imbalance within the body.

Here are examples of just two substances needed by the brain:

- Choline is the precursor used by the body to make acetylcholine, the most common neurotransmitter identified to date. A plentiful supply of choline-containing lecithin can help to support mental activity. Lecithin is found in soy-bean products.

- Vitamin C utilization is approximately 100 times more concentrated in the brain. Copious amounts of this antioxidant are burned during stress so it is important to ingest sufficient quantities. Vitamin C is found in abundance in citrus fruits, as well as in many yellow and green leafy vegetables.

As with so much else in life, balance is important in both the areas of nutrition and exercise. The brain must compete with the body for resources. If physical exertion is extreme, resources that could be used for mental exertion will suffer, and vice versa. The key is balance and moderation within a high-level-wellness lifestyle. Is it worth pursuing? You bet it is. All one has to do is scan the statistics for deaths in the United States and correlate those with the top ten risk factors contributing to those deaths. It is quickly obvious that lifestyle factors, including exercise, nutrition, and eating patterns are vital to our well-being.

CREATIVITY

When most people talk about *creativity*, they are often referring primarily to musical, artistic, or literary talents. This partial definition, however, would assign creativity to one part of the brain only. Not so. All of the thinking styles are creative in their own sphere.

- The organizing thinking style is creative in the way in which it organizes routines, pays attention to detail, handles self-care, and maintains the status quo

- The harmonizing thinking style is creative in the way in which it nurtures, encourages, develops relationships, and tries to harmonize colors, sounds, and the environment

- The visualizing thinking style is creative in the way in which it solves problems, compares diagrams and abstract patterns, innovates, and approaches artistic endeavors

- The prioritizing thinking style is creative in the way it uses words, performs analyses, sets/achieves goals, and makes decisions

Webster defines creativity as artistic or intellectual inventiveness. True creativity may really be the capacity to use all thinking styles in whatever endeavor is undertaken—each making a contribution that is both appropriate and unequaled. Developing competencies throughout the brain can definitely improve our creativity. Cultivating an inclination to use the whole brain can narrow the gap between achieving inferior and superior results; between mediocrity and genius. Studies in Western cultures indicate that ninety percent of the population under the age of five are highly creative. Only two percent of the population over eight years of age are highly creative. What, in such a short period of time, has happened to so drastically curtail their creativity?

There is a strong correlation between emotional health and the uninhibited flow of creativity. Creativity is dependent upon not only our innate giftedness, but also upon our attitude and our way of life. Furthermore, it is influenced by our ability to forge ahead even in the face of criticism. Individuals often stop being creative when they are criticized/ridiculed by others or by themselves. Truly creative people have learned to let go of self-criticism; to tell themselves that they cannot fail because creativity is inside them. Furthermore, they are not immobilized by the criticism of others. Because they choose to rise above negative, external opinions, their creativity remains intact.

Researchers at Iowa State University studied seventh- and eighth-grade students, all right-handed boys, in a gifted program. The gifted children were found to be more strongly left-brained when mentally *at rest.* When engaged in the research activities, however, their right hemispheres were more involved and differently engaged when compared to the control group. Among other things, the researchers found that all the gifted children performed verbal listening tasks with both ears simultaneously, thus actuating both hemispheres. They did not follow the usual pattern displayed by the right-handed boys in the control group, who identified verbal sounds using primarily the right ear, which is more closely linked to the left hemisphere.

This study suggests that gifted individuals may possess a profound ability to switch rapidly between the two hemispheres. This, plus notable cognitive involvement by the right side of the brain, especially in typically *left-brained* tasks, may be hallmarks of higher intelligence—and greater creativity.

DREAMING

In some cases, creative ideas surface while we are dreaming. Many individuals who have made marvelous contributions to our world (inventors and scientists like Albert Einstein), report having arrived at a solution or a new idea because of a dream. Their brains, having subconsciously continued to creatively brainstorm, communicated flashes of intuition when they had just awakened from sleep or had spent time engaging in an entirely different activity.

Dreaming is believed to happen primarily during REM (rapid eye movement) sleep cycles which occur about every ninety minutes. There is some indication that dreaming early in the night or sleep cycle may involve the right hemisphere more than the left; while dreaming later in the night or sleep cycle is more likely to involve the left hemisphere.

Dreams are believed to be more easily recalled when the mental images seen in the right side of the brain can be transferred to the left hemisphere and be translated into words.

Scientists believe that the two halves of the cerebrum ideally prefer to operate in ninety-minute cycles. That is, the hemispheres prefer to alternate in a steady rhythm. To some degree, the switching pattern continues even during periods of sleep. This might mean that, when we maintain a distinct preference for only one thinking style to the exclusion of the other three, we may be going against the natural cycles of the brain—and we may fail to realize our full creative potential.

Dreaming (versus day dreaming) presupposes that one has been able to fall asleep. Many of us were taught as children that if we were having difficulty falling asleep, we should count sheep. Some have believed that mentally picturing the pastoral scene in which sheep usually reside was conducive to sleep; others that it was the endless counting that bored one to tears and induced sleep as a respite. A recent article in *Science Digest* addressed this very topic. The article reported research by psychologists Richard Davidson

and Gary E. Schwartz on the classic method of dealing with insomnia—counting sheep. While at Harvard, they discovered that:

> *visualizing sheep prevents the brain's right hemisphere from processing anxiety-provoking imagery, while the counting itself keeps the left hemisphere from straying into problematic auditory and verbal thought . . . In effect, counting sheep ties up both sides of the brain at once to prevent insomnia-producing stimuli.*

BRAINSTORMING

Although each thinking style is creative in its own way, creativity is enhanced when we invoke whole-brained thinking. We often hear the term *synergism* applied to the use of medications whereby two drugs, given together, have a greater total effect than the sum of their individual effects. Likewise with creative brainstorming. When brainstorming synergistically, the four cerebral thinking styles produce an exponentially greater total effect than the sum of their efforts if they were each working individually (if that were indeed possible). True creativity involves the use of all thinking styles and the ability to quickly switch back and forth among them. Synergistic brainstorming is definitely a whole-brained exercise that can be done individually or collectively. Here is one way to portray this process:

1 *Insight.* Researchers believe that insight originates from functions associated with the visualizing thinking style (e.g., illumination, intuition, and the ability to see the global picture). Insight enables us not only to recognize that there is a problem, but also that it needs to be solved.

2 *Investigation.* Functions from the prioritizing thinking style now assign a label to the problem (let's call it Problem X) and begin to collect pertinent data. The data are logically assembled, categorized, labeled, weighed, and prioritized. The organizing thinking style is instructed to carefully and sequentially file the data in the memory banks for later retrieval.

3 *Incubation.* The collected data are now left to simmer while functions of the visualizing thinking style go to work again. In a very global and innovative manner, they explore options for possible solutions against the backdrop of all the accumulated data. During this process, the harmonizing functions may contribute suggestions about the data, or about potential options, based on their interest in promoting harmony. This takes time. Remember, the right side of the brain is not time-based and doesn't like to be rushed.

4 *Illumination.* Suddenly we experience a flash of illumination as functions of the visualizing thinking style (in conjunction with the other three) put everything together, arrive at a new understanding of Problem X, and provide us with a potential solution. This creative breakthrough often occurs after we have been sleeping or have engaged in some other unrelated activity.

5 *Verification and application.* Functions of the prioritizing thinking style now evaluate the creative breakthrough (innovative solution) to make sure that it is sound. Organizing functions compare the breakthrough solution with data stored in the memory banks to make sure that it does not conflict with decisions that have already been made. Harmonizing functions verify that the solution will keep as many individuals, as possible, happy. If everything is a *go*, we translate the solution for Problem X into a doable form, and practically apply it.

If we have ignored developing competencies in even one of the necessary functions, one or more of the five steps in this process may not be completed and the synergism can be lost. Consequently, there is an advantage to having developed competencies throughout the cerebrum. As the makers of a popular stomach antacid proclaim, "Your brain is brilliantly designed. Use it!" Hats off to thriving!

BRAIN BUILDERS

Points to Ponder

- Death is not the greatest loss in life. The greatest loss is what dies inside us while we live. —Cousins

- Two key concepts I have learned in this section:

  _____

  _____

- Two facts I've discovered about myself while studying this section:

  _____

  _____

- One strategy I am now using to help myself thrive:

  _____

  _____

- A competency is a _____ that has been honed through practice.

- Those at highest risk for burnout/midlife crisis may be individuals who have spent years denying innate _____.

- According to author Justice, we can give our bodies _____ through appropriate amounts of exercise and good nutrition.

- **T   F**   Adaption refers to the use of competencies from nonlead thinking styles.

- **T   F**   While temporary adaption can be beneficial, excessive/prolonged adaption can be life-threatening over time.

- **T   F**   Our self-esteem tends to increase when we select activities that match our brain lead.

Brain Teasers

1.	2.	3.	4.
GRAPH GRAPH GRAPH GRAPH GRAPH	JUS144TICE	ACCIDENT	O R D E R

Creativity Corner

Stress can be defined as a force—measured in pounds per square inch—that tends to strain or distort a body.

In 1937, Dr. Hans Selye attracted worldwide attention when he borrowed the word *stress* from the field of engineering and applied it to human beings.

IN THE MIDST OF THE STORM

Chapter Eight
The Brain and Stress

More than half a century ago, Dr. Hans Selye, of Montreal's McGill University, attracted worldwide attention when he borrowed the word *stress* from the field of engineering and applied it to human beings. These days, the word stress is part of almost everyone's vocabulary—especially as our global village becomes more frenetic. Even though the term is used quite freely, many people cannot clearly explain what stress is, although they can often describe the problems that they believe stem from it.

Webster's defines stress as a physical, chemical, or emotional factor that causes bodily or mental tension and which may be a factor in disease causation. Selye defined it as essentially the rate of all wear and tear caused by life; the nonspecific response of the body to any demand made upon it.

Based on both of these definitions, stress is a necessary phenomenon that exists at all levels of life because simply being alive requires us to continually adapt to our external and internal worlds. Anytime anything changes in life, the body must respond. Therefore, stress is the body's response to some demand; in other words, the result of its adaptation to change—whether those changes be good or bad, positive or negative, desirable or undesirable. Based on what is going on in both of these worlds, we may perceive greater amounts of stress based on the need for greater amounts of change.

Although I've never had the experience personally, those who have weathered major storms say they have been able to remain relatively calm and safe by removing themselves from the path of the storm—leaving the area or taking cover. That's a great metaphor for life. There will be, from time to time, stressful storms all around us. We need to plan our escape route. We need to build our metaphoric shelter to which we can resort in times of need. This really means that it behooves us to brush up on the topic of stress and learn strategies that can help us to manage our stressors as effectively as possible. I like to discuss stress from three different perspectives.

Eustress

The word eustress comes from the Greek root "*eu*" that signifies good. We use it in words such as euphoria, eulogy, and eucalyptus. Eustress can be thought of as desirable stress; stimuli that help us to concentrate, focus, perform, and work at peak efficiency. It can help us to feel more mentally alert and focused, to be more creative, and to successfully master

our challenges. It can motivate us to discover new options for problem solving and to achieve our goals.

Eustress can take the form of delight, excitement, challenge, or innovative creativity. Examples of desirable stress can include marriage, childbirth, a promotion, vacation, continued education, even exercise. Many of these activities represent positive situations and accomplishments in our lives. We sometimes forget that, although we may consciously choose an activity or a course of action, to the degree that this requires the body to adjust to a change, we will experience some stress. Simply turning the pages of this syllabus requires parts of the body to adapt.

Distress

The word distress comes from the Latin root "*dis*" that means not desirable. We use it in words such as dissonance, disgrace, and discharge. Distress can be defined as unpleasant, damaging stress; stimuli that, over time, can interfere with our ability to concentrate, focus, perform, and work at peak efficiency. Unmanaged, distress is a killer. In a state of distress, there is no true relaxation between one stressful episode and the next. The systems which stimulate the production of adrenalin, noradrenalin, and cortisone are stuck in the

"*on*" position, so to speak—a scenario often linked with mental, emotional, and physical ailments.

Examples of undesirable stress are relatively easy to identify because they are so common: death of a relative/close friend, bankruptcy, accidents, divorce, layoffs, and terrorism. We can think of distress as stressors that we would prefer to avoid, if that were possible. Distress is a relative concept. That is, the perception of its impact can vary according to one's gender, cultural conditioning, sensory-system preference, extroversion/introversion ratio, and innate brain lead.

Mistress

The word mistress can be defined as hidden or unrecognized stress; stimuli and factors that we tend to mislabel if we identify them at all. The prefix *"mis"* is an abbreviation of the Latin root *minus* meaning *less*. We use it in words such as misfortune, miscount, and misdeeds. On the surface, one might think that mistress is less harmful than distress.

Not necessarily so. The greatest toll from stress may not come from the major traumatic changes or misfortunes in our lives—divorce, layoff, relocation, bereavement. Rather, the greatest toll may result from the minor annoyances that we experience frequently: getting stuck in traffic; having a flat tire; trying to lose those few extra pounds over, and over again; misplacing the car keys— and a whole host of hassles that we often consider to be relatively unimportant. Other examples of unrecognized or hidden stress can include lack of sleep, improper eating habits, and in our technological age—*technostress*.

REACTION FORMS

When confronted with a stressor, we tend to deal with it through activating one of two basic reaction forms: either fight/flight or conserve/withdraw. These reaction forms are basically initiated through the autonomic nervous system, over which we do not have immediate conscious control (although we can contribute to a tendency to activate one over the other based on our thinking styles and habit patterns). Both fight/flight and conserve/withdraw are protective mechanisms designed for short-term stress management. Neither reaction form was designed to be repeatedly triggered or to have the button locked in the "on" position.

The body is able to rebalance itself from the physiological effects of one episode of either fight/flight or conserve/withdraw in approximately 18-24 hours. Physical exercise can speed up the rebalancing process of the body after fight/flight is initiated; it is not believed to speed up the rebalancing process in the conserve/withdraw reaction form.

Fight/flight

The fight/flight reaction form is designed to manage life-threatening situations when we perceive we can prevail or manage successfully. The resulting physiological changes are designed to provide us with needed energy. Most stress-management seminars concentrate on this reaction form. Selye dubbed the fight/flight reaction form the General Adaptation Syndrome—GAS for short—an acronym that really fits. When we drive an automobile, we need some type of fuel to provide the energy with which to run the vehicle. The GAS gives our bodies the fuel or energy it needs to deal with change. Almost any type of stressor can activate fight/flight.

With eustress, however, there is a relaxation phase between episodes of stimuli that activate the system to produce adrenalin, noradrenalin, and cortisone. Accordingly, Selye reported that although fight/flight could be activated with positive as well as with negative stimuli, eustress caused less harm than did distress. Repeated triggering of the fight/flight reaction form can lead to illnesses such as high blood pressure and ulcers.

Conserve/withdraw

The conserve/withdraw reaction form is designed to help us manage life-threatening or overwhelming situations when we perceive (in reality or in imagination) that we cannot manage the event or the situation successfully. It's as if a state of immobility is declared. The resulting physiological changes conserve rather than expend body energy. Thus one is enabled to survive until the event/situation has passed.

We often see the conserve/withdraw reaction form manifested in the temporary immobility or numbness that sets in after we have experienced a trauma of some sort or another (e.g., the death of a friend, a bomb scare, a hostage-taking incident). Conserve/withdraw forces us, in effect, to *take a break* or a breathing space before we have to get back to the business of daily living. It's as if the body wants to help us wait it out safely when we believe we cannot change anything through fight/flight.

Some of the behaviors we commonly see exhibited in the Post Traumatic Stress Disorder (PTSD) may relate to conserve/withdraw. When exposed to events such as major natural disasters (e.g., earthquakes, floods), war situations (e.g., Vietnam, Bosnia), terrorism (e.g., Oklahoma City, the World Trade Center), crime (e.g., robbery, abduction), or abuse (e.g., incest, rape), individuals may perceive a sense of helplessness and hopelessness—that no matter what they do, they cannot fix the situation or repair the damage. From then on until they get into recovery, these individuals may trigger conserve/withdraw habitually, especially whenever confronted with any situation that reminds them (even subconsciously) of the original event.

Not all individuals with PTSD follow a conserve/withdraw pattern— some follow a fight/flight pattern, others alternate between the two reaction forms. There is some belief that excessive/prolonged adaption can cause a type of long-term anxiety (a stressor) and induce a form of PTSD. This would make an excellent research project.

The repeated triggering of the conserve/withdraw reaction form can lead to depression. (Refer to the *Distress, Eustress & Mistress* seminar for an overall discussion of the two primary reaction forms, the differing results that can accrue from chronically triggering one over the other, *Internal Stable Globalization* self-talk patterns, practical strategies for managing a variety of stressors on a daily basis, and specific strategies for managing depression related to repeated triggering of conserve/withdraw.)

BRAIN STRESSORS

It is well documented in countless studies that unmanaged stress can adversely affect the human organism. These effects can include: decreased ability to brainstorm options, altered brain neurochemistry, physical illness, emotional distress, diminished self-esteem levels, or depression. It is also a given, that if we learn to identify stressors and manage them effectively, we can reduce the adverse effects.

There are some specific contributors and side-effects related to the way in which an individual's giftedness matches or mismatches a variety of factors such as expectations, opportunities, and environment. Some of these we can learn to manage much more effectively, thereby reducing the negative impact to our brain and body. In general, our individual response to stressors will differ based on a whole host of factors that span the spectrum from learned habit patterns to innate giftedness. Based on our innate giftedness—in combination with our specific environment and societal expectations—each of us may be at risk for different types of stressors.

With a view to prevention, it would be beneficial to check out undesirable outcomes that can accrue from the mismanagement of seven brain stressors:

1. Mismatch between innate brain lead and environment/societal expectations
2. History of woundedness in an area of innate giftedness
3. Mismatch between E:I ratio and societal rewards
4. Career not matching match brain lead, E:I ratio, or sensory preference
5. Lack of sensory-preference validation
6. Unbalanced lifestyle
7. Habitually negative mind-set

1 **Mismatch between innate brain lead and environment/societal expectations.** In general, females are rewarded for exhibiting behaviors that derive from the harmonizing functions; males, from the prioritizing. Individuals who possess a brain lead that differs from these expectations can experience stress because, at some level, they don't quite *fit in,* or they do so at great cost in terms of metabolic energy. These include males/females with a preference for using the visualizing functions, males with a preference for the harmonizing, and females with a preference for the prioritizing. In addition, individuals may experience stress when their environment doesn't acknowledge and nurture their giftedness, interferes with their ability to act upon their giftedness, or doesn't reward them (even punishes them) for using their talents.

Consider each thinking style:

Organizers

Organizers painstakingly absorb information about bounded shapes. They like to assign labels to the shapes, grasp and manipulate them, and keep them organized. Consequently, they may perceive stress when the bounded shapes within their environments are out of order (toys or clothes are strewn around everywhere); when they cannot find certain bounded shapes (their car keys); when their routines are changed (they must drive to work by a different route because of a detour); when they are subjected to a change of schedule; or if interrupted when in the midst of a project.

Being aware of this predisposition, organizers can alter their expectations or perceptions in order to reduce tension, recognizing that it's impossible to keep track of all bounded shapes all the time, or to prevent interruptions one hundred percent of the time.

Harmonizers

Harmonizers are interested in the relationship between bounded shapes. They desire harmony among colors, sounds, objects, people, and their environment. Consequently, harmonizers may perceive stress when there is disharmony in their environment, animate as well as inanimate. They are also at risk for overextending themselves in an attempt to promote harmony, a fact that can eventually increase stress as they become fatigued.

Being aware of this tendency can help them to alter their expectations or perceptions to a more realistic level in order to reduce tension, because it's impossible to achieve harmony among everyone and everything all the time.

Visualizers

Visualizers scan the environment for abstract patterns of information. They intuitively look for the *big picture* and innovatively visualize change based on identified trends. They take in copious amounts of information and tend to process rapidly and globally. They may experience stress when there is a lack of variety in their environment, or when they procrastinate necessary tasks that require the use of nonpreferred functions.

Being aware of this tendency can help them to consciously reduce tension by creating opportunities for variety in a healthy manner, balancing the need to conform to certain rules and regulations with their desire for spontaneity, humor, and adventure.

Prioritizers

Prioritizers tend to evaluate almost everything for functionality. Prompted by a desire for goal achievement, they strive to analyze, logically evaluate, and prioritize information. Consequently, they may be at risk for perceiving stress when they are unable to attain their goals as quickly or completely as they might desire. They are also at risk for failing to devote time to creating and maintaining a good social-support system; a lack that can eventually compound stress, especially in times of crisis.

Being aware of this tendency can help them to make a concerted effort to avoid workaholism, and to consciously balance their bent toward goal achievement with healthy interaction with family and friends.

The price tag on brain stressors, deriving from *mismatches,* can include:

- Decreased energy levels
- Decreased self-esteem
- Increased exhaustion
- Increased risk illness
- Increased accidents/mistakes
- Increased risk of burnout/midlife crisis

SUMMARY OF STRESSORS

Prioritizers	Visualizers
• Lack of a good support system • Workaholism • Mismanagement of emotions/feelings • Punishment for desire to lead/win • Lack of opportunity to: - make decisions - set and attain goals	• Lack of variety • Forced conformity • Expectations for detail accuracy • Punishment for spontaneity and humor • Lack of opportunity to: - problem solve freely - innovate
Organizers	**Harmonizers**
• Frequent interruptions • Disorganization in environment • Forced changes in routines • Punishment for attention to detail • Lack of opportunity to: - follow routines - maintain status quo	• Disharmony in environment • Conflict/abuse present • Emotional wounds • Punishment for sensitivity • Lack of opportunity to: - experience meaningful spirituality - establish nurturing relationships

2 **History of woundedness in an area of innate giftedness.** Sometimes individuals are punished for innate strengths. This goes beyond a lack of opportunity and moves into the arena of abuse. (Refer to Chapter Seven.) Some are tempted to play the ostrich routine, often referred to as denial. This is generally unhelpful in the long run. Individuals need to identify the maltreatment, grieve appropriately, and heal the woundedness. This will enable them to more effectively redirect and utilize the energy that has been embroiled with the woundedness.

3 **Mismatch between E:I ratio and societal rewards.** When the environment doesn't match their extroversion/introversion ratio, individuals may find themselves either overstimulated or understimulated. In such situations, they will likely not achieve the success that would be possible under favorable circumstances. Their innate extroversion/introversion ratio may also make it easier, or more difficult, for them to manage certain types of stressors.

For example, individuals with high levels of extroversion tend to be extremely competitive by nature. They consistently tend to position themselves where the action is in an attempt to obtain the stimulation that the brain naturally craves in order to feel alert. They can experience stress if the environment has no opportunities for competition or punishes them for wanting to compete. In addition, a tendency to turn all their interactions into a win/lose scenario (they intend to win, of course) can be deleterious. Unless they make conscious choices to obtain some of their stimulation outside of a competitive model, extreme extroverts can actually increase stress levels because competition not only calls for increased adrenalin, but also raises testosterone levels. Extroverts can learn to obtain stimulation through developing some noncompetitive physical activities such as running, jogging, cycling, swimming, conversations with friends, and reading.

In general, extroverts are more likely to trigger fight/flight in response to stressors and less likely to trigger conserve/withdraw. They tend to *retreat inwardly* only after a success—to identify what they did to achieve the success and to figure out how to duplicate it.

Individuals with high levels of introversion, on the other hand, are not competitive

by nature. They avoid positioning themselves where the action is on a consistent basis because their brains are superalert. They do not need the stimulation and, in fact, need to back off from activities periodically in order to process the data they have so readily taken in. They are more likely to limit their contact with others, withdraw into a corner, and read a book. Extreme introverts need to consciously program into their schedule, physical activities that will allow them to burn up energy. Otherwise, they may lie awake in bed at night as their bodies try to dissipate the energy triggered by intense mental activity.

In general, introverts are more likely to trigger conserve/withdraw in response to stressors. This is especially true after they have experienced what they perceive to be a *failure. They retreat inwardly* to analyze what went wrong. This pattern can be reinforced if they learned to concentrate on their failures instead of on their successes. Because of this tendency, they may have started triggering conserve/withdraw early in life and developed the habit of doing so. According to Blair Justice, retreating inwardly is the first step of the *Internal Stable Globalization* self-talk pattern. In his book, *Who Gets Sick,* he outlines how this learned self-talk pattern can contribute to the development of depression.

4 Career not matching brain lead, E:I ratio, or sensory preference. We dealt with this stressor in detail when discussing burnout and midlife crisis. Permit me to reiterate—spending large amounts of time engaging in tasks that primarily utilize skills outside our brain lead can consume up to one hundred times more metabolic energy second for second. This greater expenditure of energy can be interpreted as stress and, over time, can lead to a variety of problems. It can become a vicious cycle.

The cost of these mismatches can include:

- Self-esteem problems
- Fatigue
- Burnout
- Midlife crisis

- Illness
- Job hopping
- Unemployment
- Relationship problems

5 Lack of sensory preference validation. Sensory-system stressors evolve from punishment for one's preference, lack of desirable accessories in the environment to support personal preference, a lack of sensory nurturing, and/or the presence of bruising behaviors that impact one's sensory-system preference. The scenarios involving possible mismatches are endless including a lack of opportunity. For example, if one has an auditory or a kinesthetic preference and the environment is primarily visual, one can sense a loss of opportunity if not outright discomfort (although one often doesn't understand why).

In general, society appears to be somewhat unaware of the immense impact that sensory preference can have on one's life. For example, most school systems don't equally address visual, auditory, and kinesthetic preferences in the curriculum. This means that some children will thrive in the learning environment and others won't.

The lack of sensory-system validation can prove to be expensive:

- A decrease in one's ability to learn information easily
- A diminished level of competency development needed for a given task
- A decrease in self-esteem
- A sense of frustration and/or discomfort
- A halt in one's emotional development in certain areas (when abuse is involved)

6 **Unbalanced lifestyle.** Regardless of innate giftedness, any of us can be at increased risk for stress if we live an unbalanced lifestyle. Dr. Selye compared our reserves of adaptive energy to an inherited fortune from which we can make withdrawals. Although he claimed there is no proof we can make additional deposits to our energy bank, other researchers now believe that a high-level-wellness lifestyle can help us to do so, at least to some degree.

The importance of maintenance on a daily basis cannot be overemphasized. We need to adopt a high-level-wellness lifestyle. That is, everyday living that's essentially in balance, and that contains the healthiest and most timely habits we can develop. If you have not lived a balanced life, it is important to consult with your health-care

> Your life is what your thoughts make of it. —Marcus Aurelius

professional when making major lifestyle changes. For your consideration, here are several facets of a high-level-wellness lifestyle that I have incorporated into my life:

Exercise. The other day I heard a physician say, "I exercise only on specific days of the week. That is, I exercise only on the days I eat." What a great schedule! Exercise has been called a *general antioxidant*. Plan for thirty minutes of aerobic exercise every day. Walk, run, bike, skate, join a health club to work out and swim. Try jazzercise. The weather inclement? Watch your favorite TV program from your treadmill; read your favorite book from atop your stationary bike. There are limitless possibilities. Just be sure to shed that couch-potato routine.

Fresh air. Strive each day to give your body many deep breaths of fresh, clean, pure air. Avoid breathing *side-smoke* from cigarettes, cigars, and pipes; avoid busy streets and highways when exercising; change filters in your furnace/air conditioner on a regular basis. Learn to breathe with your abdominal muscles and increase your lung capacity.

Water. Dehydration is believed to be a major cause of premature aging, to say nothing of increased free-radical production. I aim to drink at least half an ounce of water per pound of my weight every day (64 ounces, for those of you who are wondering) in addition to other fluids. Many individuals find that their symptoms of *dis-ease* decrease as they begin drinking more water.

Sunlight. By now we've all heard the admonition to avoid sunburn, tanning parlors, and ultraviolet light. Nonetheless, let's not lose sight of the benefits of sunlight. Plants cannot survive without it; neither can people. Flood your home with it, but bask in it with extreme caution using sun-screen protection on exposed skin.

Sleep. Sleep deprivation, rapidly becoming a major problem for many individuals, can drain vital force. There is an optimum level for us individually; not too much; not too little. Take responsibility for getting the amount of sleep that will help you to thrive.

Relaxation. All work and no play makes for deadly, dull, and dreary. The brain loves variety. A *change* is as good as a rest. Build opportunities for relaxation, play, and laughter into your schedule. Laughter stimulates the production of endorphins that, in turn, strengthen the body's natural killer cells.

Stress management. Stress is part of life, and we wouldn't want it any other way. After all, the absence of stress is death! As mentioned earlier, however, unmanaged stress can interfere with our lives in a variety of ways. Therefore, it is important to implement effective stress-management techniques on a consistent basis.

Managing emotions and feelings. Stress often arises amid conflicts in the management of emotions and feelings (especially anger, fear, sadness, worry, and anxiety). Many of us try to manage this sphere of life using strategies based on attitudes and beliefs absorbed prior to the age of five, thus creating distress for ourselves. Learning to effectively manage our emotions and feelings can pay unbelievable dividends. We would do well to take a lesson from Winston Churchill who, on his deathbed, lamented, "I had a lot of trouble in my life—most of which never happened."

Taking charge of the brain/body connection. All stressors interact with the brain because it's the nucleus of our being. Communiqués move out from the brain through the endocrine system to the immune system—and back. Thirty minutes of challenging mental stimulation, on a daily basis, in combination with a positive mental attitude, can have a beneficial impact on the brain/body connection. If you have an *enemy outpost* of negativity inside your head, get rid of it! In the words of McWilliam's book title, *You Can't Afford the Luxury of a Single Negative Thought*.

Me, worry?

Humor. There are study reports, as well as anecdotal accounts, of the positive relationship between humor and health. We need to learn to laugh at ourselves and at the vagaries of life. This is easier for some individuals (based on brain lead and background) than for others. We can learn to look at the funny side of life, however. We can watch for opportunities to smile and to laugh. Laughter can exercise the body organs as well as boost immune-system function. It can also stimulate the release of endorphins, the body's natural pain-killer. No wonder patients have reported several pain-free hours after watching a hilarious video.

Support system. We all need a support system, a core group of individuals with whom we can share nurturing and encouragement, with whom we can celebrate as we make strides toward high-level-wellness living. Studies show that individuals who have a support system generally are healthier and live longer than those who don't.

Spirituality. Emerging research points to a connection between spirituality and health. The bodies of runners who meditate (or pray) while they exercise, for example, function more effectively; individuals who attend church regularly have less illness over time. Develop a personal connection with your Higher Power and be thankful. As the old proverb states, *a grateful heart nourishes the bones.*

Nutrition. Develop eating patterns that emphasize low-salt, low-sugar, low-fat, high-fiber, unrefined, caffeine- and additive-free foods. Pay attention not only to what you eat, how much you eat, when you eat, but also to your mind-set while you are eating. Remember that the word *stressed* is the word *desserts*—spelled backwards. Although most of us need to watch our caloric intake, we can all enjoy our meals and laugh our way to improved digestion. (I also include a synergistically-balanced herbal supplement in my wellness program.)

7 **Habitually negative mind-set.** A positive approach to life in general can help us to minimize the deleterious effects of stress. This means increasing the presence of positive factors in our lives—not simply reducing the negative factors. If keeping a cost/benefit balance sheet works for you, do it. Rather than dwelling on the possibilities of defeat, we can plan for success. If we have fallen into the trap of thinking more about negatives than about positives, we are actually accentuating the negatives and increasing the level of distress in our lives. Developing a positive approach to life involves defining our beliefs and, as necessary, learning to look at happenings from a different perspective. We regularly choose to focus on the positive, to find the *gift* in every situation.

The high cost to individuals of a habitually negative mind-set can include:

- Increased fatigue
- Decreased options
- Decreased energy levels
- Increased risk of illness
- Self-esteem problems
- Boundary problems
- A failure to thrive
- Altered neurotransmitter ratios

Remember

the

20:80

rule!

PRESCRIPTION FOR SUCCESS

Most of us have been taught to believe that the stressor causes the consequences; that due to a particular situation, we feel or act in a certain way. All stressors interact with the brain in a two-part equation: twenty percent of the consequences to the human organism is due to the stressor effect—eighty percent, to one's perception. Other studies have suggested an even greater split: that up to ninety-five percent of the time, the consequences (whatever we perceive them to be) come from our own belief about the stressor, rather than from the stressor itself. We may not always be able to control the stressor—we can do something about our perception. Since our belief systems are learned, we can learn a new way. As the philosopher Epictetus pointed out centuries ago, it's not so much *what* happens to us that creates havoc, as what we *think* about what happens to us.

MUSIC AND HUMOR

In 1994, the National Institutes of Health sponsored a landmark public symposium. I was intrigued by edited summaries of some of the presentations on Psychoneuroimmunology, a scientific field of study that focuses on the relationship between the mind and the body. Studies show that unmanaged stress, especially emotional stress, can impair immune system function. A variety of strategies have been identified as immune-system boosters. Music for one; humor for another.

As far back as the 1940s, American investigators showed that music could raise the spirits of depressed patients almost as effectively as amphetamines. In 1980, Dr. Goldstein of Stanford University discovered that in some music lovers, the thrills triggered by specific musical passages could be impeded by giving them naloxone, a drug that blocks the brain's natural morphine. (He actually discovered one of these endogenous opioids, known as dynorphin.) The data suggest that some types of music may raise levels of beta-endorphins.

Personally, I find music to be very therapeutic. So much so that I watch for the dates of special concerts and pencil them on my calendar. Besides attending the event, I reap the added benefit of pleasurable anticipation.

As to humor, there's nothing quite as satisfying as hearty laughter. Emerging research connects laughter with health. Dr. William Fry, a Stanford researcher, found that humor directly opposes emotions (e.g., fear, rage) associated with the precipitation of a heart attack. What a great reason for us to hone a sense of humor—as well as to manage our emotions and feelings effectively. The more we have adapted, due to a mismatch between innate giftedness and societal expectations, the more important this may be.

Combining humor with music can be a great stress-management technique. Not long ago, following a weekend seminar presentation, I found myself in Anchorage with a free Sunday evening. Imagine my delight to discover that Victor Borge was in town. Even more exciting was the fact that tickets to his concert were still available. Two friends attended with me. Not only did we thoroughly enjoy the music, we laughed until our cheeks hurt. For weeks afterward, the very memory of that treat could trigger a hearty laugh. No question about it, laugher is the best medicine. Look for humor in your life. Make time for laughter. Create ways to trigger it.

Instead of chocolates, try some chuckles. For starters, here are some *brainitions*.
See what you can come up with.

BRAINITIONS

Artery	a museum of paintings	Hypogastric	a gasoline shortage
Autopsy	a car with an attitude	Innuendo	hemorrhoid medication
Barium	what you do if CPR fails	Kidney	a young goat's knee
Beta-carotene	a lure for rabbits	Limbic	a large tree branch
Betadine	gambling with dimes	Lumbar puncture	a knothole
Cardiogram	a wool sweater	Medical staff	a doctor's cane
Cardioplasty	all-plastic vehicle	Metricephalic	math-induced headache
Cerebellum	before Sarah was born	Minor operation	excavation of coal
Cesarean section	a district in Rome	Morbid	a higher offer
Colic	a sheep dog	Mushroom	a pit stop for huskies
Coma	punctuation mark	Neurosis	fresh cut roses
Congenital	amiable	Nitrate	second shift differential
Counterirritant	a shopper who doesn't buy	Nitrates	cheaper than day rates
Cornea	even crazier than this	Node	aware of
Corneal	prairie humor	No kidding	birth control
Defibrillator	a lie detector	Outpatient	one who has fainted
Diagnostic	to die an atheist	Oxygen	the plural of ox
Diarrhea	two arias in an opera	Paralyze	two untruths
Dilate	to live a long time	Palsy	friendly
Enema	the opposite of a friend	Peduncle	beloved relative
Erogenous	a zone for errors	Recovery	an extra blanket
Fahrenheit	quite tall	Rhinitis	a Rhino phobia
Ferrous	a carnival ride	Serology	study of knights
Fester	quicker	Surgery	a cutting-edge experience
Fissure	a fisherman	Syndrome	detention arena
G.I. series	games soldiers play	Terminal illness	sick at the airport
Grippe	soft-sided luggage	Umbilicus	naval profanity
Gynecologist	operator of a cervix station	Varicose	nearby
Hangnail	a coat hook	Vein	conceited
Hippocampus	a school for hippos	Venereal	with respect

In summary, we can choose to:

- Avoid mistress and distress when possible
- Reframe (change) our perception of the event/situation
- Transform distress into eustress (look for the silver lining)
- Learn to laugh at ourselves and the vagaries of life
- Minimize brain/body damage by using effective stress-management strategies

Regardless of the stressor, we can usually be more successful when we approach the situation from a whole-brained perspective.

USE

YOUR BRAIN—

FOR SUCCESS

PRIORITIZERS

- Create and set goals
- Prioritize activities
- Select best options
- Manage willpower/conscience
- Develop bona fide boundaries

VISUALIZERS

- Brainstorm options
- Visualize outcome
- Be willing to *risk*
- Embrace efficacious change
- Approach life with humor

ORGANIZERS

- Build and follow routines
- Pay attention to details
- Attend to self-care
- Stay organized
- Practice, practice . . .

HARMONIZERS

- Connect with your Higher Power
- Build nurturing relationships
- Create an effective support system
- Manage emotions and feelings
- Grow personally

BRAIN BUILDERS

Points to Ponder

- The most universal form of stress is pain . . . it's part of the human condition. —Richard M. Restak

- Two key concepts I have learned in this section:

  _____

  _____

- Two facts I've discovered about myself while studying this section:

  _____

  _____

- One way in which I am now applying stress-management strategies:

  _____

  _____

- Rather than dwelling on the possibilities of _____, we can plan for success.

- Remember that the word stressed is simply the word _____ spelled backwards.

- Regardless of innate giftedness, any of us can be at increased risk for stress if we have an _____ lifestyle.

- **T F** Extroverted individuals are more likely to trigger fight/flight when confronted by stressors.

- **T F** Repeated triggering of conserve/withdraw can lead to depression.

- **T F** Dr. McGill was the first to apply the word stress to humans.

Brain Teasers

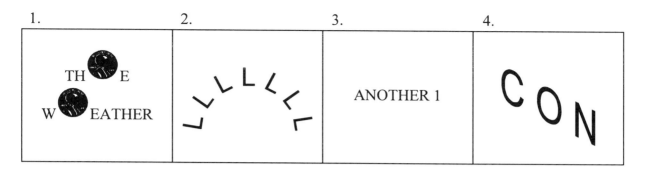

1.	2.	3.	4.
TH⬤E W⬤EATHER	LLLLLLL	ANOTHER 1	CON

Creativity Corner

MORON & COMPANY

Other than that one little mistake, Mr. Morton, what do you think?

EMOTIONS VERSUS FEELINGS

Although the words *emotions* and *feelings* are often
used interchangeably, they are not synonymous.

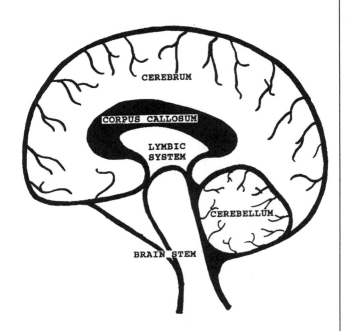

◆ Emotions—arise in the limbic
system and trigger physiological
changes throughout the body.

◆ Feelings—are cerebral interpretations of the physiological changes
triggered by emotions.

◆ While we are not always responsible for the surfacing of every
emotion; in most cases, we are responsible for our feelings because
we create them.

*To change the
way you feel,
change the way
you think . . .*

Chapter Nine
Managing Emotions and Feelings

My husband and I see flags almost everywhere we travel. The majority are of the orange highway variety. Recently, in Louisiana, we were driving from the airport to a seminar appointment. Sure enough, before very long, there was a flagger with his attention-getting flag waving in the breeze. It was a cue that something ahead would require extra attention. We didn't yet know, however, anything about the specific situation or what action would be required.

As we drew nearer, we could see that a section of roadway was undergoing reconstruction. Slowing down, we assessed the situation and prepared to take appropriate action. We obediently followed the detour signs, drove around the construction, and continued safely on our journey. Notice, neither my husband nor I ever considered rolling down the car window, and snatching up the flag that had first commandeered our attention.

I think of emotions as little *flags* that signal us to pay attention to stimuli impacting our lives, and to take appropriate action when necessary. Most of us would think it rather ludicrous to see motorists plucking up highway flags. What about the emotional flags that so many individuals are painstakingly gathering up and, in some cases, waving for years?

James Weber, in a crisis-resolution course he prepared for the National Christian Counselors Association, put it very well when he wrote: "Emotions are like the oil light on the dashboard of our car. There is nothing wrong with the light; it does not make the car go wrong. It is the lack of oil. There is nothing wrong with emotions. They are God-given and they are indicative of something else."

Emotions are powerful and purposeful. They can have an organizing, or a disorganizing influence on our lives. They

are not characteristics that we simply turn on or off as we do light switches. In fact, they were designed to be our best friends. Often they remember what our conscious minds have chosen to forget. In and of themselves, emotions are neither good nor bad; they just are. Used wisely, they can help us to be relatively safe and successful. Used un-wisely—repressed, neglected, degenerated, or allowed to run riot—they can contribute to much unhappiness, illness, and even our own destruction. The problem is that emotions rep-resent an unknown quantity to most of us. Not unknown in that we don't know they exist; unknown in terms of our understanding and our skill in managing them.

Emotions are believed to arise because of some change, as a reaction to some stimulus. The stimulus can be from the external environment (animate or inanimate) or from the internal environment; from our perception of what is happening outside us, or from a thought that is created or recalled within the mind. Some people surmise that exter-

nal stimuli cause the strongest emotional response. In reality, the strength of the emotion elicited can be equally strong from external or internal stimuli. Hopefully, as we mature emotionally, our re-sponses will be increasingly appropriate.

For example, at the age of three a child may cry or scream in protest when someone snatches his/her book, whereas in adulthood, the same stimulus may evoke only mild surprise. At the age of five, a child may shout and jump for joy when the parents announce a trip to Disneyland; in adulthood, the same information may be acknowl-edged with a smile and perhaps a verbal affirma-tion such as, "What a great idea. I can hardly wait!"

In addition, what were once external stimuli can become internal stimuli. On their honeymoon to the Bahamas, Dick and Teresa heard a song they both especially enjoyed. From then on, whenever they heard what they had labeled *our song*, they both experienced strong emotions of joy. Eliot must have rec-ognized this connection when he wrote: "The only way of expressing emotion in the form of art is by finding an objective correlative; in other words, a set of objects, a situation, a chain of events which shall be the formula of that *particular emotion;* such that when the external facts, which must terminate in sensory experience, are given, the emotion is im-mediately evoked."

PAIN/PLEASURE CENTER

The limbic system, also known as the pain/pleasure center, consists of a group of structures that surrounds the top of the brain stem like a cap. It includes brain organs such as the amygdalae which help us to process emotional information; the hypothalamus which functions as the liaison between the limbic system and the cerebrum, and as the regulator of rage, aggression, and pleasure; as well as the hippocampi which help us to store and retrieve long-term memories. The limbic system is not part of the cerebrum, and is not believed to contain conscious thought. Watch for studies published by Paul MacLean, perhaps the world's foremost living researcher on this brain system.

Emotions are referred to as limbic-system reactions to life because they are believed to arise within the limbic system. Upon surfacing, they elicit strong physiological changes throughout the body. While not identical in every case, these changes are very similar: our heart and breathing rates increase; we break out in perspiration; we may experience a queasy sensation in the pit of the stomach; our hands may shake; we may even lose our voice and be temporarily unable to speak. Initially, we may not clearly recognize what the specific emotional flag is trying to tell us. However, we need to stop, look, listen, and pay attention to what is going on inside in order to expeditiously and accurately identify the emotion(s).

FEELINGS

Although many people use the words emotions and feelings interchangeably, they are not synonymous. Feelings are different from emotions. Certainly there are hundreds of feeling-descriptive words for every emotion. Metaphorically speaking, feelings add *color* to our lives; to what would otherwise be somewhat of a black-and-white existence. In one sense, human beings are really like fountains of feelings. Sometimes the fountain overflows; sometimes it dries up. Learning how to manage our feelings, with equipoise, will create a pleasing pattern in the fountains of our lives.

As previously stated, the surfacing of an emotion in the limbic system causes a variety of physiological changes in the body. Although not part of the cerebrum, the limbic system is connected to it by the cingulate gyrus which transmits information about emotions (physiological changes) to the thinking part of the brain. Once this information reaches the cerebrum, we begin to cogitate upon these changes in an attempt to assign meaning or weight to them. Our interpretations eventually become our feelings, with the personalized label we apply to them.

Sometimes individuals have difficulty accepting this concept. It's so much easier to blame someone else. We hear, "If you had only done such and such I wouldn't *feel* this way," or "If you hadn't done such and such, I wouldn't feel this way." Though this may sound plausible on the surface, it isn't true. The exhibited behaviors of others may trigger our emotions, but we, ourselves, create our feelings. What an empowering concept! No one else can ever force us to *feel* a certain way. We determine not only *what* we feel, but how deeply and for how long.

METAPHORICAL STAIRCASE

Evidence shows that at least some of our emotional reactions occur before higher centers in the brain even deliberate upon them. According to Goleman, author of *Emotional Intelligence,* the amygdalae (part of the limbic system, remember?) can trigger an emotional response before the cerebrum has fully understood what is happening. A person may sense fear, for example, and not be able to recognize why—at least initially. Combine this with the fact that the anterior lobes of the cerebrum may not be completely myelinated until somewhere between the ages of eighteen and twenty-one, and we can catch a glimpse of the reason it can take years before we learn how to successfully manage our emotions and feelings—most of the time.

Drawing a metaphorical staircase is a helpful way in which to depict the range of emotions. We may move up and down several times each day as emotional flags signal us to pay attention to particular incidents. The goal is to spend the majority of our time at the level of enthusiasm. The core emotions fall along the tone scale in a predictable sequence.

EMOTIONAL TONE SCALE

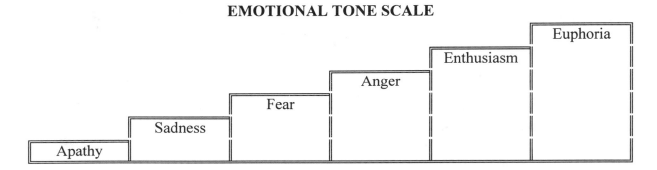

No one knows how many innate emotions exist. Let's briefly consider several:

- The flag of euphoria was designed to periodically add spark and intensity to our lives. We were not designed to live at euphoria. Individuals who, for some reason, don't understand this dictum, may become involved in mind-altering behaviors (that can turn into addictions) in an attempt to constantly maintain an unnatural high.

- The flag of enthusiasm (joy) alerts us to the fact that everything is basically going well with us; that our needs, and some of our wants, are being met. We are enabled to rejoice and give thanks; to experience the strengthening of the immune system through the effects of this positive emotion.

- The flag of anger was designed to alert us that our boundaries are, or are in danger of, being violated and to motivate us to take appropriate corrective action. Individuals often have more difficulty with this emotion than with all the others combined.

- The flag of fear was designed to alert us to a potential threat. Managed appropriately, it can help to protect us from any number of dangerous situations. Mismanaged, fear can turn into terror, phobias, immobility, or paranoia.

- The flag of sadness was designed to help us to grieve losses and to heal woundedness.

- The flag of apathy alerts us that we may have unadvisedly collected bundles of flags, when it would have been more advantageous, and energy-efficient, to take appropriate action as each emotion surfaced.

We need to be able to move freely up and down the staircase as needed. If we don't understand the role of these various emotional flags, and have not learned how to identify and utilize the cues they offer, we may find this difficult to accomplish.

EMOTIONAL TONE

Emotional tone is a term describing a person's usual position on the scale. Is it high or low? Positive or negative? A variety of factors can influence our position. These include:

- A mismatch between brain lead and societal expectations

- A high level of extroversion within a nonen-riched environment, or within one that rewards only moderate levels of extroversion

- Excessive/prolonged adaption

- Forced conformity to the expectations of others

- A high level of introversion

- A history of past or present abuse (living and/or working in a dysfunctional system)

- The repeated triggering of the conserve/withdraw stress reaction form

DOC SPOOF'S GLOSSARY

Emofeeliology - the study of emotions and feelings

Emotec - one who is skilled in managing emotions and feelings

Emogage - a device for measuring one's emotional tone

Efability - a knack for expressing emotions/feelings appropriately

Emofee - the penalty for losing one's *cool*

- Woundedness in an area of innate giftedness. For example:
  - Organizers are blocked from maintaining the status quo
  - Harmonizers are unable to achieve rewarding/nurturing relationships
  - Visualizers are thwarted in their attempts at innovation or artistic creativity
  - Prioritizers are prevented from making decisions or are unable to achieve goals.

CLIMBING THE STAIRS

It took me a long time to buy into the concept that we create our own feelings. (As human beings we have a compelling tendency to want to blame others for the way we feel!) Once I finally got the picture, taking complete responsibility for my position, on the emotional tone scale, became one of the most empowering brain-function tools in my repertoire. The more time goes by, and the more consistently I apply this information to my daily life, the smoother my ride. This doesn't mean that I won't need to move up and down the stairs, perhaps several times a day. It does mean that I climb the stairs more quickly and easily.

People often ask me what is involved in *climbing the stairs*. Allow me to share a personal experience. My father died in 1990. As he was my nurturing parent, his death left a large void in my life. Gradually, I learned to carry him in my mind, so that, even though he is no longer tangibly present, his memory is ever present. Talking about him, however, can quickly evoke deep emotion. With a visualizing brain lead, I tend to express deeply-felt emotion through tears. In fact, *Niagara* was one of my childhood nicknames.

Several years after he died, I was walking through the hospital lobby toward my office when I was intercepted by a woman. "Are you Warren Taylor's daughter?" she asked. When I replied in the affirmative, she said, "I knew your father years ago, and something about you reminded me of him." She began to tell me some of her recollections. They were so interesting, and I was enjoying our conversation thoroughly. As thoughts of my father triggered emotions in my limbic system, however, it wasn't long until tears welled up in my eyes and spilled down my cheeks. When she noticed them, she became quite agitated. "Oh, dear," she lamented. "I've made you cry. I'm so sorry."

Smiling through my tears I responded, "You didn't make me cry; that's how my brain lead expresses emotion. I'm enjoying our conversation. Please continue." She went on, but was obviously uncomfortable with my tears. Soon her family arrived and as we parted, I thanked her for sharing with me.

Back in my office, I dabbed my cheeks with a tissue, and pondered what had just happened. For one thing, I regretted being unable to get across to this delightful woman that she had not caused my tears; that I was responsible, not only for my feelings, but also for my behaviors related to them. For another, I took a moment to identify my current position on the emotional tone scale, and then immediately took action to move back up to the level of joy (enthusiasm). I *talked the talk* and *walked the walk*, like this:

Here I am at the level of sadness. Talking about my Dad reminded me of my loss. I'm sad that I have been deprived of his tangible presence in my life. I cannot change that, however. I have the choice to remain here at sadness, or I can use the energy this emotion generates to head toward joy. (Note: I must work through each step on the way up—can't skip any!)

I take a step up to the level of fear and acknowledge that I am afraid. Sometime again in my life I may lose someone very special and significant. I dread that possibility. However, I cannot control the possibility of future loss. I know that, in combination with my Higher Power and support system, I can handle whatever the future holds.

I take a step up to the level of anger—and am I angry! Angry that in this world death happens. It wasn't meant to be like this. It's actually the pits! Why, why, why? I can't change the way things are. I can choose how I respond to these events and, in this case, how long I will remain angry.

I resolutely take another step up. What do you know? Here I am back at the level of joy (enthusiasm). This is where I choose to spend most of my time. However, I wouldn't have missed gleaning new insights about my father for anything. The benefits far outweighed the cost.

How long did this process take? Just a few minutes. The climb can happen very quickly once we understand the emotional tone scale, accept personal responsibility, and develop the necessary skills. Depending upon what's happening in our lives, we may run up and down several times a day.

MISLABELING

Many of us have a tendency to mislabel certain emotions (a tendency often learned through societal-gender expectations). Even though, men and women are believed to experience basically similar physiological responses to various emotions, they differ in their perception of what they sense, in their labeling of those physiological sensations, and in their exhibited behaviors. This is particularly true of the emotions of anger and sadness.

In research situations, groups of men and women were shown pictures designed to elicit the emotion of *anger.* When asked what they *felt,* males responded that they felt angry; females said they felt hurt or sad. Society has taught us that it's okay for men to acknowledge anger. Consequently, males are more likely to accurately label anger as anger. Women, on the other hand, don't.

When the research participants were shown pictures designed to elicit the emotion of *sadness*, men denied they felt sad; women acknowledged they felt sad. Here we see an example of opposite socie-

> The strangest and most fantastic fact about negative emotions is that people actually worship them. —Ouspensky

tal conditioning. Our culture has taught us that it is okay for women to feel sad. Consequently, females are more likely to accurately label sadness as sadness. Men tend to deny the emotion of sadness or to mislabel it (as *indigestion* perhaps). This tendency to mislabel is not very helpful when trying to develop healthier patterns of expression. It is helpful to recognize, and to take into account our societal conditioning.

In general, our society has not come to grips with the emotion of anger. Individuals are usually told one of two extremes: stuff it, or let it all hang out. When embarking on the study of emotions and feelings, I recalled a Bible passage related to anger and discovered

175

that it is congruent with current research findings. The Apostle Paul (Ephesians 4:26) admonishes us: *in your anger, do not sin.* This biblical injunction was not meant to deny that anger exists; rather, it indicates that this emotion is regularly felt by human beings, and that it should be dealt with constructively and appropriately. The text goes on to remind us to resolve our anger before the sun goes down. I jokingly say that, at the most, we have twenty-three hours and fifty-nine minutes to resolve each episode of anger. To do otherwise places us at risk of living *in a state of anger*, the exact condition we wish to avoid.

EMOTIONAL INTELLIGENCE

French psychologist Alfred Binet is credited with devising the first intelligence test. Many individuals have taken one or more IQ tests. Recently, they have been falling into some disfavor, especially as a method of predicting success. Researchers now believe there are several types of intelligence. (Refer to Chapter Six.) According to Dr. Goleman, emotional intelligence is at least as important as IQ in determining individual achievement.

Hallmarks of emotional intelligence include:

- Self-awareness. The ability to identify emotions and feelings accurately. If you can't tell the difference between being angry or hungry, you may eat whenever you're upset. It's important to feel all our feelings. If we live from the neck up, we'll likely miss vital cues.

- Mood management. Take control of your feelings. There are many more options than the traditional three: fight, stuff it, or flee. This means taking responsibility for our feelings and decreasing any tendency to ventilate rage. We can learn strategies that include exercise, meditation/prayer, and taking appropriate action to distract ourselves whenever necessary. We can reframe events and look at them from the perspective of mature adulthood, rather than from an old childhood script.

- Self-motivation. The trusty adage that practice makes perfect is as true today as it ever was. Motivate yourself to succeed; develop a positive mind-set. Picture your desired outcome in your mind's eye and then bend every energy to move toward it. Train as for the Olympics!

- Impulse Control. It is vitally important to learn to delay gratification. If we can't do that, it will be much harder to stick to a practice schedule. Part of impulse control involves identifying all available options and their probable consequences before deciding on a course of action.

- People Skills. If you would develop high emotional intelligence, learn to listen to yourself and others. Become comfortable verbalizing your feelings, as appropriate, rather than allowing them to pepper everyone. Don't expect others to *read* your mind. Observe body language, yours as well as that of others. Exhibit congruence between words and actions.

- Education. Learn the difference between emotions and feelings; between feelings and actions. Take care to practically apply the knowledge you gain. Study topics such as nutrition and aging; or any subject that might provide you with helpful tools.

- Stress Management. Develop effective skills for managing stressors. Avoid wasting vital energy with potent brain suspenders such as worry and anxiety.

MOODS

According to David Berenson, moods are an attempt to manage emotions *intellectually*—thoughts trying to deal with emotions. In his *map of emotions*, he places moods at the very bottom. Cognitively translating emotions into feelings is one thing: trying to manage emotions directly through logical thought, bypassing the feelings step, will simply move a person down into the *moods* level. Moods can be insidious and can actually be harder to manage than the emotions themselves. In order to get out of a mood, we have to consciously *let go* of it in order to get to the underlying emotion, correctly identify it, and translate it into a feeling which is more readily manageable.

You can change

the way you feel—

just change the

way you think!

Many individuals act as if they are helpless in the face of *moods*, or blame others for the way in which they feel or don't feel. While we may not always be responsible for the surfacing of every emotion, by and large, we are responsible for our feelings because we create them. This means that, outside of some physiological imbalance within the brain, if we want to change the way we feel, we need to change the way we think.

CHEERFUL OR DOLEFUL

Some studies have linked activity in the frontal lobes of the brain with various emotions—especially cheerfulness and dolefulness. You may have read some of their conclusions. For example, in research situations, people with more activity in the cortex of the left frontal lobe tend to have a cheerful temperament. Typically they reacted with delight and interest to people and situations of all sorts. In general they showed a positive outlook and were easily cheered. They were social, ebullient, had a strong sense of self-confidence, and saw themselves as rewardingly engaged in the world.

People with more activity in the cortex of the right frontal lobe, on the other hand, were found to sometimes shrink from encounters with people or situations and were easily fazed by setbacks. They tended to reflect a more negative outlook, and were more likely to be vulnerable to depression. Only about fifteen percent of subjects in research studies showed no tendency one way or the other.

On the surface, these studies would lead one to associate happiness with the left side of the brain and depression with the right side of the brain. However, other researchers believe that these observed emotional differences may relate more to societal conditioning and expectations. Benziger supports this position, suggesting that the apparent connection between positive feeling states and the left hemisphere may have a basis in societal expectations, and may reflect that there are generally many more opportunities in our society for individuals to succeed at (and be monetarily rewarded for) tasks that derive from the left side of the brain. For example, people with a harmonizing or visualizing lead (especially males) are not rewarded in the same way as are those with an organizing or prioritizing lead. In addition, individuals often find it difficult to earn a decent salary unless they are working in left-brained jobs. Expectations, rewards, and conditioning, therefore, may account (at least in part) for the cheerfulness/dolefulness differences.

In some studies, subjects who suffered from depression were found to have decreased blood flow to the brain. The studies also found that depression could often be relieved when the participants were put on a regular exercise program—perhaps, in part, because exercise helps to increase blood flow to the brain.

Some researchers believe that emotional balance may depend not only on the balance of the right and left hemispheres, but also on the balance between the anterior and posterior lobes. It is also believed that when individuals exhibit (so called) *highly emotional* behaviors over a long period of time, and without any identifiable medical or stress-related cause, there is a distinct possibility that their innate giftedness is not being honored, encouraged, and rewarded. They may be experiencing pressure to abandon natural preferences in order to conform to the expectations of family and society. In such situations, it can be helpful to evaluate what is happening in the life.

In general, the more we know about who we are, and the more we are able to match our activities to our innate giftedness, the higher our emotional tone. When who we innately are doesn't match societal expectations or opportunities in life, or when we experience high levels of stress/trauma/crisis, our emotional tone may slide.

Individual brain lead can influence the ease with which we stay in touch with and identify emotions, as well as the way in which we exhibit them. The following summary is not intended to suggest that some of us cannot learn to manage emotions and feelings effectively. Rather, its purpose is to stimulate discussion, and to point out that, congruent with innate preferences, we may also have innate weaknesses—which necessitate different management strategies.

BRAIN LEAD AND EMOTIONS SUMMARY

Prioritizer	Visualizer

● Oblivious to emotion in self/others and does not *read* nonverbal body language well (often due to a lack of access to the diagonal harmonizing mode)
● May be threatened by emotions, as they represent a potential for loss of *control*
● Expresses emotion through sarcasm, criticism, and *blowing up*
	◆ Perceives emotion in self, but may not *read* it very well in others
	◆ More comfortable with *change,* so less threatened by emotion
	◆ Expresses emotion through:
	  - Gesturing
	  - Tears/laughter
	  - Humor/prosody/drama/stories

Organizer	**Harmonizer**

■ Tries to avoid emotions, as they represent a potential for *change* from the status quo
■ Not innately skilled at reading emotion in others
■ May habitually maintain the emotion most often experienced
■ Expresses emotion minimally
	◆ Very sensitive to emotion in self/others
	◆ Skilled at reading emotion/nonverbals in others
	◆ Expresses emotion through:
	  - Affective speech/tonality
	  - Nonverbals (body position, smiles, frowns, touch)
	  - Drama/stories

VIOLENCE AND EMOTIONAL SENSITIVITY

Research indicates that our emotional sensitivity can be affected through exposure of the brain to raw emotion. To a large degree, our society is filled with violence. We have, as citizens of America, the option to view, on an almost continual basis, the portrayal of violence via television, movies, videos, and the newspapers—to say nothing of personal experience in connection with riots or other disasters. Restak points out in his book, *The Brain Has a Mind of Its Own:*

The human brain was designed to process only so much raw emotion at one time. Watching a personal tragedy or a natural disaster on the morning news is a qualitatively different experience from merely reading about the tragedy. The video image is processed primarily with the right hemisphere of the brain; it by-passes language, reason, and logic...We cannot cope with a sustained assault of elemental emotions like fear, horror, and outrage. If enough horrors are repeatedly depicted with sufficient graphic impact, in a self-protective reflex the brain simply shuts down. Hideous images cease to arouse any emotion except, perhaps, boredom. The pornography of violence is every bit as ugly and brutalizing as sexual pornography—probably more so. TV news violence can be dangerous to your mental health.

This may be one reason for Paul's admonition, in Philippians 4:8, that we are to think about things that are true, noble, right, pure, lovely, admirable, excellent, and praiseworthy. What we think about, what we see, can affect not only our ability to experience our own emotions, but also our ability to be sensitive to the emotions and feelings of others.

If we are going to be able to understand ourselves and to offer encouragement to others, it is important to maintain our ability to feel. We also need to learn to interpret our emotions correctly and manage our feelings appropriately. The fourth chapter of Ephesians describes individuals who are past feeling and who, consequently, have given themselves over to undesirable behaviors. Unfortunately, there are individuals who are unable to experience feelings. Such people would undoubtedly find it difficult to empathize with others.

MANAGING EMOTIONS AND FEELINGS

We are all strongly influenced by our emotions and feelings. Even the words themselves are loaded with intensity. They evoke as many different responses as there are different individuals. Authors try to preserve them on the printed page; composers try to translate them into sound; actors try to bring them to life through drama; dancers try to express them through motion; artists try to capture them on canvas; poets try to fit them into meter and rhyme. Unfortunately, many of us did not learn how to manage them effectively. Fortunately, it is rarely too late to learn a better way.

In order to manage emotions and feelings successfully, we must learn to tell the microscopic truth about them. I was talking about this one day with a woman who said, "Oh, I couldn't tell the truth about what I feel; I'd be too embarrassed." We can only be *embarrassed* if we choose to accept and foster embarrassment. John Gray in his book, *What You Feel You Can Heal,* emphasizes the need to be honest in these words: "The first step in telling the complete truth in your life is knowing what it is. Most of us are unaware of the complete truth; this phenomenon is called the Iceberg Effect."

Just as we see only a small portion of an iceberg, many people are aware of only a fraction of their emotions and feelings. In order to see the complete iceberg, we would have to don a diving suit and go underwater. Metaphorically, we have to do that with ourselves; don a diving suit, as it were, and look deep inside of us. We need to *surface* feelings that have been repressed and denied over the years. Often the process of repression and denial began in childhood as a safety mechanism. We must exhume the hidden treasure; *treasure*, because we can learn so much about ourselves by uncovering it.

I asked you to tell me what you're feeling, Harold. *Really hungry for some chicken* is not a feeling . . .

181

Understanding the difference between emotions and feelings can help us to realize how important it is for us to manage them effectively. We need to learn to identify emotions as quickly and as accurately as possible, and then translate them into appropriate feelings. We can *feel* all of our feelings without taking action on any of them. This frees us to experience the entire range of emotions and feelings without fearing that, if we do so, we may exhibit inappropriate behaviors. If we cannot correctly identify our emotions and feelings, we may engage in unhelpful behaviors. Indeed, studies of some eating-disorders-program participants revealed that many of them had not developed prerequisite skills for identifying feelings accurately. If you can't differentiate your being angry, fearful, anxious, sad, or hungry, you may eat whenever you feel upset. Or you may avoid food for the same reason.

GRIEF RECOVERY

Grief is a natural response to loss. It can be defined, simply, as intense emotional suffering related to a loss, misfortune, injury, or an evil of any kind. It can also include conflicting feelings that are experienced following any major change to a familiar *state of affairs*. Unresolved grief from the past can accumulate and can increase the intensity of our reaction to a present situation.

In our culture, we have a tendency to interpret the concept of loss too narrowly. The roster could include divorce, the death of a loved one, or displacement due to a natural disaster such an earthquake. It could be a mastectomy or the amputation of a limb; the loss of sensory perception (e.g., sight or hearing). It could be a hoped-for event that does not materialize (e.g., failure to conceive) or the diminishment of our options (e.g., inability to follow a certain career path).

There are many reasons for our inability to deal with loss effectively. For example:

- We have learned ineffective ways of coping with grief/loss

- Our culture has taught us how to be adept at *acquiring* but not at *losing*

- We have not learned what to say in situations involving loss and grief

- We tend to intellectualize grief instead of truly working through it

- We learn myths such as:

    - Grieve alone or bury your feelings
    - Replace the loss as soon as possible
    - Just give it enough *time* and the pain will resolve on its own
    - Don't *trust* in the future, there's only today
    - Recall only the good times and events in order not to be *disloyal*
    - *Regret* the past and wish that it had been different
    - There is only one way to grieve, one path to recovery

- We haven't learned how to manage stress or our emotions and feelings effectively

When engaged in grief recovery, do something special for yourself— even if all your ducks aren't in a row yet...

GENDER DIFFERENCES

Typically, the genders exhibit different coping strategies in situations involving loss and grief. Some of these behavioral patterns reflect innate gender differences; others reflect experience, education, and cultural conditioning. In general, males approach grief in a *goal-oriented* style. That is, they want to *fix* the problem quickly. When this doesn't work—grief recovery is not instantaneous—they may try to put the experience behind them by, figuratively or literally, running away. Almost any venue can be used as an escape (e.g., work, sexual activity, jogging, video games, religion, politics, sports, food, drugs, alcohol).

Because of societal expectations, males often struggle to remain in control of their emotions at all times (essentially be silent about them), and fail to articulate their grief. The unexpressed pain can trigger violence, a retreat into stony silence, or even suicide attempts.

Because of their socialization, many males grow up desiring control. Since emotions represent a potential for loss of control, men often tend to repress their emotions. They may act them out instead of trying to accurately define and label them, and may even avoid trying to translate them into words.

In addition, many males grew up without seeing emotions expressed positively by their male role models and/or were not encouraged to learn an appropriate emotional vocabulary. They were not coached to verbalize feelings appropriately, and thus avoid doing so. Rather, many of them seem to prefer *acting out* their emotions, which is not always the preferred option.

> We are healed of a suffering only by experiencing it to the full. —Proust

According to Tanenbaum, men usually try to resolve their emotions as quickly as possible because it takes a great deal of energy for them to feel. This may mean that men tend to jump to conclusions about their emotions instead of taking time to learn to label them accurately.

Women, on the other hand, have been socialized to express grief aloud. They face fewer taboos against crying. They can become stuck in recounting the loss, however, and develop the habit of brooding. This enmeshment can delay acceptance and resolution. They may avoid taking constructive action, believing that talking is enough even when taking action could help them to cope more effectively.

These differences between the genders can and have formed the basis for a great deal of misunderstanding, and have prevented men and women (in many cases) from offering appropriate nurturing and support during situations of grief. We need to learn from each other. We can share the burden of grief. We can recognize stereotypical gender tendencies and encourage one another in recovery strategies. Unresolved grief can remain bottled up inside and can later explode when a similar, but unrelated incident, triggers the emotion of sadness.

Because of the great disparity in grieving patterns between the genders, it is no surprise that many relationships break up when loss occurs. Even when the partners do not separate, they may misread each other's messages and fail to offer the support, acceptance, and nurturing that are needed for healing and recovery.

In general, males need to learn to articulate their grief rather than assuming that emotional pain will somehow go away on its own. They need to act out their feelings in appropriate ways.

GENDER GRIEVING STYLES SUMMARY

♀ FEMALES	♂ MALES
STEREOTYPICALLY:	**STEREOTYPICALLY:**
◆ Exhibit a process-oriented grieving style ◆ Tend to want to articulate their loss and grief, to verbalize it to friends and family ◆ Have often been socialized to be more comfortable expressing grief through tears ◆ Overprocess and begin to brood ◆ Endlessly rehearse the incident believing that *talking* about it is enough, even though taking some action could help them to cope more effectively	◆ Exhibit a goal-oriented grieving style ◆ Want to *fix* the predicament ◆ Tend to *run away* (literally or figuratively) when they can't fix it ◆ Avoid verbalizing grief (are silent) but may act it out in their behaviors ◆ Allow unresolved grief to build up inside where it can explode later on when a similar (but unrelated) incident triggers the emotion of sadness
NEED TO:	**NEED TO:**
◆ Learn to take constructive *action* whether or not they feel like it at the moment ◆ Avoid perpetually indulging negative feelings *and* brooding endlessly	◆ Learn to *articulate* grief and act out feelings in an appropriate manner ◆ Realize that emotional pain won't truly resolve on its own

Females need to learn to refrain from perpetually indulging their feelings, from brooding endlessly and becoming totally enmeshed in their grief. They need to learn to take appropriate constructive action.

GRIEF RECOVERY TIPS

Once the flag of sadness alerts us to a loss, we can take appropriate action and progress through the grieving process. Grief recovery is the process of learning to *feel better* and to achieve a condition of balance following a loss. Before we can truly help anyone else, we must resolve the grief episodes in our own life. That does not necessarily mean forgetting about the loss. In actuality, grief recovery enables us to retain our memories—without the immobilizing sting of the emotional pain.

Here are several grief recovery tips:

- Give up denial. Admit there has been a loss. Assert that you are now willing to deal with your grief. Give up blaming yourself and others, and focus on recovery.

- Talk with a same-gender friend; consider joining a support group. It is more difficult to recover alone. Be honest about your episodes of loss, and require confidentiality of friends/support group.

- Develop a spiritual relationship with a Higher Power. This can help you to work through feelings of guilt, shame (including false guilt/shame), hopelessness, or depression.

- Learn to journal. Write a *loss history* or create a graph of specific personal losses, noting the dates when they occurred so you can clearly visualize them.

- Move beyond the loss. Tap into your support system, increase your awareness, look for the *gift* (the positives), and continue the healing process.

- Start to take action. Instead of just thinking about recovery, begin to act.

- Find a grief-recovery group and attend regularly.

- Utilize the *Grief Recovery Pyramid* to increase your awareness and understanding.

GRIEF RECOVERY PYRAMID

STAGE I — SHOCK
Symptoms may last from a few days
to several weeks

STAGE II — DISTRESS
Symptoms may last from a few
weeks to two years

Stage III — ACCEPTANCE
Time lines will vary for each person

STAGE I - SHOCK SYMPTOMS

Agitation, confusion
Collapse, crying
Denial or disbelief
Euphoria or hysteria
Insomnia
Lethargy or weakness
Loss of appetite, nausea
Numbness or unreality

RECOVERY STRATEGIES

Feel and show grief
Do not make major decisions
Allow others to help you
Rest and survive
Avoid substance abuse
Talk it out
Spend time in nature
Spend time around *living* things

STAGE II - DISTRESS SYMPTOMS

Anger, anguish, anxiety
Crying, confusion
Fear, guilt, mood swings
Hopelessness; life seems to be in limbo
Insomnia, restlessness
Low self-esteem
Irrational decision-making
Loneliness, isolation
Pain, physical illness
Poor judgment
Overeating, undereating, improper diet
Slowed thinking
Suicidal thoughts

RECOVERY STRATEGIES

Beware of rebounding
Acknowledge and verbalize emotional pain
Keep decision-making to a minimum
Avoid substance abuse
Allow yourself to mourn; try journaling
Accept the support/assistance of others
Check decisions with others
Return to career or volunteer work
Get a physical examination
Heal at your own pace
Plan for good nutrition
Get plenty of rest and exercise
Seek and accept counseling

STAGE III - ACCEPTANCE SYMPTOMS

Distress becomes less acute
Feel stronger and more energetic
Interests return
Comfortable with the self
Have only periodic *crashes*
Loneliness surfaces intermittently
Physical symptoms decrease
Nostalgia replaces emotional pain
Return to optimum functioning

RECOVERY STRATEGIES

Cut final ties to loss and grief
Exercise consistently
Let go of *might-have-beens*
Pamper yourself regularly
Forgive yourself and others
Socialize; include new people
Take control of your own life
Develop new interests
Learn to *act* rather than *react*

BRAIN BUILDERS

Points to Ponder

- I control my thoughts.
  My feelings come from my thoughts.
  I can control my feelings.
  —Wayne Dyer

- Two key concepts I have learned in this section:

  _____

  _____

- Two facts I've discovered about myself while studying this section:

  _____

  _____

- One way in which I am applying this information in a practical way:

  _____

  _____

- The emotional flag of _____ alerts us to the fact that everything is basically going well with us.

- If we are going to be able to understand ourselves and to offer encouragement to others, it is important to maintain our ability to _____.

- Grief recovery is the process of learning to feel better and to achieve a condition of _____ following a loss.

- **T   F**   Emotions and feelings are synonymous concepts.

- **T   F**   To change the way you feel, change the way you think.

- **T   F**   Emotional intelligence may be at least as important as IQ in determining our individual achievement.

Brain Teasers

1.	2.	3.	4.
ALL　　　ALL 　　TOWN ALL　　　ALL	DOINORS	DOSE	*Listing Listing Listing*

Creativity Corner

INDIVIDUATION

the state of totally and uniquely being oneself

Achieving
bona fide
individuation
is a
lifelong journey.

It involves an
inner progression
to wholeness*
while remaining
true to one's
innate giftedness.

*Wholeness can be defined as valuing, developing, and
utilizing with a degree of comfort:

♦ all four thinking styles
♦ all three main sensory systems
♦ extroverted and introverted processing

Chapter Ten
Family-of-Origin Work

There's all the difference in the world between living a life of quiet (or not so quiet) desperation and enthusiastically embracing life in its fullness. Believe me, I know the difference! Many decades ago, standing at my kitchen sink, up to my elbows in dishwater, up to my ears in a dysfunctional marriage, to near-exhaustion in my job, and over my head in stepparenting, my life was definitely not working well. I just didn't know why. I couldn't identify the reason. Most likely, at that time, I wouldn't have recognized functionality even if it had jumped up and splashed me in the face. Like so many others, somewhere in my early childhood I had absorbed the belief that if I was a good girl—worked hard, followed all the rules, and tried to be perfect—life would be fine. I'd done all of those things to the best of my ability, but life was definitely not a bowl of cherries—more like Erma Bombeck's portrayal of *pits*.

Having always been interested in the *brain* and sincerely wanting answers to a myriad of *why* questions, I embarked on a course of in-depth study. My selected sisters-of-choice joined me in this adventure, and together we made discoveries that were exciting,

> Family trees are always trees of knowledge and often they are also trees of life. —Rabbi Friedman

healing, energizing, and empowering. Eventually, I was introduced to the Benziger Thinking Styles Assessment (BTSA). It answered many questions, and thus proved to be an invaluable addition to the resource pool for sorting and putting together the puzzle pieces of my life. Seriously embracing a high-level-wellness lifestyle, I began to move from a position of barely surviving to one of enthusiastic thriving.

Over time, the obvious improvements in my own life were so dramatic that others began asking me to share what I had learned; to help them develop healthier patterns of living. I traveled around the world presenting a variety of seminars (refer to Appendix). Years of lecturing, writing, and hosting radio programs have honed my belief that every one of us can learn to thrive if we're given the right tools and are willing to invest the time and energy. In order to accomplish this, however, we have to risk a peek backstage into our generational inheritance.

In order to move to a position of thriving, I had to engage in some *serious* family-of-origin work (FOOW). Many times I've joked that the acronym sounded like *phew*. Indeed it does take commitment and work (sometimes *blood*, *sweat*, and *tears*). It's more than worth it, however.

I define FOOW as the process of getting to know who we are, individually, against the backdrop of our generational inheritance and our environmental history. In some ways, it's really a journey of awareness. We want to determine where we came from and identify where we want to go.

It has been said that awareness is the first step on the road to positive change. Being *aware* is a concept that has been recognized down through the ages by a variety of individuals. They may have used slightly different terminology, but I believe they were all talking about awareness. For example:

- The unexamined life is not worth living. —Socrates
- Know thyself; to thine own self be true. —Shakespeare
- The truth will free you. —Christ. John 8:32 (TM)

I recall a group leader asking each one of us to repeat after her, "I promise to tell the truth, the whole truth, and nothing but the truth." There isn't much point in putting in the time and energy to do FOOW if we are going to pretend, deny, or lie about our past. We often interpret scripture very narrowly and assume that it's only spiritual truth that can set us free. Wrong. The truth about who we are can free us to become the individuals we were intended to be.

One of the Ten Commandments tells us to avoid bearing false witness. Most people think of the truth issue in terms of their relationships with others. Next to our own relationship with our Higher Power, however, the most important relationship is the one we have with ourselves. Some individuals try to hide from themselves. In effect, they tell lies—bear false witness—to themselves about themselves. They are not honest about what they think and feel, they are not honest about their personal history, and, consequently, they live lives that are only partially fulfilled. And in the bigger picture, if we cannot be honest with ourselves, how can we hope to be honest in our relationships with others?

When I engage in FOOW, I like to think of myself as looking in four directions. I look *behind* me to discover where I have been; *within* me to discover who I innately am; *ahead* of me to write and live out my personalized script; and *above* me to develop a personal spiritual relationship with my Higher Power and tap into that boundless energy source.

192

ERROR PREVENTION

People sometimes ask, "Will family-of-origin work keep me from making mistakes?" The answer is a resounding no! Family-of-origin work will not prevent us from making mistakes. However, the knowledge we gain on our journey can help us to break the cycle of repetitive generational mistakes.

Others ask, "Why can't I just start from here?" That question reminds me of a conversation I overheard at a filling station. It went something like this:

Motorist: *I need some directions.*

Attendant: *Where do you want to go?*

Motorist: *I'm not exactly sure.*

Attendant: *Where did you come from?*

Motorist: *Um, well, again, I am not sure.*

Attendant: *How can I give you directions when you don't know where you've come from and aren't sure where you want to go?*

Many of us live our lives exactly this way. It is extremely difficult, if not downright impossible, to arrive at a desired destination in life when we are unsure of where we are headed, to say nothing of where we have been and what has happened to us along the way.

My husband and I recently purchased a new house. We made several visits to the property, measured the rooms, marked up a floor plan and, in general, thoroughly investigated the house. When the movers arrived with our furniture, almost all of it fit exactly where we had planned.

On the other hand, imagine that we had looked at the outside of the house and knew what it looked like—but were basically unaware of what was inside; that we didn't investigate carefully to be certain of the number of rooms, their size, or the floor plan. It would be very difficult in such a situation to have the movers unload our furniture and have everything come together pleasingly and functionally. How silly, you say. No one would do that. We do just that when we neglect family-of-origin work.

Unless we know who we are, where we have come from, what happened to us along the way, and where we want to go, we may do little more than mark time throughout life. We can be the inventor of our own future; but we can't invent a healthier, more functional future for ourselves until we know ourselves. I've always liked the statement attributed to Christ (John 8:14), "Even if I testify on my own behalf, my testimony is valid for I know where I came from and where I am going." What a role model! Talk about awareness, responsibility, and functionality!

BENEFITS OF FOOW

I have actually heard some individuals pooh-pooh FOOW, saying, "I'm going to let sleeping dogs lie." That's an unfortunate position to take. If we choose that route, we may temporarily avoid some emotional pain, but we likely will never achieve the level of thriving and success that it's possible for us to attain. Sleeping dogs can hold us back.

Why

not

just

let

sleeping

dogs

lie?

Family-of-origin work can help us to:

- Manage our energy more effectively. Grief, anxiety, sadness, dysfunctional patterns of behavior, and excessive adaption all drain vital energy

- Enhance the brain/body connection. Writing and living out our own *script* can often decrease addictive behaviors and improve our health and well-being

- Improve our relationships. We cannot be truly intimate at any level unless we are truly *real*. Unhealed woundedness can block our spiritual connectedness, as well, and place us at increased risk for addictive behaviors

- Invent a healthier future. Breaking the cycle of dysfunction, and role-modeling more functional behaviors, may be our greatest gift to the next generation.

There are several exciting reasons for us to begin this journey of awareness. Only by identifying who we are, where we came from, and what happened to us, do we have the opportunity to make healthier choices in terms of our behaviors. When we honestly take responsibility for who we are and where we are going, we become empowered. Reaching our potential, becoming the person we were intended to become, is possible only as we learn who we are. In this investigation we become, in effect, our own Sherlock Holmes.

- Discover what you learned
- Define specific roles you played
- Recall abuse (if any)
- Heal woundedness
- Identify more functional behaviors
- Develop a map for desired change
- Learn how to thrive

The benefits that can accrue to us are innumerable. For example, we can:

- Discover what we were taught, as well as what we actually learned. Were we a wanted or unwanted addition to our family? Our current responses to life are usually directly related to our childhood and the learning that took place—consciously and perhaps even more importantly, subconsciously. Since actions speak louder than words, we usually learned what we saw role-modeled rather than what we were told to do.

- Define the specific *role(s)* we played. Some of us played several roles, changing them as the need arose. Shakespeare said that life is a stage, and we are actors playing roles. The specific roles we adopted in childhood are often similar to the ones we are currently exhibiting. Identifying these roles can help us to make informed choices about which roles we will accept in the future.

- Recall abuse (physical, emotional, mental, spiritual, sexual) if any was present. We must identify what needs to be healed in our lives, and then get serious about healing that woundedness so we can move more easily through life. Some of us are lugging baggage accumulated over several decades; others are actually grappling with baggage from generations past.

195

- Identify the *script* that we were handed at birth and evaluate how well it matches who we innately are. Ninety percent of our adult personality is believed to be in place by the age of six or seven. This doesn't mean our personality is cast in concrete. It does mean, however, that in adulthood many people continue to *act out* their childhood scripts. Portions of those scripts may be very functional but some portions may need serious revision.

- Learn from our mistakes, discover new ways to think, and identify new options. As we progress, we can evaluate whether or not there are healthier and more desirable ways in which to behave. After taking stock, we may need to refocus. We may need to initiate more functional living patterns—not only for our own benefit, but also for the benefit of others who can learn, through our role-modeling, how to achieve improved outcomes for their expended energy.

- Develop a *map* for desired change. Instead of continuing to struggle through life, sometimes successfully, sometimes despairingly, we can learn to reparent ourselves in areas where we are not achieving desired outcomes. As we break some of the generational dysfunction and role-model differentiated actualization, we can exponentially improve our legacy to those who come after us. While prevention is always better than treatment, treatment is next best. Part of our treatment means that prevention strategies can be available for the next generation.

- Achieve a position of thriving instead of just surviving. Effective family-of-origin work can move us toward a position of thriving, and from my point of view, that's the best way to live! Of course it takes work, but the benefits that accrue are universal and exponential. They rub off, so to speak, on our family members, friends, coworkers, pets, and everyone with whom we come in contact.

In this process there need not be any blaming. We are on this journey of discovery to identify *patterns* of behavior. I have found it helpful to approach family-of-origin work from the premise that I am the problem, I am the resource, and (in cooperation with my Higher Power and support system) I am the solution. For me, that removes any tendency I might have to blame others for any deficiencies in the way my life is progressing.

Of course, sometimes bad things happen to good people, as the title of a popular book suggests. In general, however, it has been suggested that at least half of our problems are of our own making, deriving largely from the way we think. If we took care of fifty percent of our problems just by changing the way we think (about the past, the present, the future), imagine how much more energy we'd have to work on the other fifty percent!

A WORD ABOUT CONFIDENTIALITY

Individuals are often concerned about confidentiality. That's smart. Bona fide boundaries—appropriate guides, or self-identified limits that enhance our health and safety—can help us to be politically smart in this arena. We need to be judicious about what we share, with whom, and under what circumstances. Silence is a characteristic of dysfunctional systems. The opposite stance is motor-mouthing all over everyone and in every situation. Neither position is healthy. As John Bradshaw says, 180 degrees from dysfunctional is still dysfunctional. We need to choose the healthy medium.

When discussing what we are learning in family-of-origin work, here are a couple of important confidentiality guidelines:

> Time—our youth—
> it never really goes, does it?
> It is all held in our minds.
> —Santmyer

- Remember the eleventh commandment: *thou shalt not explain*. You do not owe explanations to everyone about everything. Personal information should be disclosed judiciously and only to individuals you trust. Avoid triangling.

- Share information about yourself only—nothing about anyone else. A next-door neighbor of mine had a favorite expression: *tend to your own rat-killing*. Anything we might be tempted to share about someone else will be only our perception and nothing more. It's much safer and more functional to avoid any temptation to gossip.

FAMILY-OF-ORIGIN WORK

I look at family-of-origin work as involving at least three major tasks. These are to discover our:

- Innate personal collage
- Personal history
- Generational history

> You can't change the past
> but you can find out what
> to avoid in the future.
> —Anonymous

Let's look more specifically at each of these major discovery tasks.

Our Personal Collage

I recently observed a small child being gently questioned by a store security officer. The child, obviously lost, must have been about three years old and was blubbering in a bewildered manner. He was apparently so frightened he wasn't cooperating with the officer at all. Instead of answering questions to the best of his ability, he was crying and screaming and striking out at the man who was trying to help him. (I could understand his terror. It triggered a childhood memory of my being lost for a couple of hours in a huge Hudson's Bay Trading Company store in Canada.) In adulthood, when we don't fully understand who we are, we may wound the very people who are trying to help us. We do this through our dysfunctional communication and behaviors.

One way to begin to get to know who we are as individuals is through a variety of personal tests. These tests will give us some assorted labels that can help us to describe our characteristics. Labels are simply reference points that help us to quickly describe specific entities. With a computer, for instance, when inputting, we must assign labels to data if we ever hope to retrieve them. The labels do not change the data that we have entered, they only provide a mechanism by which we can later recall and put the data to use.

Some people are afraid of personal testing. One said, "I don't want to take any of these newfangled brain or temperament tests. I don't want to be stuck in a box!" Another said, "I am just fine the way I am. Why should I let someone else poke around in my mind?"

Each to one's own viewpoint. Mine is different, however. I have learned a great deal of valuable and immensely helpful information about myself through testing. The Benziger Thinking Styles Assessment (BTSA) has been the single most helpful instrument. The knowledge I gained so notably changed my life that I became licensed to score and interpret the BTSA so I could help others more effectively. I developed both the *Whole-brained Success Strategies* seminar and the *Brainworks Unlimited*™ program for the same reason—as well as a dozen other seminars and related resources (see appendix).

So our first task is to identify who we are and who we were meant to be. Think of yourself as a little plant. Your goal is to ascertain as much as possible about the environment in which you grew up. A good starting point in this discovery process, is to ask yourself some general questions. For example:

- What was the *garden* like in which I found myself planted?
- Was I affirmed for who I was, or primarily for conforming to expectations?
- Was my innate giftedness nurtured and rewarded, or was I punished for being different?

- Were appropriate tools, accessories, and learning opportunities available to assist me in developing competencies within my brain lead?
- Did my environment match my extroversion/introversion ratio?
- Was my sensory preference similar to, or different from, others in my family?

My Personal Collage

We can only invent a more functional future—
for ourselves—when we know ourselves

✔ Thinking style
✔ Sensory preference
✔ E:I ratio
✔ Gender
✔ Body image
✔ Health status
✔ Joys and fears
✔ Level of adaption
✔ Innate aptitudes
✔ Weaknesses
✔ Intelligence quotient
✔ Emotional intelligence
✔ Emotional tone
✔ Likes and dislikes
✔ Needs and wants
✔ Personal vision
✔ Goals
✔ Lifestyle

*I promise to tell the truth,
the whole truth,
and nothing but the truth . . .*

It is also helpful to identify at least the following specifics about yourself:

- Preferred thinking style (brain lead)
- Primary sensory preference
- Extroversion/Introversion ratio
- Aptitudes (innate giftedness, developed talents, and weaknesses)
- Intelligence quotient as well as emotional intelligence
- Lifestyle and health status
- Level of adaption (if any)
- Gender and personal body image
- Likes and dislikes (some of us were taught to be quiet about any dislikes and *do it anyway;* others never learned to define any likes and, therefore, when asked what they would like to do in a given situation have no idea)
- Needs and wants (they're often very different, you know)
- Personal vision (some of us grew up knowing either a parent's vision or none at all)
- Goals that can help us achieve our personal vision

Our Personal History

The second major task is to discover our personal history. Remember that this is a *journey*. While we are building our personal collage, we often uncover bits and pieces about our personal history, as well. Finding out more about our personal history can give us new insights into who we are, and who we were meant to be. Try to view this as an adventure!

You may want to begin by systematically asking yourself questions such as:

- What important events have occurred in my life?
- What type of environment surrounded me in childhood? What were the similarities and differences between my environment and who I am in terms of brain lead, sensory preference, and extroversion/introversion ratio?
- What type of home atmosphere did I experience? Was there a sense of happiness, gloom, unease, anxiety, fear, suspicion, anger, acceptance, comfort?
- What kind of resources did I (and my family) possess and in what amounts?
- What is my financial history?
- What did I hear people say about me?
- How was I treated by others?
- What losses did I experience?
- What joys did I experience?
- What were my educational experiences?

- What advantages have I had so far in life? What disadvantages?
- Was I abused in any way? Physically, mentally, sexually, emotionally, spiritually? Some individuals were abused and know it, some have *forgotten* the abuse, still others have mislabeled or denied the abuse. (Refer to *Back to Basics* for assistance in identifying different forms of abuse. In terms of damage, there may be little difference among physical, sexual, and emotional abuse; nor between vicarious and actual abuse.)

It can sometimes be difficult to maintain a semblance of order when you are trying to fit everything together in your mind only. Therefore, it can be helpful to actually write down the answers to these questions, and others that you may think of—it's much easier to put a puzzle together when you can actually *grasp* the pieces. You will likely be discovering new pieces about your personal history, and adding layers to your personal collage, for as long as you live.

Our Generational History

The third task is to discover our generational history. This important step in the recovery process involves learning about ourselves against the backdrop of our progenitors and their history.

Different family systems have different giftedness, different strengths, different weaknesses, different risks, and on and on. Good people sometimes exhibit dysfunctional behaviors because they are enmeshed in a dysfunctional system.

We need to identify the system that spawned us. It will usually have some desirable characteristics. Just as likely, it will contain some systems problems that have influenced our beliefs and expectations, to say nothing of the behavior patterns we exhibit. We cannot begin to deal with our own dysfunction efficaciously, until we pinpoint the dysfunctional issues and patterns exhibited in our *line*.

Exploring our family tree helps us to discover the types of behavioral patterns—functional and dysfunctional, healthy and unhealthy—common to our generational inheritance. Recognizing the patterns and characteristics frequently exhibited in our lineage helps to provide a baseline of information as well as some objectivity. It helps us to identify the particular behavioral patterns that have influenced us or are actually operational in our own lives today.

Some therapists estimate that seventy percent of all dysfunctional patterns in a family system are behaviors that can be explained in terms of unfinished generational issues—problems that were hidden, denied, or not dealt with for generations before us. These problems and problem behaviors have an uncanny way of reappearing regularly in the lives of descendants.

Every person is an omnibus in which his/her ancestors ride. —Holmes

Just as we looked for patterns in our own personal history, we now need to look for patterns in our generational inheritance. Consider factors such as:

- Culture
- Education
- Marriage
- Finances
- Careers
- Abuse
- Vision

- Service
- Addictive behaviors
- Presence or absence of children
- Unwed pregnancies
- Presence or absence of characteristics common to dysfunctional family systems (e.g., denial, silence, isolation, rigidity)

We can explore our generational history in a variety of different ways. For example, we can talk with family members and close family friends. Don't interrogate them, but use nonthreatening personal interviews. Ask them what they remember about you. If you aren't comfortable talking to family and friends in person or by telephone, write letters and ask pertinent questions. The more clearly I was able to articulate that the purpose of my discovery journey was to help *me* exhibit more functional behaviors, and that there was no blame involved in my search, the more willing the individuals were to share their recollections, observations, and impressions with me.

Look through old photo albums; revisit childhood homes, schools, and towns. Sometimes looking through newspapers in your home-town library can jog your memories of childhood events. I've found it helpful to draw genograms, visual diagrams of important events and relationships over at least three generations. Think of a genogram as a jigsaw puzzle in which you are one of the pieces, or as a road map that tells you where you have been and where you might be headed. (Refer to Marlin's book, *Genograms*, for useful tips.)

As I continue this process, I'm constantly amazed (and even somewhat entertained) at what I discover about myself and my family. Some of the information I like; some I dislike; some is humorous; some is sad. It's all interesting, however—and helpful!

RECALL OF MEMORIES

What is memory? Despite decades of research, the precise mechanisms driving memory are still somewhat elusive. We can define it, however, as the ability to recall thoughts. This is an active mental process. Recalling, processing, and sometimes reframing memories from our past is important in family-of-origin work and recovery. Both what we can and cannot recall, offer us important clues (keys) to who we are today. In order for an experience to be recalled, it must have produced an engram (memory trace) within the brain. Several portions of the brain are believed to be involved with memory including the association cortex of the cerebral lobes (e.g., temporal, parietal, occipital, frontal), parts of the limbic system, and the diencephalon.

There are many factors that influence whether or not we can recall specific memories. Here are just a few to consider:

- Innate preference. Depending upon our own unique giftedness, we may have a tendency to pay more attention to certain information. Organizers tend to focus upon facts, figures, details, rules, labels, routines, and the location of bounded shapes (e.g., car keys). Harmonizers may pay more attention to information about relationships, nonspeech

203

sounds (e.g., music), emotions, and feelings. Visualizers tend to pay attention to the big picture, to patterns of abstract information, to innovation, and to visionary concepts or ideas. Prioritizers may concentrate on data that can help them to set and achieve goals, and on information related to how things function.

In order for us to recall a memory it had to be laid down in the first place. Fortunately, the brain screens out much of the stimuli with which we are bombarded; otherwise it might be overwhelmed with information. Short-term memory, the ability to recall bits of information, generally lasts only a few minutes or hours. For example, we can locate an unfamiliar number in the telephone book and remember it long enough to dial. Short-term memory is believed to depend a great deal on the brain's electrical and chemical regulation. There are a variety of conditions that can interfere with electrical activity within the brain, and therefore, inhibit short term memory and its possible transfer into long-term memory. These conditions can potentially include general anesthesia, coma, electroconvulsive shock, and any event that reduces blood supply to the brain. Chemical activity can be disrupted by a variety of factors (e.g., use of street drugs, Alzheimer's Disease). The loss of one's ability to recall information is a key symptom in Alzheimer's disease. One of the research findings is the disappearance in certain parts of the brain of a key enzyme required to synthesize acetycholine, a neurotransmitter that plays a part in memory.

With the help of brain organs located in the limbic system, about one percent of the information that comes to our consciousness is transferred from short-term memory into long-term memory. Long-term memory can last for years, although over time, we may not accurately recall everything about the memory. Sometimes we lose the details while retaining the concept or main idea. Long-term memory may depend more on structural changes—anatomical or biochemical—that influence the formation of new synapses. Electron micrographic studies of neurons that have been subjected to prolonged, challenging mental activity show changes that include an increase in the branching patterns of dendrites and enlargement of the synaptic end-bulbs.

> When you get right down to it, the root meaning of the word *succeed* is basically to follow through on becoming the person you were intended to be. —Anonymous

- Life experiences must be identified with labels that can later be retrieved. In childhood, prior to the development of the left frontal lobe that possesses the ability to label abstract experiences, we may be unable to retrieve stored data at will. Memory fragments may pop up from time to time, however, especially in situations that are in some way reminiscent of the original situation or event. The form a memory takes depends upon our age at the time. Experiences that occurred prior to the development of verbal language may return in memory only as a vague emotion or as a bodily sensation rather than as a detailed recollection that we can describe in words. In addition, the limbic system hippocampi (that mature at about the age of four) record memories in terms of time and space. Therefore, according to Dr. Carnes, some memory traces for experiences prior to the age of four may be recalled in fragments without the facts that would specifically relate them to time and place. As adults, we need to pay attention to these memory fragments. We also need to be very conscious of the taxon system (helps one to register memories of feelings and sounds), especially in dealing with children. Even during gestation, we are already absorbing and registering such information.

- We tend to store experiences that have a great deal of meaning to us. In other words, most of the time we actually record only the highs and lows of childhood. For example, we are more likely to recall the summer when we broke a leg, or the trip to Disneyland with a favorite aunt, than the times we went shopping with mother. In addition, experiences tied to strong sensory cues are more likely to be retained in long-term memory. Smell may be the sense most directly linked to memory because scent perceptions are processed in the limbic system of the brain—the same area involved with emotions, the creation of new memories, and their transfer to long-term memory banks.

- Situations that are tied to emotionally-charged events such as a divorce, the birth of a sibling, and starting school are more likely to be recalled. If nothing happened to distinguish one experience from another, it may be difficult, if not impossible, to bring it to mind. Events related to abuse can involve a whole kaleidoscope of emotions. As with events leading to PTSD (post traumatic stress disorder), these memories may be temporarily buried (blocked from conscious thought). They can and do profoundly influence our lives, however, which is one reason that recovery is so vitally important.

Taken together, these and other factors are reminders that none of us recalls everything. In general, based on the comments already made about brain maturation, the absence of early childhood memories doesn't necessarily indicate that something horrible happened to us. Nevertheless, there definitely are exceptions. One of God's gifts to children is the ability to repress unpleasant, painful, or puzzling incidents of childhood. Consequently, children from dysfunctional families often *forget* much of their childhood or specific time periods of their childhood, especially if abuse (e.g., physical, emotional, sexual, intellectual, spiritual,  ritual) was present. Sometimes they forget events associated with certain individuals (e.g., alcoholic/drug-addicted parent), with one particular environment (e.g., a specific house, room, or town). This defense mechanism of forgetfulness helps the child to cope. The same defense mechanism routinely used in adulthood is generally unhelpful.

Recalling specific memories can give us reasons for the way we act now. By the age of five or six years, we've already made some very important decisions about who we are, based on what has happened to us so far. In their book, *Unlocking the Secrets of Your Childhood Memories*, the authors suggest that we should try to recall our earliest childhood memories—below eight years of age, if possible—because the earlier the memories the more significant they are. The more recent the memories, the more likely they have been skewed or altered by who we want to be.

In order to be helpful, the memories must involve *specific* events; and the more detail we can recall, the better. Generalizations are not as useful in helping us to view ourselves clearly. Think of these memory pictures as mental minivideocassettes. The more scenes or snatches of scenes we can recall, the more puzzle pieces we have to assemble into a collage. Some researchers believe that stored memories tend to return to us when we are ready to deal with them.

There has been much ado recently, in some quarters, about real versus false memories. To be as sure as possible that what we recall are *real* memories, we must try to recall what *we* remember, not what someone else has told us. In other words, the memories must be ours, and not incidents that were merely related to us. Sometimes it can be difficult to tell the difference.

Try asking yourself:

I'm looking for a counselor—one who has done personal family-of-origin work . . .

- "What did I see, hear, or actually experience?" If we cannot in our mind *see* a specific scene, or *hear* words that were spoken, or identify some *kinesthetic* sensation, we may merely have been told about the event.

- "What did I *feel?*" To be our own, the memory should have some emotion attached to it (e.g., joy, fear, anger, sadness). When we can recall a specific incident, that has an emotion attached to it, there is a strong likelihood that it will be our own.

If you are having difficulty deciding whether a memory is real or false, it is important to consult a skilled counselor. Look for someone who has experience in this field. Interview your potential counselor as carefully as you would a potential investment banker. I strongly recommend consulting with a same-gender counselor.

Now, get busy and put it all together. Rewrite *your* own script as necessary. Picture yourself on the stage of life, following your well-planned script, being the *real* you, achieving success beyond your wildest dreams, giving the performance of a lifetime. What a way to live!

PRESENTING: THE PERFORMANCE OF A LIFETIME

BRAIN BUILDERS

Points to Ponder

- Those who cannot remember the past are condemned to fulfill it.
  —Santayana

- Two key concepts I have learned in this section:

  _____

  _____

- Two facts I've learned about myself while studying this section:

  _____

  _____

- One way in which I am now applying this information in my own life:

  _____

  _____

- Awareness is the first _____ on the road to positive change.

- Exploring our family tree can help us to discover the types of behavioral patterns common to our _____.

- It is important to be _____ _____ about what we share about ourselves, with whom, and under what circumstances.

- **T   F**   We can be the inventor of our own future but we can only invent one that is healthier and more functional when we know who we are.

- **T   F**   Family-of-origin work will prevent us from making mistakes.

- **T   F**   There need not be any blaming in this discovery process.

- **T   F**   One hundred and eighty degrees from dysfunctional is still dysfunctional.

Brain Teasers

1.	2.	3.	4.
1 3 5 7 9 WHELMING	IS IS IS IS IS IS IS IS IS IS	ALL_{WORLD}	OINSIDEUT

Creativity Corner

THE UNIVERSE OPERATES BY NATURAL LAWS

Caution: we violate them at our own risk

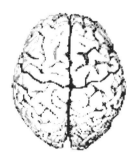

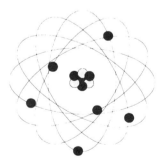

INTERNAL UNIVERSE

EXTERNAL UNIVERSE

BRAIN LAWS AND RADAR TRAPS

Chapter 11
Taking Charge of Your *B/BC*

Although it is our greatest asset, researchers estimate that most of us stimulate less than ten percent of our brain potential on a daily basis. We're definitely missing the mark if we settle for that! I like to use the analogy of my hands with their ten fingers. Suppose I primarily used only one finger most of the time. There are many things I could do: use an adding machine, a telephone, even a computer.

But suppose that I decided to use two fingers on a regular basis, my thumb and forefinger on one of my hands. Imagine the possibilities now! I could grasp and manipulate objects and on and on. And, if I decided to add the use of a couple more fingers on my other hand, my ability to function digitally would increase exponentially.

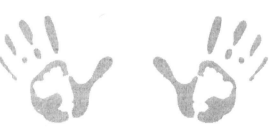

Unless we possess fewer than ten fingers for some reason or other, most of us use all of our fingers on a regular basis. We do this, in part, because we have been taught to do so, but, in addition, we have found that we can be more efficient and can accomplish more in life that way.

Now just imagine what we could accomplish if we each chose to stimulate closer to one hundred percent of our brain's potential on a regular basis! Why does the average person stimulate less than ten percent of his or her potential brain power? There may be endless reasons and, no doubt, they differ for different individuals. For example, they may:

- Be preoccupied with the cares of everyday living
- Be uninformed in reference to brain function and potential capabilities
- Be lazy and don't want to put forth the effort required
- Have learned less-than-optimal behaviors
- Be locked into a box of lowered expectations
- Have never caught a vision of what is possible
- Never have learned to manage stress, emotions, or feelings
- Be expending large amounts of energy in excessive/prolonged adaption
- Not grasp the value of working within the brain's natural laws

NATURAL LAWS OF THE UNIVERSE

Natural laws? What do you mean we need to work within the brain's natural laws? Hold on a minute and I'll explain. The universe operates by natural laws, rules that pro-scribe predictable outcomes. Most of us realize that we violate these laws (e.g., gravity, heredity, spontaneous combustion, the tides) at our own risk. One of science's dramatic discoveries has been the awareness that natural laws also govern our internal universe (e.g., cardiovascular, respiratory, digestive, and nervous systems).

"GOTCHA RADAR TRAP"

Through understanding the ways in which the brain functions most effectively and by cooperating with its natural laws we can often avoid many metaphorical *radar traps*—traps that can diminish our chances for success. In other words, we can often avert problems, reduce misunderstandings, alleviate stress, enhance desired outcomes, and increase our enjoyment in life. I refer to this process as *taking charge of our brain/body connection (B/BC)*.

I have no idea as to the number of natural brain laws. Identifying and understanding some of them, however, has positively impacted my life. As you review the following six examples of brain laws, you may think of others.

1 The brain readily responds to challenging mental exercise. Consider the following quote from, *Care and Feeding of the Brain*: "Uncultivated cortical functions diminish in strength when they are not used, much as muscles weaken when they are not exercised." Brain tissue is not a muscle in the usual sense of the word. Like muscle, however, brain tissue can decline with lack of use. Without stimulation and regular use, the axons and dendrites, the connecting fibers of the neurons, can shrivel up—like pulling the fingers of your hand into the palm. The neurons actually atrophy with disuse.

On the other hand, neurons become stronger with regular mental exercise. The number of synaptic connections between neurons increases when the brain is exposed to challenging mental stimulation. No one knows how many neurons the average brain contains. Numbers like one hundred billion are often used, however. This is an enormous number and I have trouble picturing what it really means. In addition, these billions of neurons interact with each other in thousands of different connections. It has been estimated that the number of interconnections (synapses) is represented by the number ten, followed by eight hundred zeros. Perhaps some math genius can fathom that number! According to one researcher, the number of connections is potentially greater than the number of atoms in the entire universe. Suffice it to say, most of us haven't even caught a glimpse of our potential brain power and what we could accomplish if we tapped into it appropriately. My brain has the potential for creating more interconnections than there are atoms in our universe. Staggering concept!

The number of interconnections is believed to be directly related to the way in which the brain is challenged, and can be a factor in delaying the onset of symptoms of aging. Researchers have identified two strategies that help to prevent and, in some cases even reverse, mental decline. The first is thirty minutes of daily physical exercise, preferably aerobic exercise. The second is a consistent daily program of

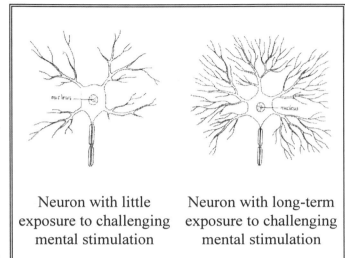

Neuron with little exposure to challenging mental stimulation

Neuron with long-term exposure to challenging mental stimulation

challenging mental exercise. In a healthy individual, mental gymnastics can actually stimulate the neurons to grow more dendrites; to stretch out their axons; to modify old pathways; to create new pathways.

Making specific provision for including challenging mental exercise in our lives may be more important than you might think. Research in three countries has shown the same conclusion. For every year of education we have completed beyond college, our risk

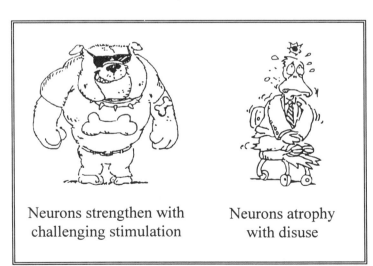

Neurons strengthen with challenging stimulation

Neurons atrophy with disuse

of Alzheimer's Disease decreases by twenty percent. The stimulation of education causes the brain to create more synaptic interconnections. This suggests that even if Alzheimer's should strike us in our later years, an enriched brain may exhibit less impairment in cognitive function. Just picture the difference between a barren tree in midwinter and a fully-leafed tree in summer.

"What constitutes challenging mental exercise?" It can be different for different individuals. Some love difficult and complex crossword puzzles; others enjoy going to classes at the local junior college to study music or a foreign language, to take an acrylic painting class, or to learn how to balance their checkbook. Still others like to write, compose music, or read to shut-ins. The mental exercise must stimulate active mental picturing, however. This means that *watching* the *soaps* on television doesn't qualify.

Whatever you select, a mental exercise routine is certainly worth a shot. To some degree, the term *use it or lose it* can apply to maintaining mental ability. And beyond the stimulation to your neurons, just think of all the new friends you'll make and all the enjoyment you can receive from what you learn! So *think*—and reap a rich harvest.

2 **The subconscious recognizes little difference between rehearsal and actuality.** Inherently, the subconscious mind recognizes little difference between rehearsal and actuality. That's why practice makes perfect, why individuals rehearse before they perform in public. Many athletes have capitalized on this enigma. They have learned to create mental pictures and thus enhance their performances. Those of you who enjoy watching the winter Olympics on television as much as I do will recall seeing some of the athletes, the downhill skiers in particular, pause at the top of the run. Eyes closed, they were picturing the course and seeing themselves traversing it successfully. Greg Louganis, arguably the greatest male diver in Olympic history, engaged in the same type of mental preparation before executing nearly-flawless dives that won him four gold medals.

THE ONE PERCENT ADVANTAGE

Rate of improvement:

- Group one - actual rehearsal
  24% improvement

- Group two - mental rehearsal
  23% improvement

- Group three - no rehearsal
  0% improvement

You may have heard about an experiment with some basketball players who were fairly evenly matched in ability to accurately shoot baskets. They were divided into three groups. Each group received different instructions. The first group was directed to show up at the gym every day for three weeks. They were to actually practice shooting baskets for one hour each day. The second group was told not to show up at the gym for the next three weeks. Instead, they were to spend one hour each day *imagining* they were shooting baskets in the gym. The third group was instructed to stay away from basketball for the next three weeks entirely. In fact, they were to told to banish all thoughts of shooting baskets.

When the three weeks were over, the groups reassembled at the gym and were tested. Not surprisingly, group number three, the players that neither practiced at the gym nor thought about basketball, showed no increase in their ability to shoot baskets. The players in group number one, who had consistently practiced at the gym for one hour each day, showed a twenty-four percent increase in their accuracy rate.

Now get this. Group number two, composed of players who only imagined shooting baskets (who practiced in their minds), showed a twenty-three percent increase in their accuracy rate. That's incredible! Only one percentage point less than their sweat-laden counterparts in group one!

My father deserves the credit for helping me learn this lesson when I was eleven years old. I don't know if he had heard about the basketball players and really knew what he was doing, or whether he just wanted me to stop complaining. I had wanted to learn to play the harp for as long as I could remember. Regularly I alluded to how nice it would be if we could just own a harp. Finally my father purchased a vibraharp. It didn't look like a harp at all. It looked much more like a marimba but with metal keys and electrical vibrators to enhance the sound. Part of me was disappointed; part of me realized Dad was right when he explained, "It will be much easier to transport between home and church than would a harp." Of course, he was anxious for me to learn to play it well enough to provide special music for church.

To be perfectly honest, I was not very excited about the vibraharp, although I tried not to let that show. And then there was the problem of finding a teacher. No one in our neck of the woods seemed to have ever heard of a vibraharp. (Indeed, my father had ordered it from the Deagan company—by mail. Wherever he had learned about the instrument I never knew.) Consequently, I set about trying to teach myself to play. It felt very strange, trying to hold two mallets in each hand. Even stranger was attempting to get all four mallets to strike four correct keys all at the same time. My fingers cramped and my hands perspired as my nerves and muscles struggled to learn this *foreign language*. Repeatedly one of the mallets would decide to take a break during a crucial chord and fly off to a distant part of the room.

I persisted. For one thing I didn't want to admit that four sticks of wood, with one end of each wrapped in yarn, could get the best of me. For another, my father persisted—in an encouraging sort of way. When I practically fainted at the thought of playing in public, he offered to play a duet with me. It truly was much easier holding only one mallet in each hand and we did a credible job that first time. Somehow he was always too busy to practice after that, but did find time to listen to me. Opportunity for practice seemed somewhat limited, however. My mother was frequently ill and I would have to take over the cooking and housecleaning and even represent her at certain functions. Funerals, for instance.

> Your brain is a work in progress. —Taylor

One day my preacher father and I were driving home from a funeral. As we drove by the Eastman School of Music, Dad commented, "Reminds me of the vibraharp. I sure wish you'd hurry up and learn to play it."

"I don't have enough time to practice," I retorted. "Just take today, for example. I had to spend three hours attending a funeral, for someone I didn't know, in a parlor that gave me the creeps." Dad chuckled and then rather casually remarked, "So learn to practice in your head. That way you won't be limited by your environment."

I was really irritated by his obvious lack of sympathy. I was also curious, however. So curious, in fact, that I closed my eyes right then and there just to see if I could *picture* the vibraharp. It took me awhile, several minutes, actually. Of course, I had some interruptions. Who wouldn't open their eyes with the car skidding around on the icy highway in northern Canada?

I clearly recall the feeling of amazement that swept over me when I finally *saw* the vibes in my mind's eye. When I actually visualized myself standing in front of the instrument, mallets in hands, I was so surprised that I forgot to be irritated any longer.

"I can do it, Dad." I laughed aloud.

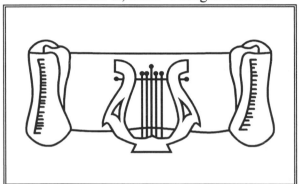

"Do what?" he asked, his mind obviously on something else. (His driving for one, I hoped!)

"Practice the vibes in my mind!" I closed my eyes to make sure it hadn't been an accident. Sure enough, in just a few seconds I could do it again. In response, Dad said something to the effect that he knew I could do it, and would I be ready to play a selection in church the following week.

That was the first time I ever consciously realized the resourcefulness of mental imaging, and what it could enable me to accomplish, if I just tapped into it. Too bad I didn't translate this realization into other areas of brain function more quickly! And yes, whenever I play the vibes, although that is much less frequently now, I do practice in my mind.

The brain does *push us* toward the outcomes we internally picture. In order to cooperate with this natural law, we need to picture a desired outcome and then practice, practice, practice. This ability can help us in countless ways. The old adage *fake it till you make it* speaks to this. We act *as if* we have already achieved the desired outcome even as we move toward it and continue to build skill and confidence.

> They can because they think they can. —Virgil

3 **The subconscious readily understands *positives* but processes *negatives* (the reverse of an idea) less effectively.** While we may not understand exactly how we think, most of us quickly realize that the process involves imagining or picturing an idea. For example, say to yourself, "I'd like an ice cream cone." (I don't particularly like ice cream but most people do, so I'll use it as an example.) Stop for a moment and metaphorically pull down the movie screen of your mind. Most likely you will project a picture of your favorite flavor perched atop a sugar cone. What color is the ice cream? What does it feel like on your tongue? What does it taste like? Can you smell the flavor as well as taste it?

Now try this. Say to yourself, "I *don't* want an ice cream cone." What happens this time? Your brain again creates a picture of an ice cream cone—and then must try to erase it. Negatives utilize a two-step process that, of necessity, requires more energy expenditure..

Imagine that one lovely afternoon you step out into your back yard to see the five-year-old from next door trying to walk along the top of the fence. Your heart leaps up into your mouth. The fence is over six feet high. How ever did the child get up there to begin with? You fear there's going to be an accident. In typical fashion, the first words out of your mouth are, "Don't fall!" Now think about those words for a moment. In order to process what you have just said, the child's mind must first create a picture of falling, and then try to picture the reverse of that idea. The first picture (of falling) will usually result in the very outcome you are trying to prevent—because the mind has a

> The growth of the human mind is still high adventure, in many ways the highest adventure on earth. —Cousins

tendency to *act out* what it envisions. Suppose, however, you say instead, "Stretch out your arms to balance yourself. I'm coming over to help you safely down." There is every possibility that the child will create a mental picture that will reduce the likelihood of a fall.

Many of us were told at one time or another during childhood, "Stop laughing right now," or "Don't laugh, whatever you do." In my case, those words almost guaranteed that I would practically die laughing, no matter how hard I strove to hold back the giggles.

Let's suppose that it's the end of a very rough day. Some truly insignificant thing happens and you growl at your partner; or worse yet, shout. A few minutes later, remorseful, you say to yourself, "I don't want to shout at my partner anymore." It would be much more effective to say instead, "I speak patiently to my partner." Why? Because messages

that use a negative (e.g., *don't*), can actually be misinterpreted. In order for the brain to understand "do not shout," it first has to create a picture of you shouting. Then it must try to erase that picture, and replace it with an image of you speaking kindly, at a reasonable decibel level. It takes less energy and is more effective to create the positive picture initially. Every time we say *don't* to ourselves, we risk the possibility that the subconscious can miss the *don't* or the message can get lost as the brain tries to reverse the mental image.

Here is another example. You have decided that it is time to shed fifteen pounds from your frame. If you say, "I don't want to be fat," or "I don't want to overeat," your mind sees a picture of you overeating and looking overweight. Instead try words such as, "I enjoy weighing one hundred and thirty-five pounds" (or whatever is realistic for your body frame). Create an internal picture of what you want your body to look like at the desired weight. You might also add

statements such as, "I like the way my body looks when I am wearing size ____ clothes," or "My food intake has decreased to help me achieve my optimum weight," or "I eat less at each meal and feel satisfied," or "I feel full after half a slice of pie."

Janeen, a single woman, used to frequently say, "I'm so lonely. I just hate living alone." Of course that created a mental picture of her being alone, of hating it, and of feeling dreadfully lonely. When she changed this sentence to, "I choose to find a friend to connect with today," even she was surprised at the way in which her life improved. Somehow, creating a positive picture of connecting with a friend allowed her to see open doors where before she had seen nothing. She used the telephone more often and got into the habit of writing more cards and letters. Most of the time she is still alone. But being alone is different from being lonely. As Janeen puts it, "I'm rarely lonely any more. Even when I am by myself, I carry my friends around with me in my mind."

We can apply this to almost any situation in life. Rather than saying, "I hope I don't have a car accident," try, "I am arriving safely at my destination." Instead of, "I can't do that," try, "I can learn to do that with some practice."

You may have noticed that many of my examples are phrased in the present tense. That is an important technique to develop. When we speak about the past, the subconscious hears our words and knows that nothing can be done to change what happened. Therefore, it elects not to put any energy into the process. In a similar way when we speak about the future, the subconscious knows that the time for action has not yet arrived. The only thing that can be actually dealt with is the present, the now, this moment.

Understanding this perspective enables us to utilize our brainpower to help us exhibit desired behaviors and accomplish goals. We do that by telling the subconscious that the action is happening now. For example, let's say that you have just snapped at one of your children. This behavior is not on your top-ten list of all-time favorites and you make the decision to discontinue it.

If you say, "I want to speak kindly to my children in the future," this is not perceived by the brain as demanding any action at the present time. Consequently, it will not prompt you to think about taking action. If, on the other hand, you say, "I speak kindly to my children," the present-tense picture created is processed by the subconscious as requir-

ing action right now. It records that thought and plays it over and over again, whether or not you are aware of it. And it will help to *push* you in the direction of speaking kindly to your children.

You can further increase your chances of success by mentally rehearsing the situation in which you just snapped at your child. This time, see yourself speaking kindly and patiently. Play that video a couple of times, watching yourself being successful. Just as with the basketball players, the mental rehearsal will predispose you to appropriate action when the next incident occurs.

In his book, *Unlimited Power*, Anthony Robbins tells the story of Karl Wallenda. For years as the creator and head of the Flying Wallendas, Karl had performed aerial routines with outstanding success. Some considered him the greatest high-wire acrobat of all time. He never even considered the possibility of failure; certainly falling was not part of his mental makeup. One day, however, Karl mentioned to his wife that he had begun to see himself falling. She was predictably horrified. Nothing she could say, however, helped her husband to stop seeing himself falling. Sure enough, three months later, Karl fell to his death. Some people might say that he had a premonition. Robbins takes another view. He believes that by dwelling on the possibility of falling, Karl gave his brain a new path to follow. In that way, he had helped to foster his own disastrous demise.

The brain hemispheres talk to each other and to us all the time. We can capitalize on this communication by creating internal pictures and recording internal tapes that instruct the brain in the way we want to behave—now. The good news is that we can learn to speak and to act *as if* we are already realizing our goals. This is especially important in childrearing. Haim Ginott said it very well, "Treat a child as though s/he already is the person that s/he is capable of becoming." The same principle holds true at any age. The positive messages, in pictures and words, play back in our subconscious and help influence us to act out—to become—what we envision is possible.

4 **Mind-set can alter neurotransmitter ratios and influence immune system function.** In order for us to be able to sense pleasure and to experience joy or enthusiasm, certain neurotransmitters must be present in the brain in appropriate amounts. Serotonin, for example. When individuals are unable to experience pleasure, we say they are depressed. Some researchers believe that the levels of both serotonin and norepinephrine are implicated in the imbalance common to depression. There may be disregulation in the release mechanism for these neurotransmitters. There may be disruption in receptor regulation or reuptake.

Negative thinking styles, especially when combined with chronic anger and bitterness, are associated with diminished levels of serotonin, as well as alterations in other neurotransmitters. This means that there can be a connection between a negative mind-set (a negative approach to life) and depression. Science has not decided which comes first: depression resulting in altered neurotransmitter ratios, or altered neurotransmitter ratios followed by depression. Likely, one scenario may be true in some cases, the opposite in others.

In cases of severe or chronic depression, individuals sometimes need to take medication, at least temporarily. Many of the medications available for use in such situations affect neurotransmitters in one way or another. Prozac, for example, is designed to increase serotonin levels in the brain. Some studies suggest that cognitive/behavioral therapy (helping an individual to change unduly pessimistic ways of thinking and to learn effective coping skills) can be as effective as medication for some people. Certainly the risk of relapsing into severe depression appears to be lowered in individuals who are treated with antidepressants in combination with talk therapy.

> The chief function of your body is to carry your brain around. —Edison

Not too long ago, I was presenting a seminar on the connection between stress and depression. After I mentioned the importance of positive self-talk, one of the participants interjected, "Self-talk? What's that? Everyone knows that people who talk to themselves are crazy!" Another participant rejoindered with the flip comment, "You're not crazy when you talk to yourself, only when you start answering!" After the laughter subsided, we focused on the fact that we not only talk to ourselves most of every waking minute, we answer as well. True, much of this conversation occurs silently, but this is the process that has been labeled self-talk. The average person may speak at rates of between one and two hundred words per minute, may listen at rates of a thousand words per minute, and may think thoughts at rates of three thousand per minute. Therefore, the question isn't, "Do we hold conversations with ourselves?" but rather, "What type of conversations do we hold with ourselves?"

Since our thoughts can actually influence the level of certain neurotransmitters within the brain, it is signally desirable to maintain a positive mind-set instead of regularly

engaging in negative thoughts. When we think negatively, we basically rehearse thoughts that reinforce how miserable life is; how hopeless the situation is; and how helpless we are to take action. It is truly difficult, if not impossible, to develop a positive mind-set if we regularly engage in negative self-talk.

In addition to affecting neurotransmitter ratios, the quality of our self-talk can contribute to the development, or persistence, of depression. In his book *Why Zebras Don't Get Ulcers,* author Sapolsky wrote: "On an incredibly simplistic level, you can think of depression as occurring when your cortex thinks an abstract negative thought and manages to convince the rest of the brain that this is as real as a physical stressor." When we are depressed, we certainly do tend to see life from a negative point of view. Thus the vicious circle gains momentum. Even our level of self-esteem is tied to our self-talk.

Unfortunately, much of our learned self-talk is negative. Human beings, in general, are programmed for negativity. For one thing, our culture has educated us to focus on areas in which we do not do well instead of rewarding ourselves for the undertakings we do well. For another, studies estimate that during our childhood and youth, most of us heard from seven to nine negative comments for every positive one. The bad news is that because of this input, many individuals have developed negative self-talk patterns. The good news is that we can learn a new way. Simply changing the way we talk to ourselves can, in and of itself, reduce stress and diminish the possibility of neurotransmitter alteration.

On the other hand, when we think positively, we rehearse thoughts that reinforce the abundant, exciting, and joyful adventure known as thriving. In his book, *You Can't Afford The Luxury of a Single Negative Thought,* Peter McWilliams provides an excellent description of what it means to emphasize the positive (versus the superficial positive-thinking bandages that some recommend). When we develop a positive mind-set, we:

- Take note of the information (including negative data)
- Decide what to do about it
- Take necessary action
- Focus on the positive aspects

This simple prescription is not a recommendation to deny reality. Let's say you trip over a stool that was not put away after it was used, and sprain your ankle. If you say, "I didn't really sprain my ankle; the pain is only an illusion," you are not facing reality. You did fall, after all. Some physical consequences have resulted to your ankle. But here's the rub—are you going to face reality from the perspective of a negative or a positive mind-set?

A negative mind-set might say, "I'm so clumsy. Here I go again, falling. How stupid! I'm going to spend the rest of my life stumbling over objects. One of these days I'll really get hurt." You might also focus on the idiot who left the stool out in the first place (assuming it was not you) and expend a great deal of energy on anger and blame.

A positive mind-set does not deny what happened, but it looks for ways to turn the situation into a blessing, if you will. From this perspective you might say, "Oops, that was a most unfortunate accident. Is there something I can learn here that might prevent a similar occurrence in the future?" If, by chance, *you* were the *idiot* who left the stool out in the first place, you might make a decision to learn a new way, to become more responsible in the future. You might also focus on the fact that, since you need to stay off that ankle for a couple of days, this will be a great opportunity to finish reading a book, listen to a personal-growth tape, or spend some one-to-one time with a close friend or family member who has been shortchanged on quality time lately.

How you choose to respond will influence the messages that are transmitted between the brain and the body; messages that can strengthen or suppress immune system function; messages that can change the level of certain brain neurotransmitters. If you have an *enemy outpost* inside your head, created by a habitually negative mind-set, take steps to get rid of it by focusing on the positive.

We can begin this process by *listening up.* Many of us haven't given much thought to *thought.* That is, we are often quite unaware of the thoughts that continually circle around inside our minds. It can be most enlightening to identify our self-talk immediately after a stressful situation. Do you hear negatives? *People always dump on me. I'm such a failure. I'll never succeed.*

Once we are aware of our personal self-talk patterns, we can begin the process of moving in a more positive direction by identifying one self-talk expression that reinforces negative behavior or a poor self-image. Next, we can create an alternate expression that will help to reinforce the positive type of behavior or attitude that we choose to exhibit. Every time we hear that negative self-talk, we follow it immediately with the positive. In addition, we can practice turning down the volume on the negative and turning up the volume on the positive.

Thinking is when the picture is in your head with the sound turned off . . .

I have been pleased to discover in my own life just how quickly this process can be accomplished if one really wants to work on it. When I first began speaking in public, I was terrified—and that's putting it mildly. It didn't help a bit when I learned that public speaking was the number one fear of the average American. Not only would I experience anxiety for several hours prior to my speaking appointment; sometimes I felt nauseated, as well. There were times when I felt so miserable that it was a challenge to keep from bolting to the next county.

It may interest you to know that once I actually began my presentation, I truly enjoyed the experience. Over time, I came to the conclusion that the recurrence of my presentation anxiety was dysfunctional—to say nothing of tiresome—and that something had better be done about it. No one else offered to do anything about it. The ball was squarely in my court.

I read the book *Feel the Fear and Do It Anyway,* and realized that I needed to face up to my fear. In reality, it was only an illusion, but it took me a while to discover that. In the process of confronting my anxiety, I decided to *listen up*—and was truly amazed at what I heard. There was a whole collection of negative self-talk CDs playing through my brain's stereo system. Titles included:

- The speaker who forgot—everything.
- The toilet-papered shoe.
- The trip that escalated into a fall off the podium.
- The audience that went elsewhere.

When I finally *tuned in* and became aware, I made some changes. Every time I heard negative self-talk, I would follow it with a line that described the outcome I hoped to achieve. I recorded some original CDs with lines that went something like this:

- I'm recalling the information I want to present. (I'll forget to forget.)
- Most people are fairly polite. (Plus I'll pack my presentation so full of timely information that they'll stay to the very end—and applaud. Their time will not be wasted!)
- I'm very sure-footed. (I'll purchase some lower-heeled shoes just to up the ante.)
- At least one person desperately needs to hear what I have to share. (It's quality, not quantity. Plus, I remember many times in life when I'd have given almost anything to hear someone tell me what I now have to share.)
- Toilet paper on one's shoe does create chuckles in the audience. (Nevertheless, I'll make a point to check!)

In addition, I started turning *down* the volume on the negative thoughts and turning *up* the volume on the trailers. Gradually, many of the old CDs disappeared from my internal self-talk library or their messages became so faint I could hardly hear them.

My husband and I recently had the privilege of traveling in Alaska. It was a fantastic trip, and we learned all manner of new information. For one thing, we discovered that they grow some pretty healthy mosquitoes up there, at least during certain parts of the year. One little girl with an unsightly facial bump the size of half a hen's egg said she had just been bitten by a mosquito. I shuddered. (For me, an auditory, hearing a mosquito humming around my ear is almost as bad as fingernails on a chalkboard!)

Imagine that you have decided to take a vacation in Alaska. Assume that you do have control over the time of year when this trip will occur. Information about the possibility of huge mosquitoes has come to your attention. Negative self-talk patterns might go something like this:

I hate those bloodsuckers. They always find me. I am going to be disfigured within seconds. Their viscous attacks might leave me sick for the duration of the whole trip. In fact, I'm sick right now just thinking about it. I know I won't have any fun. I think I'll just stay home. Nothing ever works out right for me. Now I'm losing out on a trip to Alaska, too, all because of those miserable bugs. I never have any fun. Life is truly the pits. Rats!

It certainly would be quasi-positive thinking to ignore the possibility that mosquitoes exist or to pretend that, if bitten, there wouldn't be any swelling or itching. A positive mind-set, on the other hand:

- Acknowledges the information (mosquitoes do exist.)
- Decides what to do (I don't want to change my vacation to the winter when those little varmints are dead. I prefer a summer vacation.)
- Takes appropriate action (packs insect repellent and some long-sleeved shirts.)
- Focuses on the positive aspects (I have dreamed of visiting Alaska for years. I will love seeing the *last frontier* with its magnificent mountains, endless tundra, glaciers, and wild life—surely outweighs a few mosquito bites!)

Some individuals have had the type of role models that enabled them to learn some of these lessons earlier in life than I did. Recently, I watched one little boy walk up to another and say "You're a dummy." The demeaned child replied, "I know I'm smart, but you're free to have a different opinion if you want to." What a fantastic response! That boy obviously had received some wonderful role-modeling, not only in the art of positive self-talk, but in terms of optimum self-esteem, as well. The messages playing in his head enabled him to acknowledge what was said, choose not to internalize it or to expend needless energy in angry reaction, and to graciously allow the other child to have a different opinion. Regardless of our age, we can learn to do the same. The choice is ours.

5 **Information stored in the brain can later return as a stimulus to action..** Barring injury to the brain or the presence of disease such as a tumor, every action is the result of a thought. Sometimes the thought is conscious, sometimes subconscious. If we want to exhibit positive behaviors we need to take responsibility for the thoughts we dwell upon. It's that simple.

That's why it is so absolutely essential to think on what we *want* to accomplish, and the ways in which we want to behave, instead of thinking about what we do not want to have happen. We can effectively prepare for certain events in life (at least to some degree) by imagining ahead of time how we plan to act. Otherwise, we may be at increased risk for falling for almost anything, for exhibiting undesirable and ineffective behaviors, and for failing to reach our individual potential.

Electrical recordings of brain activity have shown a flurry of activity about three hundred and fifty milliseconds—a full third of a second—before a person's conscious awareness is triggered. "A third of a second isn't very much time!" one seminar participant commented.

Actually it's a great deal of time within the brain in which information flies along neuron pathways at upwards of four hundred feet per second. A lot can happen in a third of a second! An understanding of the predictable sequence that occurs reinforces a belief that, in the main, we can choose to have control over our actions:

- A stimulus (external or internal) occurs.
- Neuron activity is triggered by the stimulus.
- Conscious awareness of neuron activity (a thought) occurs approximately three hundred and fifty milliseconds (a third of a second) later.
- We are presented with a choice. We can continue to think the thought, or we can think a different thought; we can take action based on the thought, or we can refrain from taking action (which in and of itself is an action).

A thought process is actually in operation before we have the opportunity to initiate a conscious act of the will. *Free will* operates in several arenas: choosing to continue to think a thought or to think a different thought; choosing to take action based on the thought or to refrain from taking action; and, of course, carefully screening the type of information to which we will expose our brain. The so-called *temptations,* which the Bible says are common to everyone, are indeed very different from actions—the behaviors we choose to exhibit based on thoughts that arise within the brain.

In this light, the Ten Commandments consist of a call to positive action. The fourth Commandment tells us to *remember* the Sabbath day and to plan ahead for the types of activities that we'll enjoy on that day. The fifth reminds us to *honor* or respect the position that our parents hold in our generational inheritance. The other eight remind us that if our thoughts prompt us to worship another god, to make graven images, to blaspheme, to murder, steal, covet, lie, or commit adultery, we are to refrain from acting upon those thoughts.

Information can be stored in the brain even when the information never actually enters our awareness. The author of *The Amazing Brain* points out:

It seems that at least some visual information, like that about faces and scenes, may pass directly into permanent memory.

> The ancestor of every action is a thought. —Emerson

Furthermore, when information comes to the brain in two modalities at the same time, the probability that the information will bypass conscious deliberation and go directly into long-term memory is enhanced. In other words, when the mind is exposed to stimuli that combine words and music, or sounds and sensual images that invoke deep feelings or emotions, the information presented may bypass the conscious-decision-making portion of the thought processes—and pass directly into the brain's long-term memory banks.

Music can be a powerful stimulus. Depending on its mood, rhythm, intensity, and perhaps even volume, music can serve as a trigger of a variety of emotions (e.g., joy, anger, fear, sadness, euphoria). When the music is combined with sensory images (as in rock videos), it can influence an individual to lust for sexual activity, to choose to experiment with drugs, to seek power and control. The rhythmic beat of the music can suspend judgment-making abilities. The combined potential impact on the person's behavior can run the gamut from slightly embarrassing to devastatingly disastrous.

Research also suggests that information with a strong emotional component, especially when it appeals to two or more senses, may bypass selective choice and pass directly into long-term memory. Most TV programs, movies, videos, and even TV games employ multimedia. The pictures, sensory images, visual variety, music, rhythm, nonspeech sounds, and feeling components of the content (often a story) appeal to the right hemisphere of the brain.

The verbal and written words may be processed in the left hemisphere, but the majority of stimuli attract the right hemisphere which does not clearly recognize the difference between staged scenes and real-life occurrences. The left side of the brain is capable of this logical processing. It may believe intellectually that the murder which just took place on the screen was staged. The palms of the person's hands may still become sweaty, however, because the scene is processed as literal and plausible. Logic is often overridden by the potent sensory input.

The subconscious definitely responds more readily to emotional amplitude. That is, we tend to store and recall information more readily when our emotions have been involved. For example, speaking to ourselves in emphatic statements stimulates the brain to pay closer attention. Mumbling the words, "I'm only eating one piece of pie at Thanksgiving dinner," will not *grab* its attention as it will if you stand in front of the mirror, smile, take a deep breath and say in a loud forceful voice: "Pay attention now. I am eating only one piece of pie today. I am satisfied and happy!"

As an aside, the understanding, tracking, and management of time is a function of the left cerebral hemisphere; the right hemisphere is less oriented to time. Consequently, it may be very easy for some (especially right-brainers) to stay glued to the TV screen for hours—quite oblivious to the passage of time.

Sometimes a particularly grisly movie will be shown in the theaters or on cable television. A few days later, the news media will often report similar crimes that were committed at various locations throughout the nation. The perpetrators may have watched the movie; the scenes passed directly into their long-term memory banks to subsequently become a potential stimulus toward action.

I recall reading the story of a child who witnessed a murder. That traumatic experience served as a basis for certain behaviors that were exhibited in adulthood. It took a great deal of mental prodding in a safe environment with skilled counselors and therapists before the person was able to consciously recall the experience, heal from the trauma, and exhibit different behaviors. Although not recalled for years, the stored memories had deleteriously impacted the person's behavior.

To recap, information that has a strong emotional component, especially in a multi-media presentation, may pass directly into the subconscious memory. Because of the nature of the stimuli, conscious decision-making control over what is going to be stored in long-term memory is bypassed. Stored sensory impressions can return later on as a subconscious stimulus toward behavior. The individual may, at the conscious level, be totally unaware of them and may not even be able to recall or verbalize any memory of the original incident.

It *is* important to monitor and control the type of information to which the brain is exposed. There is a great deal of difference, for example, between scanning the headlines and watching the news portrayed on TV in living color. The brain was not designed to witness twenty thousand murders on TV by the age of twenty! Continual exposure to large amounts of raw emotion can cause the brain to shut down its sensitivity to emotion. This phenomenon may explain, in part, how individuals can take part in riots, loot businesses and homes, and even kill other human beings—without showing any remorse.

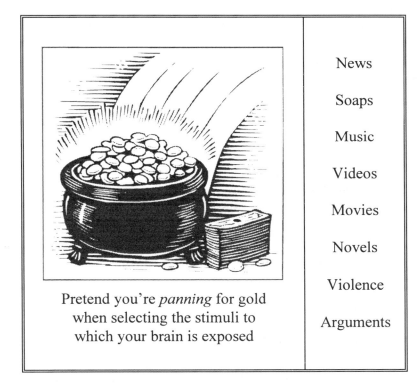

News

Soaps

Music

Videos

Movies

Novels

Violence

Arguments

Pretend you're *panning* for gold when selecting the stimuli to which your brain is exposed

The brain tends to play and replay its *recordings,* consciously and sub-consciously. It has, in effect, its own metaphorical video camera/projector and CD recorder/player. The recordings playing inside our heads definitely influence who we are and how we react to daily-life situations. Emerson was correct, the ancestor of every action is a thought. It is vitally important to pretend that we are panning for gold when selecting the stimuli to which our brains are exposed. It's equally important to take conscious control of our thoughts, once they come to conscious awareness, and carefully select the behaviors we choose to exhibit.

We may not be responsible for every thought that is triggered within our mind. We are responsible for some of the stimuli that trigger neuron activity; specifically, stimuli deriving from information to which we have deliberately exposed our brain. In any event we certainly can and need to take responsibility for our thoughts at the point of conscious awareness, and for our actions related them.

6 **Chemical messengers keep the brain and body in close two-way communication.** Western Medicine has traditionally emphasized the position that mind and body are separate (contrasted to Eastern Medicine that has generally assumed a more global approach). Consequently, many professionals have concentrated on treatment rather than on prevention. Some, to the detriment of many, have even ignored the inseparability of the brain and body. They are one, in constant communication with each other, linked by way of nerve pathways and chemical messengers that are bi-directional. This means that what goes on in the brain can influence the health of the body and what goes on in the body has an effect on the brain.

As mentioned earlier, Psychoneuroimmunology, PNI for short, is a field of scientific investigation that is exploring what I like to refer to as the *brain/body connection* (B/BC); the relationship between the mind and the immune system. PNI is providing us with convincing evidence that a positive mental outlook can help to strengthen immune system function. Even though it is not a *new* field of study, in that it can be traced back to ancient Greece and Rome, PNI has been receiving widespread attention.

In an article published in *Psychology Today*, Marc Barsh described, in cleverly crafted words, what many people are now calling the brain/body connection:

> *Mind and body have their hands so deep in each other's pockets it's hard to tell whose car keys are whose . . .(the) brain, nervous system and immune system, far from being incommunicado, are at this very second hunched elbow-to-elbow at the expresso-bar of the Chatterbox Cafe, animatedly sharing your most intimate particulars.*

Dr. George Solomon (professor of psychiatry and biobehavioral sciences at UCLA) is widely acclaimed as the father of PNI. The first scientific evidence of a link between emotion, immunity, and disease was published in 1964. Researchers Solomon and Moos studied women with rheumatoid arthritis, and found that symptoms developed earlier, and were more serious, in women who were passive, self-sacrificing, and unable to express anger. Other studies conducted during the eighties, with patients infected with the Human Immunodeficiency Virus, showed over and over again that *assertiveness* had a positive effect on the immune system.

Some research focuses on a group of hormonal messengers called neuropeptides—molecules composed of short chains of amino acids whose job it is to modulate the response of various neurotransmitters. Some five dozen of these neuropeptides have been identified. Brain neuropeptide messengers include the enkephalins and endorphins. Research has found evidence of these brain messengers in immune system organs such as the bone marrow, where most blood cells are produced, and in the thymus gland, the master organ of the immune system.

In turn, the immune system also secretes substances similar to neurotransmitters. These immune system messengers, such as the interferons and the interleukins, feed information back to the brain. Brain tissue has been found to contains receptor sites for immune system messengers.

Marion Woodman, a Canadian Jungian analyst, uses a wonderful metaphor to describe this brain-body connection. She compares neuropeptides to little hand-held mirrors, that reflect our mental attitudes. Subsequently, the reflections are translated into chemical messengers that travel throughout the entire immune system. (Refer to my *Immune System Smarts* audiotapes for more information.) It behooves us to carefully monitor the type of attitudes that are being mirrored.

Karen Bulloch, neuroscientist at the University of California at San Diego, has traced direct neurological pathways between the brain and the immune system. This research indicates that the brain and the immune system are joined in an intricate feedback loop by which each one influences the other. In reality, this rich, two-way communication system links the brain, the immune system, and potentially all other body systems.

The body is only too ready and willing to act out what it hears the brain say about it; the brain is susceptible to whatever is going on within the body. Thus, emotional states, behavioral patterns, and mental attitudes are central issues in health and disease. There are some who believe that up to eighty percent of all illnesses begin in the mind. Estimates project that approximately seventy-five percent of all visits to doctors are for illnesses that relate to stress and anxiety, and/or that could ultimately be resolved without treatment.

Because of this close mind/body connection our thoughts, attitudes, and feelings can have measurable effects on our physical health. Decades ago, Ellen White, the author of the book *Education*, mentioned this connection: ". . . the influence of the mind on the body, as well as of the body on the mind should be emphasized. The electrical power of the brain, promoted by mental activity, vitalizes the whole system and is thus an invaluable aid in resisting disease."

As mentioned earlier, my Dad was a preacher, so I heard a great many sermons during my childhood. Because of that, I can't help referencing a few Bible texts that suggest a brain/body connection. The book of Deuteronomy (26:11) encourages us to rejoice in every good thing. There is life-giving power in cheerfulness and gratitude. The famous proverb, *a happy heart does good like a medicine* (Proverbs 17:22), certainly describes the effect of a positive attitude on the immune system. The best way I know to manage this brain/body communication network is to develop a mind-set that accentuates a positive mental attitude.

Of course the flip side is a negative mental attitude. No doubt that is why the Bible also advises us (Philippians 4:6 and Matthew 6:25-34) to avoid anxiety and worry—brain suspenders that create a form of stress that can suppress immune system function. Worry decreases the number of B and T cells within the body. One school of thought suggests that fear (e.g., viewing very *scary* movies and videos) may generally suppress immune system function much in the same way as worry and anxiety.

Studies at Ohio State Medical School and Harvard University discovered that stress related to examinations measurably reduced the level of a specific antibody (IgA) in the saliva of students. Examination stress can also decrease the effectiveness of natural killer cells and the ability of the body to produce interferons. No wonder college students sometimes get sick after exam week. Fortunately, it is possible to modulate our individual response to stress; to learn to manage it more effectively.

We have all heard lines such as *he who laughs—lasts.* Did you know that it is biochemically impossible to get sick or sicker while we are laughing? King Solomon, billed as the wisest man who ever lived, must have known this because he is quoted as saying: "I know that there is nothing better for people than to be happy and to do good while they live" (Ecclesiastes 3:12). Dr. Fry at Stanford Medical School compares laughter to exercise. Laughter, a physiological response initiated by the brain, causes us to breathe more deeply.

This in turn brings more oxygen into the body while the shuddering internal action stimulates various organs. Fry says that twenty seconds of vigorous laughter can double the heart rate for three to five minutes; the equivalent benefit of three minutes of strenuous rowing.

Several studies have demonstrated that the use of humor can enhance immune system function. Dr. Lee Berk of Loma Linda University found that the activity of disease-fighting cells increases after hearty laughter. He reports that having participants view a sixty-minute humorous film decreased their level of cortisol, a hormone that has immune-suppressing capability.

Psychologist David McClelland from Boston University showed that levels of antibodies in the saliva increased after a group of medical students watched an amusing movie. In another study, he documented significant increases in Immunoglobulin A (IgA) concentrations in students who viewed a fifty-minute Mother Teresa film designed to induce a positive, caring, emotional state. In her research, Dr. Dillon also documented significant protective increases in salivary IgA after students viewed a humorous thirty-minute videotape.

Norman Cousins was convinced that he helped his body to recover from several life-threatening illnesses through the use of humor. Genuine laughter stimulates endorphins, the body's own morphine. With laughter, a measurable increase in endorphins can help to decrease a sense of physical pain. Vigorous laughter can burn up as many calories per hour as can brisk walking or cycling. In theory at least, we could burn calories and strengthen our immune systems by relaxing on the sofa watching a humorous video.

Perhaps some of the decreased immune response as we get older may be related, in part, to something as simple as smiling less frequently. Babies smile an average of 280 times a day and baby girls smile even more than baby boys. As adults, we smile fewer than eight times a day. It takes thirty-four muscles to frown and only thirteen to smile. Why take the extra effort to frown?

Biofeedback and mental-imaging techniques are being used successfully at centers throughout the country. The story is told of a woman who was sent to consult with Dr. Norman Cousins at his UCLA Medical School office because she was resisting the efforts of medical professionals to talk her into having a mastectomy for breast cancer. Cousins reportedly thought there would be no harm in teaching her a few visualization techniques, which he proceeded to do. Two weeks later, when she returned to his office, he found to his amazement, that the tumor had completely disappeared.

Harvard psychiatrist Dr. George Vaillant maintains that mental health is the most important predictor of physical health. His study, reported in the book *Adaptation To Life*, found that men with immature coping styles, when subjected to stress, became ill four times more often than men with healthier coping styles. Studies have shown that emotions do have an effect on symptoms of illness such as those seen with the flu, colds, and genital herpes. Who knows what our minds are capable of and what can be accomplished through successfully managing our B/BC?

Take		Eliminate
charge		all enemy
of your		outposts
brain/body		inside your
connection		head

Our brain is our *best bet*. When we cooperate with its natural laws, we can enhance our lives immeasurably, and have fun in the process. We can laugh our way to success!

BRAIN BUILDERS

Points to Ponder

- The only person who never makes a mistake is the one who never does anything. —Theodore Roosevelt

- Two key concepts I have learned in this section:

  _____

  _____

- Two facts I've discovered about myself while studying this section:

  _____

  _____

- One way in which I am now applying my favorite brain law:

  _____

  _____

- Brain tissue can _____ with lack of use.

- Those who _____, last.

- It is important to monitor and _____ the type of information to which the brain is exposed.

- The mind has a tendency to _____ _____ what it envisions.

- **T F** Watching the *soaps* on TV qualifies as challenging mental exercise.

- **T F** Our self-talk is definitely tied to our self-worth.

- **T F** We can choose to remedy negative self-talk patterns.

Brain Teasers

1.	2.	3.	4.
LEVEL LEVEL LEVEL	SHE/HERSELF	T O U C H	GI GI GI CCCCCCCCCC

Creativity Corner

Guess what? I've got the key to another door . . .

Chapter Twelve
Staying Geared Up

In and of itself, simply learning new information is not enough. To make a difference, we need to practically apply the information in our own lives and interactions on a daily basis. The influences of our innate preferences are all-embracing. They impact what we think, feel, say, do, or don't. This includes the choices we make in every arena. Here are three suggestions to consider.

1 When there is a difference of opinion about a course of action, take time to observe. Often you can quickly recognize the probable thinking-style perspective that is driving the disagreement. This awareness can reduce a tendency to take things *personally,* as well as help to smooth troubled waters and re-solve misunderstandings.

2 When you have a personal de-cision to make, spend a few minutes imagining the way in which the problem could be ap-proached from the perspective of each thinking style. This can help you to be more creative, and to generate additional options.

3 When you want to practice your application skills, select almost any situation and create four scenarios, one for each thinking style. This exercise can potentially increase your level of discernment in a variety of interactions.

COMPARISON EXERCISE

A worksheet is included (refer to appendix) to help you identify relationship differences and similarities. Fill in information about yourself on the first line. Then write in the names of several individuals for comparison purposes. You may want to include your best friend, your worst antagonist, significant family members, and work associates. As you complete the worksheet, the emerging pattern can help to explain why some of your relationships work better than others.

Use the worksheet as a catalyst for discussion in your family circle and with your friends. The more we openly talk about this information the better we tend to accommodate differences, to become less defensive when they occur, and to value the contribution of each perspective. When we truly understand that, just as the blind men who went to visit the elephant, each of us possesses only part of the picture and none of us possesses the whole, we will be less likely to invest large measures of energy into convincing others that ours is the only point of view. For some individuals, that behavioral change alone will free up voluminous amounts of vital force.

In general, we teach others how to treat us. Therefore, as we begin to role-model

Understanding this brain stuff has made such a difference . . .

healthier behaviors, as we become more meticulous in being *real,* some of our relationships will, of necessity, also change. Others will observe the positive changes in our life and applaud our efforts. Some will be curious enough to investigate what made the difference and may even decide to join us on the journey of discovery and growth. Others may hold back in an attempt to maintain the status quo, or out of their own discomfort and fear, try to sabotage our personal growth journey. A few may even decide to terminate their relationship with us. Knowing who we innately are, making a commitment to wholeness, and developing a strong support system of individuals who have a similar vision can help us to remain centered regardless of the choices made by others.

We need to design a personal script that concentrates the bulk of our energy on identifying who we are, becoming the person we were intended to be, and using our innate giftedness to make this world a better place. As we validate and nurture this process individually, or with others who are into personal growth, we must take care to refrain from trying to develop an agenda or a script for anyone else. That is neither our right nor our responsibility. We can change only ourselves. The best way to encourage others is to accept them as they are.

CRAFTING YOUR OWN FUTURE

You can be the director of your own expedition—the architect of your own future. As Dr. Stiles indicated in the foreword, this information can assist you in finding the keys to many unopened doors. These practical strategies are designed to help you to progressively gain a broader understanding of who you are as an individual, to enhance your life-management skills, and to craft your own future. As you add discovery to discovery, and victory to victory, you will be amazed at your truly sterling qualities and talents.

On this journey, expect to repeatedly circle through at least four important phases:

1 Awareness. Information is power—power to maximize your potential and to nurture and support others in their quest. Once exposed to a new idea, the brain never returns to its original dimensions, however great those dimensions were. This exposure to brain-function information has already increased your cerebral synaptic connections. These can serve you well in the future. Continue to keep abreast of emerging research data.

2 Understanding. Our grasp or comprehension of the information turns into knowledge when we make it our own. Zig Zigler reportedly said, "Most people do not like to change their minds. However, given new information, many people are more than willing to come to a new conclusion." Through increased understanding, we can be willing to come to some new conclusions that can benefit us the remainder of our lives.

3 Desire. How much we want to grow, and the degree to which we are willing to personally internalize what we learn, will definitely influence the extent to which we actually improve. Some individuals are content to vegetate, to expend the least possible energy in everyday living. Others truly thirst for knowledge and cultivate an inclination to learn, to grow, and to realize positive change.

4 Application. In order to achieve positive outcomes, we must actually apply the information—we must choose to act. The ageless adage still applies—*practice makes perfect.* Application definitely requires practice. What we can conceive, we can achieve. Don't only *think* about scaling the summit. With thought alone you'll never get beyond base camp. Get out on the slopes and conquer summit after summit.

Although the concepts presented herein will neither remove all differences nor solve all problems, their consistent application can minimize frustration, and promote patterns of acceptance and tolerance. We can create an environment wherein, instead of trying to become either critics or clones, we can be enriched through each other's uniqueness. As we emphasize whole-brained living, individually and collectively, we come to the realization that, with all working together in equality, and with all of us contributing our innate giftedness, something special, something exponentially greater than ourselves, something exciting and honoring to all can be achieved.

THE EAGLE THAT THOUGHT IT WAS A CHICKEN

Once upon a time, so the story goes, a rancher was hiking through some very rugged mountains. Hearing a sound he paused and looked around. At the base of a towering giant of a tree he discovered a baby eagle. It was obvious that the tiny bird was very hungry. Had it tumbled out of the nest several stories above? Had its parents been killed? After deliberating for awhile, the man carefully tucked the little orphan into one of his roomy pockets and headed for home. Back at the ranch he placed the eaglet in the pen with a flock of chickens and, for all intents and purposes, forgot about it.

Weeks later, when a distant neighbor stopped at the ranch, the two men happened to walk by the chicken pen. "Ho," said the neighbor. "What have we here?" What they had was an eagle, nearly grown, scratching for food on the ground with the chickens.

After some discussion, the rancher agreed that it would be a good plan to release the eagle. They stepped into the pen, picked up the eagle, and carried it outside. Rather than launching itself into the wild blue yonder, however, it sat quietly for a time looking around. Soon it hopped down to the ground and walked to the door of the chicken coop and waited to be let back in.

"Can you beat that?" the rancher exclaimed! "Poor bloke doesn't want to be free." They talked about the bird at dinner and decided to take it to a bird sanctuary some distance away.

"Maybe they can teach the eagle how to fly," the neighbor suggested.

Within a month, the rancher realized that his work would take him in the direction of the bird sanctuary. In a carrying cage, the magnificent bird bounced and jounced over the mountain roads to its new home. Preoccupied with his duties, the rancher gave little thought to the bird. Once, when he was hiking in the high country, he saw an eagle soaring overhead and briefly wondered if it might be the bird he had rescued.

Imagine his surprise, when several years later he met the sanctuary volunteer at a county meeting. The two men struck up a conversation and the rancher asked where the eagle had been released. "Oh, it's still at the bird sanctuary," the volunteer replied. "We've tried absolutely everything to get that bird to fly. No luck. We even dropped him from a helicopter once, and he all but flattened himself when he hit the ground. Luckily we were over a freshly plowed field!" The man shook his head. "Put him in with a couple of chickens, however, and he's as happy as a clam."

"But has he never even offered to fly?" the rancher persisted.

"There was one time when I had hoped it might happen," the volunteer replied. "Oh, how I had hoped!" He then related how once, while he was cleaning the sanctuary coop, a wild eagle had flown overhead and screamed its call. The tame eagle had paused for a moment, looked up for a fleeting second, and then continued scratching on the ground. "You just can't imagine how I felt," the volunteer offered, his voice choked with emotion. "I wanted to jump up and down and shout, *Fly! Fly! You were meant to fly!*"

Nevertheless, the eagle was making a wonderful contribution to education. The volunteer was very busy filling request after request from school principals who wanted to schedule his popular *show and tell* exhibit. Many of the students had never seen a live eagle up close. They were awed by its regal appearance and amazed at its expansive wing-spread. Now, they understood why it had been selected as a symbol of their nation.

"What does the eagle do during the presentations?" the rancher asked.

"Nothing," the volunteer replied. "He sits calmly on my arm, looks around the room, and eventually hops down onto a desk when I throw a bit of chicken feed out there. It's the strangest thing," the volunteer continued, shaking his head, "I actually believe the eagle thinks it's a chicken."

The volunteer went on to recall one particular school he had been at with the eagle. Halfway through the presentation one of the students interjected, "I saw an eagle once at my grand-dad's place. It was amazing to watch him soar and dive. Can this bird do that?"

The volunteer explained that, while the eagle had the potential to exhibit this behavior, never in all the years he had been at the sanctuary had the workers been able to help it catch a vision of how eagles behave.

One of the other students offered, "How I wish I could become an eagle for just one day. If I could just speak *eagle-ese* I'd try to tell this bird what he is missing in life and what he could become if he only would!"

The rancher drove home very slowly. In his mind's eye he recalled seeing countless eagles soaring high above the mountain peaks. It was hard to picture one sitting contentedly on the volunteer's arm and hopping down to scratch for dinner. *What a waste,* he thought. *What a waste!*

We humans have the potential to easily accomplish much more than the majestic eagles. Yet in many cases, we have been acting like chickens for a variety of different reasons: some economic, some cultural, some out of fear, some because of an absence of role-modeling and encouragement, some for lack of understanding. We were meant to soar. Instead, metaphorically, we have been living as banded bantams just scratching the surface.

It's time to write that new chapter in our lives. That's what this journey is all about—learning about brain functions in general, and about ours in particular.

It's time to figure out who we are, and become the person we were intended to be. Our potential is virtually unlimited. Let's catch the vision. Let's seize the opportunity. Let's spread our wings and soar!

You'll never know how high you can fly— until you spread your wings and try . . .

BRAIN BUILDERS

Points to Ponder

- How easy it is to drift at times in yesterday's shadows and fail to live in the light of today's joy. —Ball

- Four phases I can expect to repeatedly circle through on my journey:

  _____   _____

  _____   _____

- One new goal I have set for myself:

  _____

  _____

- One specific step I am taking today to help move me closer to this goal:

  _____

  _____

Brain Teasers

1.	2.	3.	4.
ODDSUS	ILBCNGU	? RAINRAINRAIN	UR EXTENDED
T T O O W W E E R R	GOLDEN GATE	FOCAL FOCAL FOCAL	PARK

MONEY MANAGEMENT SUMMARY

Prioritizer

*I know how to make money work for me;
I like to see my bank account growing;
I spend time learning how to invest wisely;
I do a cost-benefit analysis before I spend;
I want the best buy . . .*

Visualizer

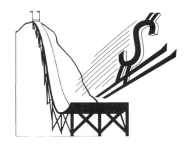

*I just can't seem to focus on money and
budgets; balancing my checkbook is
definitely not a priority; fortunately my
accounts eventually seem to turn out
all right most of the time . . .*

Organizer

*I have a budget and meticulously stick to it;
I know exactly how much money I have to
spend and where it goes—to the penny;
I am a very methodical spender . . .*

Harmonizer

*I need money as a medium of exchange for
the things I want to do and the gifts I want
to buy; somehow I always seem to run out
of money before I run out of month . . .*

APPROACH TO CHANGE

Prioritizers

Avoid Change

- Will embrace change if it is necessary to *win* and if it is *logical*
- Once the decision has been made, want to expedite, direct, and maintain control
- Can be insensitive and dictatorial in the process

Visualizers

Seek Change

- Initiate change to solve problems and to avoid boredom
- Usually want to innovate intuitively and spontaneously
- Can be inspiring but may be impatient with details

Organizers

Generally Oppose Change

- May accept change if it's a life and death issue and if it is practical/proven
- Want to deliberate before taking any action
- Can incorporate change into an existing routine but may sabotage the process through procrastination

Harmonizers

Acquiesce to Change

- Tend to accept change it it's beneficial to all and promotes harmony
- Want to discuss the change, minimize conflict, and smooth the process
- Excessive concerns about harmony issues can delay implementation of the change

ABOUT THE AUTHOR

A brain-function consultant, radio talk show host, and presenter of *Brainworks Unlimited*[TM], Arlene is founder/president of Realizations Inc/Success Resources International, and is the executive editor of *SynapSez,* an educational newsletter. Taylor holds doctorates in Health and Human Services as well as Clinical Counseling, a Masters degree in Epidemiology/Health Education, and a Bachelors in Nursing. She and her husband make their home in the Napa Valley. Audiences around the world have found her an engaging and imaginative speaker as she presents seminars on health, motivation, and personal growth. Seminar titles include:

- Bona Fide Boundaries
- Brain & Bedside Manner
- Brain/Body Connection
- Brainworks Unlimited[TM]
- Brain Reward Systems (addictions)
- Cancer Prevention
- Conquering Codependency
- Cross-Gender Teamwork
- Distress, Eustress & Mistress
- Eight Basic Energies
- Gender Graphics (M/F differences)
- High
- Imm

- Managing Difficult People
- Managing Holiday Stress
- Mars, Venus & the Brain
- Minding Emotions
- Myths of Aging
- Optimum Self-Esteem
- Patience of Job in the 90's
- Sexuality & Compatibility
- Superwoman Syndrome
- Watch Out for the SuperBugs
- What's Your E.Q.?

Strategies

Century

RESOURCES

For inform

P.O.

Information about Dr. Taylor's seminars, the brain function assessment (BTSA), *The Brain & Innate Giftedness* weekend program, and the quarterly newsletter, *SynapSez,* is available from:

Realizations Inc/Success Resources International

Web Site
www.arlenetaylor.org

E-mail
thebrain@arlenetaylor.org

P O Box 2554
Napa CA 94558 USA
707-554-4981
Fax 707-648-1965

resources, or to

648-1965

s

THINKING STYLES ASSESSMENT

The *working model of brain function* is based on a physiological update to the work of C. G. Jung. In its present form, the model represents the synthesis of work by Dr. Katherine Benziger of Texas, Dr. Karl Pribram (formerly) of Stanford University, Dr. Hans Eysenck of London, Dr. Richard Haier of San Diego, and others. The Benziger Thinking Styles Assessment (BTSA) grew out of the working model of brain function. The BTSA was designed to assist individuals in identifying key components of Jung's therapeutic approach, and provides the missing link between one's neurochemistry and social environment. Feedback information is presented in a twenty-page personalized profile. The knowledge gained can help individuals increase their general effectiveness, collaborative skills, life-management skills, and overall well-being through enhanced self-awareness.

The BTSA uses value-free labels, thus making it easier for individuals to view all four different cerebral thinking styles as of equal value. BTSA validation reports have been summarized in a document entitled: *The BTSA User Manual. A Guide to the Development, Validation, and Use of the BTSA* (Benziger). A high positive correlation has been established between the BTSA and the Myers-Briggs Temperament Indicator (MBTI).

The BTSA also holds promise as a tool that can enable organizations to create *whole-brained* teams with enhanced potential for collaboration and sufficient diversity to solve problems effectively and to accomplish group objectives. It can potentially enable treatment programs to structure their therapeutic modalities in a way that can predict not only individual success rates, but can also assist participants in achieving desired outcomes on a consistent basis over time.

The BTSA is available by mail. Order from:

Realizations Inc/Success Resources International
P.O. Box 2554 Napa CA 94558-0255   707-554-4981   FAX 707-648-1965

The BTSA is also available as a component of *Brainworks Unlimited*^{TM}. This weekend program is offered at the Health Center at St. Helena Hospital located in the world-famous Napa Valley of Northern California. Thirty (30) hours of continuing education credit for nurses; California BRN Provider #08580.

Who attends Brainworks? Those seeking:

◆ Career direction
◆ Recovery strategies
◆ Options for thriving
◆ Adaption resolution
◆ Personal growth tips

◆ To enhance relationships
◆ To augment management skills
◆ To avoid burnout/midlife crisis
◆ To reduce excessive energy expenditure
◆ To manage stressors and avoid depression

For more information and to register, call **1-800-358-9195**

ANSWERS TO BRAIN BUILDERS

CHAPTER ONE

Blanks:	• Cerebrum	• Pain/pleasure	
True or False:	• True	• True	• True
Brain teasers:	1. Grandstand 2. Block head	3. Upside down 4. Circles under the eyes	

CHAPTER TWO

Blanks:	• Thinking	• Value	• Gender
True or False:	• True	• False	• True
Brain teasers:	1. F (Friday) 2. Ninety-one	3. I understand 4. Scrambled eggs	

CHAPTER THREE

Blanks:	• Cerebral callus	• Stimulation	• Emotional
True or False:	• True	• True	• False
Brain teasers:	1. Reading between the lines 2. Crying over spilt milk	3. A backward glance 4. E (Eight)	

CHAPTER FOUR

Blanks:	• Meditation	• Left	• Female	• Imagine
True or False:	• True	• True	• False	
Brain teasers:	1. Mind's eye 2. Tricycle	3. Mind over matter 4. Just between you and me		

CHAPTER FIVE

Blanks:	• Visual, auditory, kinesthetic	• Preference

True or False:	• True	• False	• True	• True

Brain teasers:	1. Left brain	3. Square dance
	2. The underworld	4. Badly overdrawn

CHAPTER SIX

Blanks:	• Learning	• Gender	• Giftedness
		• Brain lead	
		• Sensory preference	
		• Extroversion/Introversion ratio	

True or False:	• True	• True	• False

Brain teasers:	1. Six feet under ground	5. Down hill
	2. 35	6. Laid back
	3. Three degrees below zero	7. Undermine
	4. J (January)	8. Union Square

CHAPTER SEVEN

Blanks:	• Skill	• Giftedness	• Love

True or False:	• True	• True	• True

Brain teasers:	1. Polygraph	3. Accident prone
	2. Gross injustice	4. Tall order

CHAPTER EIGHT

Blanks:	• Failure	• Desserts	• Unbalanced

True or False:	• True	• True	• False (Selye)

Brain teasers:	1. Change in the weather	3. One after another
	2. Elbow	4. Condescending

CHAPTER NINE

Blanks:	• Enthusiasm (joy)	• Feel	• Balance

True or False:	• False	• True	• True

Brain teasers:	1. All around town	3. A single dose
	2. Indoors	4. Multiple listing

CHAPTER TEN

Blanks:	• Step	• Lineage	• Politically smart

True or False:	• False	• True	• True

Brain teasers:	1. Odds are overwhelming	3. It's a small world after all
	2. Tennis	4. Inside out

CHAPTER ELEVEN

Blanks:	• Atrophy	• Laugh	• Control	• Act out

True or False:	• False	• True	• True

Brain teasers:	1. Trilevel	3. Touchdown
	2. She's beside herself	4. Three GIs overseas

CHAPTER TWELVE

Brain teasers:	1. The odds are against us	5. Twin towers
	2. I'll be seeing you	6. Golden Gate Bridge
	3. Somewhere over the rainbow	7. Trifocals
	4. You're overextended	8. Central park

NOTE: visualizing functions enable us to see options in 3-D figures (e.g., pages 26-27). In the past, dictionaries have sometimes referred to these types of figures as *optical illusions*.

COMPARISON WORKSHEET

Part I: Brain Lead and Emotional Tone

Enter your data. Use the remaining lines for family members, best friends, and associates. You may want to include names of individuals with whom you have had conflict. Use this information to help you better understand/improve your relationship interactions.

Name	Organizer	Harmonizer	Visualizer	Prioritizer	Innate Brain Lead
Me					
1					
2					
3					
4					
5					
6					
7					
8					
9					

COMPARISON WORKSHEET, CONT'D

Part II: Brain Lead and Emotional Tone

E:I RATIO: EE = extreme extrovert   HE = high extrovert
B = Balanced E:I ratio   EI = extreme introvert   HI = High introvert
EMOTIONAL TONE: Positive (P)   Negative (N)   Determined (D)

Visual	Auditory	Kinesthetic	E:I Ratio	Emotional tone, past three years	Emotional tone, past three months

SELECTED BIBLIOGRAPHY

Andreasen, Nancy C. *The Broken Brain* (Harper & Row:NY)

Bandler, Richard. *Using Your Brain for a Change* (Real People Press:UT)

Benziger, I. Katherine. *Falsification of Type—Dissertation Summary* (KBA Publishing:TX)
_____. *Overcoming Depression* (KBA Publishing:TX)

Benziger, Katherine and Sohn, Anne. *The Art of Using Your Whole-brained* (KBA Publishing:TX)

Benson, Herbert, with Proctor, William. *Your Maximum Mind* (Avon Books:NY)

Blakeslee, Thomas, R. *The Right Brain* (Anchor Press/Doubleday:NY)

Blevins, William. *Your Family, Your Self* (New Harbinger Publications Inc:CA)

Bricklin, Mark; Golin, Mark; Grandinetti, Deborah; Lieberman, Alexis. *Positive Living and Health. The Complete Guide to Brain/Body Healing and Mental Empowerment.* (Rodale Press:PA)

Buzan, Tony. *Make The Most of Your Mind* (Linden Press:NY)
_____. *Use Both Sides of Your Brain* (E.P. Dutton:NY)

Carder, Dave, et al. *Secrets of Your Family Tree* (Moody Press:Chicago)

Cornils, Stanley P. *The Mourning After; How to Manage Grief Wisely* (R&E Publishers:CA)

Dienstfrey, Harris. *Where the Mind Meets The Body* (HarperCollins:NY)

Donahue, Phil. *The Human Animal* (Simon & Schuster Inc.:NY)

Doran, Sandra. *Raising Tough Kids in Tough Times;* a syllabus. (MA).
_____. *Attention-Deficit Disorder*; audio-cassettes.

Durden-Smith, Jo and de Simone, Diane. *Sex and The Brain* (Warner Books:NY)

Edwards, Betty. *Drawing on the Right Side of The Brain* (J.P. Tarcher Inc.:CA)

Fincher, Jack. *Sinister People. The Looking-Glass World of the Left-Hander* (Putnam:NY)

Gazzaniga, Michael S. *Mind Matters* (Houghton Mifflin Company:Boston)

Goleman, Daniel. *Emotional Intelligence* (Bantam Books:NY)

Gordon, William P. *Memory and Cerebral Dominance: A Guide For Health-Care Professionals* (Cortext:CA)

Hall, Nicholas R. S. et al. (editors). *Mind-Body Interactions and Disease* (NIH, Health Dateline Press)

Hartman, Thom. *Attention Deficit Disorder: A Different Perception* (Underwood Books:CA)

Hickman, Ruth with Meusburger, Joanne. *Hope for Hurting People* (Whitaker House:PA)

Hutchison, Michael. *Mega Brain* (Ballantine Books:NY)

James, John W. and Cherry, Frank. *The Grief Recovery Handbook, A Step-By-Step Program for Moving Beyond Loss* (Harper & Row:NY)

Klauser, Henriette Anne. *Writing on Both Sides of the Brain* (Harper & Row:CA)

Luria, A.R. *The Working Brain* (Basic Books Inc.:NY)

Luria, A.R. (edited by K. H. Pribram). *Psychophysiology of the Frontal Lobes* (Academic Press:NY)

Maguire, Jack. *Care And Feeding of the Brain* (Doubleday:NY)

Marlin, Emily. *Genograms. The New Tool for Exploring the Personality, Career, and Love Patterns You Inherit.* (Contemporary Books:NY)

Maltz, Maxwell. *Psycho-Cybernectics and Self-Fulfillment* (Bantam Books:NY)

Moir, Anne and Jessel, David. *Brain Sex* (Carol Publishing Groups:NY)

Middleton-Moz, Jane and Dwinell, Lorie. *After the Tears, Reclaiming Personal Losses of Childhood* (Health Communications Inc:FL)

Murphy, Joseph. *The Power of Your Subconscious Mind* (Bantam Books:NY)

New International Version. *The Holy Bible* (Zondervan Bible Publishers:MI)

Ornstein, Robert and Sobel, David. *The Healing Brain* (Simon & Schuster:NY)

_____ and Thompson, Richard F. *The Amazing Brain* (Houghton Mifflin Co:MA)

Ostrander, Sheila and Schroeder, Lynn. *Super Learning* (Dell Publishing Company Inc.:NY)

Pribram, K. H. *Languages of the Brain* (Prentice-Hall Inc:NJ)

_____.(Editor of selected readings). *Mood, States, and Mind* (Penguin Books:MD)

Restak, Richard M. *The Brain* (Bantam Books:NY)

_____. *The Brain Has a Mind of Its Own* (Harmony Books:NY)

_____. *The Brain. The Last Frontier* (Warner Books Inc.:NY)

Robbins, Anthony. *Unlimited Power* (Ballantine Books:NY)

Rosenthal, Norman E. *Winter Blues. Seasonal Affective Disorder* (The Guilford Press:NY)

Sacks, Oliver. *The Man Who Mistook His Wife for a Hat* (Harper Perennial:NY)

Sapolsky, Robert. *Why Zebras Don't Get Ulcers* (W.H. Freeman and Company:NY)

Smith, Joanne and Biggs, Judy. *How to Say Goodbye. Working Through Personal Grief* (Aglow Publications:WA)

Springer, Sally P. and Deutsch, Georg. *Left Brain, Right Brain* (W.H. Freeman and Company:NY)

Staudacher, Carol. *Men & Grief* (New Harbinger Publications, Inc:CA)

Strelau, Jan and Eysenck, Hans J. (editors). *Personality Dimensions and Arousal* (Plenum Publishing Corporation)

von Oech, Roger. *A Whack on the Side of the Head. How You Can Be More Creative* (Warner Books:NY)

vos Savant, Marilyn and Fleischer, Leonore. *Brain Building in Just Twelve Weeks* (Bantam Books:NY)

Taylor, Arlene. *Back to Basics* (Teach Services:NY)

Taylor, Arlene and Lawrence, Lorna. *Thresholds to Thriving* (Realizations Inc:CA)

Vitale, Barbara Meister. *Unicorns Are Real. A Right-Brained Approach to Learning* (Jalmar Press:CA)

White, Ellen Gould. *Mind, Character, And Personality,* Volumes 1 and 2 (Southern Publishing Association:TN)

Winter, Arthur and Winter, Ruth. *Build Your Brain Power* (St. Martin's:NY)

Zdenek, Marilee. *The Right-Brain Experience* (McGraw-Hill:NY)

. . . PATHS DIVERGED IN A WOOD . . .

Imagine four individuals, each representing one of the thinking styles, standing poised where paths divide. Listen to their stories:

Prioritizer

I chose the path that allowed me to get something done. It took me to a destiny where there were tools (e.g., telephone, FAX, computer). Here, among my tools, and with a few individuals who share my goals, I am on target.

Visualizer

I selected the path that matched my aptitudes, even though it was less traveled and needed some trailblazing. It led me to pursue adventure, innovation, and futuristic ideas. Of course, that has made all the difference.

Organizer

I took the most-traveled path. It led me to a traditional environment where there was little likelihood of change; where conservatism, and the status quo were emphasized. Here, among my established routines, I am secure.

Harmonizer

I found myself following the path that allowed me to be in touch with people. It took me where there is connection and collegiality, harmony and conversation. Here, among my friends, I feel nurtured and comfortable .